Reflexive Leadership

Organising in an imperfect world

Mats Alvesson
Martin Blom
Stefan Sveningsson

Los Angeles | London | New Delhi
Singapore | Washington DC | Melbourne

Los Angeles | London | New Delhi
Singapore | Washington DC | Melbourne

SAGE Publications Ltd
1 Oliver's Yard
55 City Road
London EC1Y 1SP

SAGE Publications Inc.
2455 Teller Road
Thousand Oaks, California 91320

SAGE Publications India Pvt Ltd
B 1/I 1 Mohan Cooperative Industrial Area
Mathura Road
New Delhi 110 044

SAGE Publications Asia-Pacific Pte Ltd
3 Church Street
#10-04 Samsung Hub
Singapore 049483

Editor: Kirsty Smy
Assistant editor: Lyndsay Aitken
Production editor: Vanessa Harwood
Copyeditor: Rosemary Campbell
Proofreader: Derek Markham
Indexer: Caroline Eley
Marketing manager: Alison Borg
Cover design: Shaun Mercier
Typeset by: C&M Digitals (P) Ltd, Chennai, India
Printed and bound in Great Britain by Ashford Colour
Press Ltd.

Library of Congress Control Number: 2016940012

British Library Cataloguing in Publication data

A catalogue record for this book is available from the
British Library

ISBN 978-1-4129-6158-5
ISBN 978-1-4129-6159-2 (pbk)

Reflexive Leadership

SAGE was founded in 1965 by Sara Miller McCune to support the dissemination of usable knowledge by publishing innovative and high-quality research and teaching content. Today, we publish over 900 journals, including those of more than 400 learned societies, more than 800 new books per year, and a growing range of library products including archives, data, case studies, reports, and video. SAGE remains majority-owned by our founder, and after Sara's lifetime will become owned by a charitable trust that secures our continued independence.

Los Angeles | London | New Delhi | Singapore | Washington DC | Melbourne

Contents

About the Authors

Mats Alvesson works at Lund University and also part-time at the University of Queensland and Cass Business School, City University. He has published about thirty books on critical theory, organizational culture, leadership, gender and qualitative and reflexive methods, including: *The Stupidity Paradox: The Powers and Pitfalls of Functional Stupidity* (with André Spicer) (Profile, 2016); *The Triumph of Emptiness* (Oxford University Press, 2013); *Constructing Research Questions* (with Jörgen Sandberg) (Sage, 2013) and *Return to Meaning* (with Y. Gabriel and R. Paulsen) (Oxford University Press, forthcoming).

Martin Blom is an Associate Professor in Strategic Management at Lund University School of Economics and Management. His research interests cover topics such as strategy, corporate governance and leadership/followership. His more recent publications include 'All-inclusive and all good: The hegemonic ambiguity of leadership' (*Scandinavian Journal of Management*, 2015, with Mats Alvesson); 'Less followership, less leadership? An inquiry into the basic but seemingly forgotten downsides of leadership' (*M@n@gement*, 2015, with Mats Alvesson); 'Textual objects and strategizing: The influence of documents as active objects on strategic recursiveness' (*Journal of Change Management*, 2016, with Mikael Lundgren).

Stefan Sveningsson is Professor of Business Administration at the School of Economics and Management, Lund University. He has been visiting researcher at Cardiff Business School, Melbourne University, the University of Sydney and Auckland Business School. His research interests include leadership, managerial work, and strategic and organizational change. He has published several books and articles; recent books – co-authored with Mats Alvesson – include *Changing Organizational Culture* (Routledge, 2nd edn 2015) and *Managerial Lives: Leadership and Identity in an Imperfect World* (Cambridge University Press, 2016).

Preface

Leadership is an extremely popular topic. An enormous amount of literature has appeared on the subject. It may seem as though far too much has been published already and that it is impossible to say anything new – at least anything new that is not promising a seductive, novel recipe for effective or grandiose leadership. 'Not another new book on leadership' is therefore a very understandable reaction.

The reader of this Preface can hopefully withhold a sigh when browsing through the text. In our defence of 'yet another book', we have devoted significant time and effort over the last few decades to carrying out in-depth studies of managers trying to 'do' leadership. We have interviewed managers and their subordinates, observed interactions, and tried to get a good understanding of organizational context. All this is rare and means that we are able to claim that we have actually studied leadership, not just listened to managers (or subordinates) talk about leadership or relied on their questionnaire responses. We have also critically interpreted what we have seen – considering both leadership theories and a wealth of other perspectives. We have not imposed leadership ideas and vocabulary on relationships and interactions, but have been open to other ways of understanding organizing processes.

This has resulted in a much richer and more thoughtful understanding than is perhaps common. We celebrate reflexivity – considering and challenging various departures from and lines of reasoning – and use this to question dominant leadership thinking. A key aspect of reflexivity is to consider alternatives to leadership, both in terms of understanding what goes on and when considering how to deal with organizing processes. Effective organizing sometimes also involves the use of management, power, group work or a network, and cultivating professionalism and autonomy.

The reader may now wonder about the backgrounds of the authors. We all have some experience in senior positions – research leader, senior consultant/programme director and director of undergraduate studies – where leadership is or has been an option for achieving influence. More significantly, we have studied leadership for about twenty years. Not all of that time was devoted to leadership – broader research interests are a great plus as it means that we avoid the tunnel vision and ideological commitment to leadership that more single-minded specialists may suffer from. We have also extensively and intensively studied organizational culture, corporate governance, strategic (and less strategic) change, gender, functional stupidity, knowledge work, managerial and professional work, identity in organizations, power, and many other topics. Our leadership research is part of our broader studies of organizations; that is, on the role of managers trying to 'do leadership' in the context of management of knowledge-intensive firms (high-tech, pharmaceutical and consultancy companies), organizational change or gender issues at work. We have tried to understand what is happening in organizations; leadership and/or managerial interventions are sometimes significant and sometimes less so.

We have also done a number of more focused studies of managers trying to 'do' leadership. These are typically based on a combination of methods aiming to get rich and realistic understandings of leadership efforts and their possible effects. We have: (a) interviewed managers several times; (b) interviewed subordinates; (c) observed managerial actions and interactions between superiors and subordinates (of which some can be seen in terms of leadership); and d) investigated the organizational context. We have also tried to follow managers over some time, not necessarily longitudinally but at different moments, so we are not misled by a snap-shot approach, only capturing leadership in a specific week or month. This book is not a research report, so we do not account for our specific studies. Many of these are, however, mentioned in the reference list. Some relevant and representative studies include Alvesson and Spicer (2011), Alvesson and Sveningsson (2003a), Blom and Alvesson (2014, 2015) and Sveningsson and Alvesson (2003, 2016). In many places we refer to our own studies, but do not want to exaggerate these and instead rely on extensive readings of a variety of leadership and other organization studies of literature over the years. In this way we cover a large part of the entire field of leadership, in particular within a Western European and North American context (recognizing that there are significant differences within this field).

We are however clearly influenced by our own in-depth research, which provides us with a much more realistic and rich understanding compared to research that mainly relies on managers talking about their own leadership or subordinates filling in questionnaires about their managers' leadership. We are thus more sceptical and open-minded about leadership issues than many devoted to the topic or belonging to the leadership industry who might benefit from pumping out positive and fluffy messages about the importance and goodness of leadership.

So, we believe that this book has something important and novel to say. We draw upon rich empirical material and have a number of new, provocative, critical and constructive ideas that help to develop sharper and more thoughtful thinking and practice – both in academic and practical contexts.

This is not only a matter of our own hard work, but very much an outcome of fortunate circumstances. We have had long-term research funding allowing for in-depth studies. We are very grateful to the K. & A. Wallenberg Foundation and the Jan Wallander and Tom Hedelius research foundation for their generous support of free and flexible research. We have also worked in a research group capable of doing in-depth research and producing original studies of leadership efforts. We are grateful to co-researchers Johan Alvehus, Anna Jonsson, Dan Kärreman, Susanne Lundholm and Robert Wenglén for their collaboration and use of some of their empirical material as well as their contribution to a creative and reflective research environment here at

Lund University School of Economics and Management. We would also like to express gratitude to the scholars who have read and commented on various drafts of this book: Richard Bolden, Alan Bryman, Yiannis Gabriel, Ola Håkansson, Tony Huzzard, Anna Jonsson, Per-Hugo Skärvad and Sverre Spoelstra.

Lund, 2016
M.A., M.B., S.S.

1
Leadership: The Need for a Reflexive Approach

In terms of what is presented as crucial for the success of contemporary organizations, there is hardly anything that outranks leadership. The ambition of improving leadership to address and fix individual, organizational or societal problems seems almost endless. Here for example is a voice about the perceived leadership crisis in British healthcare:

> It is for the achievement of the common goal that we all seek (and pray for) a good leadership in our country, clubs, societies and ... organizations. We crave for leaders who will bring out the best in us. We seek a visionary leadership that can see beyond the limitations of today. We seek a leadership that can organize and deploy the available human and material resources for the benefit of all. (*The Guardian*, 2014)

No doubt, leadership can make a difference. Visionary and inspirational leadership can provide purpose and broader meaning to work tasks that might otherwise be seen as repetitive and boring. Leadership may boost morale and ethos in organizations. A leader showing high ethical standards may set a good example and contribute to reciprocity, trust and goodwill among people who identify with him or her. Leadership can also contribute to emotional well-being by recognizing that people are humans rather than simply instrumental resources. Leadership can contribute to the social atmosphere in the workplace, for example by making people feel happy, included and important. Leadership can also contribute to learning and development in various ways – both on an individual and an organizational level.

But successful leadership as described above is also quite complex and calls for reflexivity and thoughtfulness rather than just following fashionable trends and popular recipes about how to act. An illustration and inspirational example could be Jan Wallander, the former chairman of Svenska Handelsbanken (one of Sweden's major and most successful commercial banks). On entering office at the beginning of the 1970s – at a time when the bank was in a severe crisis – Wallander initiated a reduction of costs at the bank's headquarters while at the same time trying to maintain and increase motivation, identification and commitment among employees (Svenska Dagbladet, 2010).

This included a range of reforms, the most significant of which were a strong decentralization to more independent regional branches and a decision to abandon budgeting and formal organizational charts as well as the introduction of a unique profit-sharing model that offered employees the possibility of becoming part-owners of the bank via a newly formed foundation. Wallander intended to change not only behaviour but primarily how people understood and related to work, saying that:

> It is not certain that a change in the outer behaviour also is a change of the inner behaviour, i.e. that people don't just act because they have to but also because they want to … (Wallander, 2003, p. 17)

A key idea behind the changes was to create an organizational context – including culture, norms, and identity – that boosted motivation, commitment and a sense of belonging among the employees. A particular part of this was Wallander's decision to decline the higher salary offered to him on joining the bank, saying that:

> If you require from the employees that they should participate in radical changes and accept cost savings it is not a good idea to start raising your own salary. I managed very well on what I had. Also ethical considerations played a role in my case. (Wallander, 2003, p. 95)

While clearly recognizing the sometimes important role of leadership as described above, it is important to be careful about over-relying on leadership as a panacea for all kinds of organizational challenges and problems. Although leadership, in one sense or another, often plays an important role, the effectiveness and results of organizations are normally an outcome of a variety of organizational and environmental contingencies as well as pure luck. For example, fans and directors of football clubs demand the replacement of coaches once the team exhibits poor performance. However, the success of a football team may be an outcome of a ball going two inches in the right or wrong direction, a key player becoming sick at a critical time or a referee's mistake. If a company's profit is below expectation, the perception is that leadership needs to change (usually by replacing the CEO). A company may however improve its results due to the oil price unexpectedly going down, or the exchange rate becoming more favourable, or a competitor facing a scandal. A CEO may be credited with good results, but might only be benefiting from wise decisions made much earlier in the corporate history that pay off at the time when the CEO is in office.

The idea that leadership is an answer to all sorts of societal and organizational problems is not without its problems. More often than not it is unclear what leadership means or actually entails in different situations. Often leadership talk is vague, naive and idealistic. 'Leadership' could mean almost everything since it is seldom defined or used in a precise or careful manner. Rather it is treated in very broad and positive terms and can refer to diverse things: from management, managerial work, collaboration and vision preaching to simply influencing, showing some initiative, massage egos or technical problem solving. The problems of the vagueness of leadership and the difficulties in sorting out its significance in relation to everything else that affects organizations does not prevent most groups from holding and expressing an almost religious belief in it. We need more leadership (leaders) and less management (managers) is a safe statement, likely to lead to agreement, praise and applause. To suggest that we need *less* leadership in organizations would probably raise eyebrows and be seen as a less serious view – perhaps even a joke – in many contexts. Particularly in a book on leadership – such as the one you are reading right now.

Nevertheless, this book suggests that we should be open to other options. Sometimes we might actually benefit from less emphasis, hope and investment (time and money) in leadership in favour of other ways of organizing work. Being aware of different options and thinking carefully about having more or less of leadership or other ways of organizing are vital. Of course this is not to say that we shouldn't also work hard to improve leadership. This book makes a strong case for reflexive leadership, which means that people – senior and junior – think carefully about how to organize work and how to use both leadership and other ways of organizing to make workplaces function well.

THE CASE FOR REFLEXIVE LEADERSHIP

It is important to acknowledge the often legitimate and important role of leadership. When we refer to leadership in this book we mean *influencing ideas, meanings, understandings and identities of others within an asymmetrical (unequal) relational context* (we will come back to this). Our point in this book is that we need to carefully consider what we mean by leadership, what it can and cannot do, when it might work, when it is not the best option and the alternative ways of organizing work. Sometimes leadership may be central, but so might management, the use of power and less hierarchical modes of organizing, including people being supported by teams, autonomy and professional networks rather than a leader. All this may be indirectly influenced by leadership that is, for example, focused on developing teams or encouraging people to use a broad set of contacts, but various modes of organizing often grow organically and are influenced by cultures, groups and individuals other than leaders.

As with 'non-leadership' approaches of organizing (e.g. bureaucracy, performance management, quality systems, entrepreneurship and professionalism) there are advantages and disadvantages to leadership. Take bureaucracy as an example – and in this context we are talking about the reliance on plans, rules, standard procedures which dominates in most organizations over a specific size and *not* red tape and rigidity. Bureaucracy often works well in standardized contexts; think of 'machine bureaucracies' such as McDonald's and airline companies (Mintzberg, 1983). It normally leads to efficiency and reliability *and* to alienation and a low degree of initiative and creativity. Professionalism is also often a good thing: there is expertise, autonomy and a common identity amongst professionals such as physicians, dentists and social workers. But there is also a monopolization of certain types of work and experts tend to be inward oriented, focused on status and group privilege and can avoid healthy competition from other groups. There is often a guild mentality, with limited openness and eagerness to distance the group from others. It is, at least sometimes, a mixed blessing.

In some contexts and in some respects leadership works well, sometimes less so. A simple example of the latter is a knowledge-intensive context where most employees are well educated and experienced, rely heavily on their judgement and work independently and/or with peers. Here the idea of emphasizing leadership is often unhelpful. People may not like it or view it as irrelevant. Leadership efforts – the boss trying to turn people into devoted followers – are often counter-productive in such situations, at least under normal conditions. Sure, there is a need for qualified administration and coordination and sometimes for a dose of policing, but this concerns management more than leadership.

So, thinking about leadership and its alternatives is important. Within leadership there are also alternatives. Later we will explore the meaning(s) of leadership and come back to alternatives. For the moment, we offer the reader an appetizer: we suggest the consideration of leadership in terms of the prophet, preacher, psychotherapist, party host and pedagogue, that is, the '5Ps' of doing leadership. These perhaps slightly playful labels draw attention to key activities of leadership: vision, values and morals, emotional support, a positive work climate, and learning and cognitive development. But more on this in Chapter 8.

Our idea is to avoid the inclination to adopt a sweeping view of leadership which equates it with everything 'good' and sees it as representing the solution to all kinds of problems. It is important to think about and use leadership ideas, but equally important to avoid being fixated on these – something that our contemporary leadership-worshipping age and the enormous leadership industry tend to seduce us into. But as the saying goes, if the only tool you have is a hammer, everything tends to be treated as a nail. If leadership is the key concept you are in love with and use then all relationships tend to be turned into leader/follower ones, which may create as much trouble and confusion as the hammer-carrier chasing nails all the time.

This leads us to the case for reflexivity. Like leadership, reflexivity is a buzzword – who does not want to be reflective (and most believe they are)?[1] But here we aim to take the concept seriously and will also discuss it (self-)critically. Being reflective essentially means that you are willing to consider what might be wrong with established ideas and beliefs, including your own. Thinking critically and considering alternatives are key. This will be more thoroughly discussed in the next chapter.

We aim to counter the habit of simply putting the good against the bad, even if we realize that many readers will not appreciate complicated messages. A simple, straightforward message is the key to all bestsellers in leadership. It is, however, also a reason for many problems. The simple solution – the supposedly superior, seductive leadership model – tends to foster unreflective mindlessness: simplistic, naive, over-optimistic beliefs. This is not typically what we need, although we do realize that we should not complicate things too much either.

LEADERSHIP: COVERING (ALMOST) EVERYTHING, BEING GOOD AND – THEREFORE – NECESSARY

In order to make sense of leadership an increasing number of writings have emerged over some three decades. This development has resulted in a large and fragmented field of concepts, models and theories that presents a rather confusing picture. As noted by Kets de Vries (1994, p. 73):

> When we plunge into the literature on leadership, we quickly become lost in a labyrinth: endless definitions, countless articles and never-ending polemics ... it seems that more has been studied about less and less, to end up ironically with researchers studying everything about nothing.

If we look at various versions and views of leadership, the list seems almost endless: task-oriented, relations-oriented, laissez-faire, charismatic, transformational, transactional, servant, authentic, practice-based, relational, emotional, distributed, shared, strategic, administrative, complex, coaching, symbolic, visionary, etc. And with this book the reader can add reflexive leadership to the perhaps already too long and complicated list. The reader may now feel that this book just adds another label and offers a pseudo-innovation. Hopefully not – we are pretty sure that we approach the topic in a rather new and constructive way and at least partly solve the problem of dealing with all this confusing mass (and mess) of leadership views and labels. But we will come back to this.

Much contemporary literature portrays leaders and leadership as strong and determined, with the ability to challenge, influence and change. In many descriptions of contemporary leaders – although not always explicit – there is a glow of heroism. These are people doing *high-powered influencing*. Success – and also failure for that matter – are regularly attributed to the leader and his/her traits, behaviour or style. Traditionally, leadership related to people expected to carry out supervision in one sense or another in relation to their subordinates. Now, the leadership industry is much more into targeting broader and more abstract organizational issues such as culture, identity, vision and strategy. The focus has moved from supervisors and middle-level managers to CEOs and other senior people. A popular variant of the hero theme is how leaders' behaviour, traits and abilities help to develop organizations in light of difficult challenges. Visionary and strategic leadership linked to radical change and development is often in focus. Leadership is about highly significant issues, forming the overall organizational direction, and is key for organizational survival.

But the field is broad and complex and there are also low-key, 'post-heroic' ideas on leadership. Leadership is here viewed as less spectacular and consisting of *more mundane actions*; the everyday managers are portrayed as humble and hardworking heroes who manage to accomplish change – or maintain high quality and efficiency – and business success incrementally. In a bestselling management book about how to be better than good it is suggested that the difference between excellent and mediocre organizations is intimately related to leader traits such as humbleness, endurance, professional will and a strong determination to contribute to creating organizational rather personal wealth (Collins, 2001).

This view is also expressed in leadership that involves listening, small talk, showing recognition, coaching and other ordinary activities. It is often suggested that leaders should have close contact with organizational reality and be engaged, supportive and positive – sometimes framed as varieties of post-heroism. Occasionally well-being among subordinates is made central – it is expected that the leader should contribute to a stimulating, fun, friendly and cosy working atmosphere. To this we can add that leadership also includes personal development, ethics, diversity, equality and organizational health.

Based on this brief overview of some common themes in leadership it is clear that there is a multitude of demands and expectations on leaders and on what leadership can (and should) accomplish. Normally we expect managers at a variety of different levels – including middle management – to exhibit a host of skills and traits to meet these demands in modern organizations. However, often there is a mismatch between demands and what the great majority of managers are capable of doing. They lack the skills, time and interest to do all this. And they are expected to do many other things, including carrying out regular managerial work in administration as well as the operative work that is necessary for complex organizations to function.

An important development over the last two decades or so is that junior and middle managers are exposed to mixed messages about what is commonly known as *micro-management*, that is, the supervision or control of detailed behaviour and predictable deliveries.[2] All managers, regardless of their position in the corporate food-chain are nowadays more or less assumed to exercise leadership. Thus they are all expected to take charge of accomplishing change, facilitating engagement and formulating vision and strategy (Alvesson & Spicer, 2011). People's work as leaders rather than traditional managers is now regarded as paramount in managerial work. At least this is the case on the level of rhetoric. In practice it is – as we will see in this book – often quite different. Making sure that everything works and that there are deliveries of products, services, reports, etc. are key for most organizations. This is often hard to do without a strong focus on operative management.

Much of the contemporary writing on leadership – authentic, coaching, transformational – focuses on trying to identify the specific traits and styles that make an effective leader in terms of *being good*. Leadership is almost always used as a 'hurrah' word. Leaders do good things such as improve business, health care, schools and generally make sure that organizations are working properly. Leaders are associated with positive things such as having vision, being bold and good at communicating, and exhibiting good judgement, integrity and self-confidence. Rather than pointing at fanatic dictators and terrorists such as Hitler, Mussolini, Stalin or Osama bin Laden as illustrations of leaders who were extraordinarily successful in mobilizing followers, we often see other more popular and positive people in business and society portrayed as leaders, even though the former fanatics were successful in inspiring and influencing followers to sacrifice their own interests and subject themselves to the cause of the leader, both enthusiastically and voluntarily. In the great majority of contemporary leadership literature leaders are assumed to be good people with noble intentions who produce excellent results (Bass & Steidlmeier, 1999). The idea of leadership as inherently good is explicitly formulated by one of the most influential leadership writers of the last decade, James Burns (2003, p. 2):

> I believe leadership is not only a descriptive term but a prescriptive one, embracing a moral, even a passionate, dimension. Consider our common usage. We don't call for good leadership – we expect, or at least hope, that it will be good. 'Bad' leadership implies *no* leadership. I contend that there is nothing neutral about leadership; it is valued as a moral necessity.

By confining leadership to good and moral things leadership writers may be able to offer lofty and beautiful stories and images of leadership in a fairly uncomplicated and positive world in which good people lead others to produce good results. The development of leadership as something inherently good and connected to some extraordinary individuals also makes people more inclined to subordinate themselves to leadership without perhaps problematizing or reflecting on how it is presented. Often it is addressed tautologically: leadership is good in terms of morality and effectiveness, and can be observed through good outcomes (problem-solving, people thinking that their needs are fulfilled, a positive meaning has been expressed and consumed by transformed followers). This reflects our inclination to avoid connecting supposedly good things – such as how we like to see leadership – with bad things such as tyranny and bullying, or people having bad ideas or being seduced by wishful thinking and excessive positivity (this will be elaborated on in Chapter 4). The result is that if we believe that leadership by definition is good, we also want to understand the result of it as good (Burns, 2003). And if we want to understand something as bad, then we search for other explanations than leadership. Or use vocabulary that this is not 'real' leadership, but 'toxic', 'inauthentic' or something else bad. We are governed by our assumptions and ideologies and tend to be reluctant to observe, interpret or remember things that contradict our worldview. This is deeply problematic.

As ideas on leadership cover so much – from vision and overall organizational direction to mundane, everyday interactions with followers – and leadership is so good and powerful, it becomes clear that *leadership is necessary*. It is extremely important; it can – if carried out according to the right formula (or done in the superior artistic, creative way) – turn the lazy, stupid and bewildered into a group of committed, competent and vision-guided people and lead to corporate excellence. In other words, leadership is crucial for people's improvement and performance and for the success of organizations as a whole. This is the overall message of the leadership industry. We are wise to take this message with some caution. It is seductive but often deceptive.

Leadership as a way to accomplish influence has its place – in a variety of forms – but so do other modes of organizing work. Rather than assuming that good things always go together in harmony, this book aims to facilitate a more reflective view of leadership, by considering alternatives and taking a more restrained and focused view of the phenomenon.

LEADERSHIP – A MORE FOCUSED VIEW

The dominance of leadership as a solution to all kinds of problems in contemporary organizations counteracts reflections on alternative ways of approaching problems of coordination and influence. Both managers and others tend to employ leadership as a means of heroism and self-aggrandizement:

> [Leadership] may be more enticing (than the nuts and bolts of the down-to-earth-manager), but that has led to an awful lot of hubris in organizations these days: heroic leadership disconnected from the requirements of plain old managing. (Mintzberg, 2012, p. 327)

What makes this view on leadership problematic is that, as already pointed out, leadership has come to mean basically anything and everything that has a positive ring to it. We need to think in more precise and differentiated ways about organizing in order to mitigate muddled thinking. The fusion of leadership and management has been mentioned above. Post-heroic concepts like delegating or distributed leadership indicate a significant level of subordinates' autonomy, but this is viewed as an outcome of the leader's decision (or lack of time or even laziness), and therefore still leadership-driven.

An alternative view is of course that autonomous, resourceful or counter-dependent people give managers little choice than to abstain from doing much leadership. That is not to say that management or even the exercises of power/brute force are irrelevant, unimportant or not requested by the same people. But leadership is usually put forth as the superior solution almost independently of what the problem is or how challenging the reality might be. Indeed, it is a label that has attained a threatening hegemony in terms of how we think about organizational processes and results. Following this dominance of leadership, we suggest that there are good reasons to be cautious and reflective about the image of leadership and its significance for the organizations that we develop. The risk of leadership, even though well-intended, being a source of stupidity is profound (Alvesson & Spicer, 2016).

In this book we therefore suggest a more restrained view of leadership that does not include everything in terms of influencing or give the impression that the choice is between leadership and leadership. We therefore restrict leadership to be about people involved in an *asymmetrical* (unequal) *relationship* (formally or informally, permanently or temporarily, but not only momentarily) *involving followers*. Leaders are *interpersonally trying to define meaning/reality for others who are inclined to (on a largely voluntary basis) accept such meaning-making and reality-defining influencing acts*.

Where people are more or less on an equal footing there is no point talking about leadership. When the focus is less on meaning and more on behaviour, rules, output and other issues, leadership is not a productive term to use. This is broadly in line with most of the literature which tries to distinguish leadership from management (e.g. Ladkin, 2010; Smircich & Morgan, 1982; Zaleznik, 1977). We do, however, dissociate ourselves from all the distinctions between leadership and management where leadership is said to be about doing the right thing or creating change, while allegedly unsexy management is about doing things right or creating stability. Leadership can mean doing what later turns out to be the 'wrong' thing and much leadership is about maintaining morale, influencing meanings, ideas, values and emotions, so that organizations function well in everyday life, not just creating radical change.

This view of leadership recognizes the social, relational and processual character of leadership. It involves both leaders and followers engaged in mutual interaction based on the influencing of meaning and understanding. It goes beyond a static attention to the individual leader and his/her ideas, convictions and personal psychology. In contrast, leadership can productively be seen as a social phenomenon, something expressed in asymmetrical but mutual and voluntary relations between individuals labelled leaders and followers, depending on the directions of influence. Management contrasts to leadership in that the latter demands efforts at influencing meaning – dealing in interpretations, emotions and understandings. Leadership as influencing meaning is thus closely related to efforts in influencing culture. This influence is intentionally directed, relatively systematic and built upon asymmetry – but not necessarily in a formal sense – between individuals. In an interpersonal relationship someone that we see as a 'high influential person' (HIP) takes on a leader role in terms of influencing, while another person, a 'low influential person' (LIP), takes on a follower role in terms of holding back independent views and opinions. Of course relations shift. A senior manager or a leading professional may be a HIP in relation to junior people, but a LIP in relation to top management or a world authority within the profession.

This view of leadership is mainly based on voluntary compliance. People position themselves as followers based not on legal requirements or out of fear of negative sanctions, but because leadership acts provide some form of meaningful as well as practical, emotionally and morally convincing, direction. In this way leadership forms the basis for motivation since it provides some sensible idea or purpose in terms of performing specific work tasks.

It is also important to acknowledge the context in which the leadership processes are situated. The local organizational or workplace context is crucial. But so are other levels; industry, professional and broader cultural, societal and ideological contexts matter. It is however important to bear in mind that when we talk about leadership in this book, we primarily refer to leadership in modern corporate and public sector organizational contexts and not to political leadership, leadership in social movements or military combat situations. This is reflected both in the practical examples provided as well as the theories and academic studies referred to throughout the book. At the same time, most of what we say is also relevant to understanding informal and 'non-regular organizational' contexts.

A key quality of this more restrained or precise view of leadership is that it becomes something distinct from management, professional autonomy, group work and other alternative forms of achieving influence. For example, the conventionally powerful hierarchical situation of managers does not necessarily imply that they are also leaders in terms of influencing people's understanding of the significance of accomplishing specific work tasks. The latter may be related to the exercise of power or the workings of professional norms. Leadership occurs when people voluntarily let themselves become led in terms of understanding and interpreting what it is necessary and desirable to accomplish. This often includes more subtle and less spectacular actions influencing social processes and organizing relations. The interaction of leaders and followers is key, not only for leaders acting but for followers responding. This restrained and contextually sensitive approach to leadership demands a more reflective and finely tuned understanding of the phenomenon rather than the assumptions that are taken for granted and pervasive in much contemporary leadership literature.

THE PURPOSE OF THIS BOOK

The general purpose of this book is to support a more reflexive attitude towards leadership in organizations. As discussed, in this context reflexivity refers to thinking broadly and critically about one's thinking and one's self in relation to others. This includes critically examining the vocabulary on important subject matters such as leadership and considering alternative positions. Even if leadership is important and relevant it still needs to be approached in a reflexive manner in order to allow for the consideration of alternatives to leadership (being one of several modes of organizing) and of different versions of leadership. In this book we refer to two forms of reflexivity: the first as 'extra-leadership reflexivity' (ELR) and the second as 'intra-leadership reflexivity' (ILR). These two concepts, as well as the very notion of reflexivity in relation to leadership, will be explored in more detail in Chapter 2.

We aim to reach three large audiences. The first is people who want an advanced theoretical understanding of leadership and other organizing issues beyond the introductory level, that is, scholars and students. The second is the leadership industry – those interested in selling leadership and claiming to improve leaders and leadership through advice, training and recipes. The third is practitioners expected to contribute to leadership in various organizations, for example managers (not political leaders and not primarily CEOs, presidents or other top executives, but rather more 'average' managers in modern organizations), senior professionals and also subordinates or junior people, who are always more or less actively and thoughtfully influencing leadership relations, that is, by taking or not taking follower positions. We thus cast a rather wide net.

The three groups overlap, many academics are also part of the leadership industry – leadership development is a source of income (and sometimes of intellectual corruption) for many – and those in the leadership industry are also often practitioners – HR Managers and publishers also do leadership. Practitioners are students of leadership on MBA programmes, in executive education and other contexts. The three groups nevertheless differ in some key respects – not least by their interest in theoretical sophistication, the time available for reading and thinking, and in their eagerness for the take-away or pay-off of reading a text like this.

The book is therefore a balance between different readers' needs and wants. Our aim is to make it a bit more provocative and characterized by strong points than is perhaps common in academic literature. We do not aim to reproduce the assumptions and seductive nature of most texts aiming to appeal to the leadership industry and managers. We hope thereby to be much more useful than most of the leadership literature.

One modest ambition of the book is to contribute more good than bad – although this depends a great deal on the efforts of the reader to think and reflect when reading the text. As we demonstrate in the book, much leadership thinking does not seem to make people smarter or organizational life easier, but rather seduces managers and others into naive and overoptimistic beliefs that lead to clashes between great hopes and imperfect reality (Sveningsson & Alvesson, 2016).

THE STRUCTURE OF THE BOOK

We start with our key concept of reflexivity (Chapter 2), before we provide a slightly critical overview of established leadership theories (Chapter 3). Reflexivity is motivated by the need to be careful about seductive ideologies and vague language use (Chapter 4), as well as the overall influence of culture on leadership (Chapter 5) and the significance of followers for leadership (Chapter 6) – how people respond to leadership efforts is partly a matter of relations and interaction within the organizational and professional cultural context. (The same leadership behaviour can be viewed as democratic or laid-back in the military and rather authoritarian in a professional organization where peer relations dominate.) In Chapters 7 and 8 we address alternative ways of organizing and doing leadership, for example extra- and intra-leadership reflexivity (ELR, IRL). Chapter 9 deals with the complexities and imperfections of organizational reality and argues for a more realistic view on leadership. In Chapters 10 and 11 the theme is how to make the people involved view relationships and organizing work in broadly similar ways and how to encourage good communication and mutual understandings as well as adjustment. The focus is on the joint doings of ELR and IRL. In Chapters 12 and 13 we address reflexive subjects and groups, both in senior and junior positions, under the labels of, respectively, reflexive leadership and reflexive followership – although we also indicate the need to be reflexive 'outside' leadership and followership and to organize in other ways than through leadership/followership. The final chapter concludes and discusses further practical possibilities. We here return to the importance of realism. Demands on reflexivity that are too high can lead to problems – 'reflexive heroism' is a trap we want to avoid. A balanced and pragmatic view is needed.

The structure of the chapters listed above is a mix of a logical order and our wish to address some key themes that do not necessarily build directly on other themes. Some chapters can therefore be read independently of others.

We have in an appendix a number of questions aimed to stimulate reflexivity for readers that are involved in leadership and/or managerial practice, as leaders or followers. Many of these can also be used in organizational and leadership development projects.

NOTES

1. Reflective for us means carefully thinking and perhaps re-thinking how to deal with a problem or how to generally relate to a theme. Reflexivity stands for multi-level or broader forms of reflections. Being reflexive addresses the issues and also how you think about issues, e.g. reflections on reflections or meta-reflections. 'How can I improve the vision? 'is reflective. 'Where is this idea of working with visions coming from and is it a good idea?', is reflexive. More about this in Chapter 2.
2. The early leadership studies mainly studied supervisors, including their micro-management, and not directly leadership as typically understood today, e.g. broader influence on ideas, meanings, values, and so forth.

2

On Reflection and Reflexivity

Reflection can be understood as: '[A]n important human activity in which people recapture their experience, think about it, mull it over and evaluate it' (Boud et al., 1985, p. 19). Most people are to some extent reflective and many probably believe they are well above average on this quality. In contemporary society we have access to a variety of information, viewpoints and experiences. We are seldom locked up in a closed world. We draw inspiration from various sources that can trigger reflection. We consult mass media, listen to lecturers, we talk to people and receive new experiences when we face various situations. We act, see what happens and try to learn. Circumstances and conditions change and can act as triggers to think a bit more deeply about various matters; from the meaning of life to what is worth doing and how I can deal with people in my surroundings – subordinates, superiors, colleagues, friends, network contacts. Sometimes things stay the same, which can also trigger reflection. Saturation, boredom, the limited effects of one's ideas and efforts may also offer food for thought. Generally, we live in an age that scores high on reflexivity in key respects (Giddens, 1991).

Reflection is important and a feature of being human, although the interest and ability to engage in it varies enormously. Besides individual cognitive capacity and ambitions, contextual conditions can also serve as important barriers to reflection. Those contextual barriers can be structural, for example narrow role descriptions, limited time to think, performance management systems that do not reward radical thinking, limited contact with other units and peers. They can also be cultural, for example strong orientation towards consensus and wanting to agree with others, respect for authorities, strong traditions. People can also deliberately refrain from reflection – even if they have both the capacity and the opportunity – in order to make life easier, which is an example of 'functional stupidity' (Alvesson & Spicer, 2012). Functional stupidity means that one complies with available truths and norms – and goes with the flow, doing things in the 'right' way rather than asking if this really is the right thing to do.

Reflective practice (Schön, 1983) is often described in terms of reflection-in-action (thinking what one is doing while one is doing it – thinking on one's feet) and reflection-on-action (after the experience one analyses one's reaction to the situation and explores the reasons around, and the consequences of, one's actions). Some also add reflection-before-action, meaning 'thinking through what one wants to do and how one intends to do it before one actually does it' (Greenwood, 1998, p. 1049).

In this book we refer to reflection but we are not interested in the more limited and narrow forms that dominate, for example whether I should use a small or big hammer or ask the boss for a pay rise before or after the weekend, or trying to find out why a subordinate is so grumpy. We aim for, and try to encourage, something more ambitious: reflection plus or even plus-plus, meaning thinking deeply *and* broadly about issues. Often reflection is based on a certain framework and some specific assumptions guide thinking. People reflect on tactics and actions, on how to reach a specific objective, or the consequences of a decision.

There is a large literature dealing with issues like this, for instance by Argyris, Boud, Kolb, Schön and others. Argyris (1982), for example, talks about single-loop learning, where people try to learn but are caught in a framework, trying to solve a problem without varying the method or questioning the overall goal. A relevant example would be how an organization that feels that the leadership is not delivering demands *more* (of the same) leadership or better performance from management, or more intensively hammers out the preferred core messages in order to get the proper effect. This tendency to think 'within the box' is often contrasted with double-loop learning, where not only the method but also the ultimate goals and assumptions you proceed from are questioned. As said, we are mainly interested in broader and more ambitious forms of reflection and a particular ideal for how to relate to reality as well as one's own thinking, values, objectives and self-view. We refer to this as reflexivity. It is, in the present context, very much about being capable and interested in both intra- and extra-leadership reflexivity.

REFLEXIVITY

We define reflexivity as *the ambition to carefully and systematically take a critical view of one's own assumptions, ideas and favoured vocabulary and to consider if alternative ones make sense* (Alvesson & Sköldberg, 2009). Reflexivity is then the antithesis of thinking as a reflex (i.e. leaning towards standard interpretations or predictable lines of thinking) and at the same time more than simple reflection (just thinking about things) since it involves interpretations of our interpretations. Reflexivity means a willingness to scrutinize and challenge one's position – image, sense-making and vocabulary on a subject matter (such as one's work and one's self) – and consider alternative positions (Bourdieu, 1992). Reflexivity means an effort to avoid cultural conventions and truths associated with tradition, fashion and what is institutionalized. It means working with – reflecting upon and problematizing – assumptions and counter-assumptions. In other words not just focusing on a specific problem but more broadly engaging in meta-reflection. How do I think about these issues? Where do my ideas come from? Am I seduced by a particular vocabulary? Are there favoured terms that may hide contradictions and problems? What may be problematic about my assumptions and convictions? Do I have fixed ideas? Do I have ideological or cultural blinders? How come I have been convinced that a particular framework, key idea or norm is the right or the best one?

Reflexivity means a willingness and capacity to switch position and think about issues from a different angle. You take a couple of steps back and carefully think about the broader issues at stake. 'Doubt' is a key component that fuels critical thinking (Schön, 1983). A 'playful frame of mind' is another:

> When we adopt a playful attitude, we're more open to possibilities. It's OK to be inconsistent [in contrast to keeping on clinging to a rigid self-concept] from one day to the next. That's not being a fake; it's how we experiment to figure out what's right for the new challenges and circumstances we face. (Ibarra, 2015, p. 11)

As a result, one might be able to see things in a new light and consider alternative problem definitions and thereby new solutions. Or realize that this is perhaps not really a problem and the possible solution may bring new and worse problems. Sometimes it can be good to simply recognize that there are imperfections and frustrations in life and this just needs to be accepted rather than turned into an object for policies, regulations, sanctions, structures or leadership. Reflexivity takes some time, but it is more a matter of an intellectual orientation, involving curiosity, openness and a willingness to rethink one's position. Reflexivity is also dependent on knowledge and frameworks. It calls for theoretical support, not so much specific models and recipes for how to do leadership, but for ideas on how to choose between different versions of leadership or to do things in organizations other than working with leadership.

Of course the self-reflection theme (know yourself) within leadership is all but new. Lately, the increased interest in 'authenticity' can be seen as an example, where your 'true self' should shine through and guide your leadership efforts. To understand and get in contact with your true self might sound like a good reflexive exercise, but in reality it can often turn out to be the very opposite. Problems arise when ready-made templates (coaching, transformational, listening, people-oriented, result-oriented) are used in a naive and context-insensitive way (Ibarra, 2015):

> [T]he notion of adhering to one 'true self' flies in the face of much research on how people evolve with experience, discovering facets of themselves they would never have unearthed through introspection alone. And being utterly transparent – disclosing every single thought and feeling – is both unrealistic and risky (p. 3) ...

> Think of leadership development as trying on possible selves rather than working on yourself. (p. 11)

REFLEXIVE LEADERSHIP AND ALTERNATIVE MODES OF ORGANIZING AND THINKING

As indicated in the previous chapter, leadership is a suggestive, fashionable and broad term that easily attracts and seduces. It is thus a source of much naivety, wishful thinking and even stupidity. Three criteria need to be met for a concept, like leadership, to be intellectually and practically useful.

1. It needs to be reasonably distinct and not cover everything and nothing.
2. It needs to aid thinking rather than just sound good and promising.
3. It needs to allow for complexity, not just set good against bad but instead acknowledge that the two actually often go hand in hand and that many things are not easy to categorize in terms of right or wrong.

Leadership is tricky in all respects – it tends to be used broadly and vaguely and is often used in ways involving and promising all sorts of good things. And it is often used for rhetorical appeal rather than to help people think through issues carefully. Therefore leadership talk often has an 'anti-reflexive' effect.

Striving for 'simplicity' is often the enemy of reflexivity, as is the case in many best-selling texts produced by the leadership industry as well as quotes and one-liners made by celebrated leaders, such as the founder of the Virgin conglomerate, Richard Branson (2013): 'Complexity is your enemy. Any fool can make something complicated. It is hard to keep things simple'. A major actor in the global leadership industry – The Ken Blanchard Companies (named after its founder and one of the architects behind the Situational leadership theory as later discussed in Chapter 3) – also describes its 'World-Class Leadership Model' in terms of simplicity (emphasis added):[1]

> Our programs are based on behavioural models that mirror this development process and are easily applied in the workplace. As a result, leaders learn how to lead in any situation, teams ramp up faster, and individuals are more empowered and effective. It is the power and the *simplicity* of the situational context that has made our model one of the most widely adopted leadership processes in the world.

Taken together, the message seems to be that leadership should be *kept* simple, and not *made* complicated. But leadership – as theory and practice – may actually benefit from moving away from (over)simplifications to instead acknowledging its complexity. The trick is to find concepts and ideas that balance complications and simplifications, so that people can grasp, remember and use ideas but at the same time recognize and acknowledge the complexities and nuances involved in human relations.

We therefore need to try to restrict the use of the term 'leadership' and to avoid uncritically associating it directly with a lot of good things (this will be further discussed in Chapter 4). Sharpness and neutrality are hard to achieve when it comes to themes and vocabulary that tend to be used in positive ways, but it is important to avoid the fluffiness and ideologization that often characterize use of leadership terminology. In particular, popular ideas regularly score high on a combination of fluffiness and ideologization – satisfying demands for entertainment, identification, fantasies and wishful thinking more than clear and realistic thinking. The former often leads to leadership ideas being more of a source of problems than a solution (Sveningsson & Alvesson, 2016). We are therefore eager to suggest alternative terms and a range of options for thinking and acting in terms of organizing work. The good versus bad set-up is to be avoided, or at least minimized. We thereby hope to be able to offer some intellectual support for reflexivity.

The case for reflexivity in leadership consists of two key themes. The first theme is leadership in relation to alternative modes of organizing and the second is reflexivity 'within' leadership as such. We thus consider *leadership and its alternatives*, which we label 'extra-leadership reflexivity' (ELR), and, within the former, alternatives *within* leadership or 'intra-leadership reflexivity' (ILR). We then take into account how managers and others may consider doing leadership in comparison to other forms of organizing, and, when leadership is viewed as the right thing, what version of leadership is considered to be relevant. We discuss these briefly below and return to them more extensively in later chapters. In particular, ILR will be presented briefly, but will later be a key theme in Chapters 5–6, and further elaborated on in terms of various 'leadership domains' in Chapter 9.

ELR – Reflection upon alternative forms of organizing

Alternatives to leadership – framed in the restrained terms of an asymmetrical influencing process focusing on meaning, as explained in Chapter 1 and elaborated on below – need to be carefully considered. In many situations modes other than leadership may actually do most of the organizing.

We suggest a framework of five practices as alternatives and supplements to leadership:

- Management;
- Exercise of (coercive) power;
- Peer influencing (via networks);
- Group work; and
- Autonomy (self-management).

In Table 2.1 we summarize and exemplify the six terms we are using, that is, the five mentioned above plus leadership.

Management, the exercise of power and leadership refer to predominantly *vertical* (hierarchical) modes of organizing. The other three can be labelled mainly *horizontal* organizing processes. Of course, almost all practices include both vertical and horizontal elements, as almost nothing is purely hierarchical or egalitarian. Also, subordinates who push for their opinions or exhibit resistance influence senior people who try to exercise management. Peers are more or less resourceful, respected and capable of making other people inclined to be influenced by their ideas. It is not always the case that peers only have horizontal or egalitarian relations. But for reasons of clarity and simplicity, we emphasize the vertical (mainly hierarchy-based) and horizontal (primarily egalitarian) forms of organizing. The vertical is based on pronounced asymmetrical (unequal) relations. At work these are often but not necessarily based on formal rights and resources and involve some degree of 'force' or pressure to comply. In leadership the vertical position is based less on formal rights and more on asymmetries in terms of intelligence, experience, overview, rhetorical skills, charisma/aura. The horizontal is

Table 2.1 Modes of organizing

Mode of organizing	Dominant orientation	Definition and meaning	Key identities	Examples of acts or settings
Leadership	Vertical Persuasion	Interpersonal influencing process in an asymmetrical relationship, targeting meaning, feelings and values	Leader (HIP) and follower (LIP)	Inspirational talk/behaviour in order to give direction, meaning and emotional and/or moral support. Exemplary behaviour
Management	Vertical Legitimate authority	Direction and control based on formal rights and hierarchy	Manager (HIP) and subordinate (LIP)	Planning, budgeting, supervision, schedules/rules/guidelines, and performance control/evaluation
Exercise of power	Vertical Anxiety	Authority based on force and/or political skills	Dominant (HIP) and less dominant actor (LIP) in a power game	Shows authority, uses threats and sanctions, promising rewards, mobilizing group pressure, use of client/patron networks.
Network (peer) influencing	Horizontal Persuasion/advice	Guidance and support from peers within the same occupational specialty/community of practice (outside one's own work group/organizational unit)	Respected and receptive colleagues (MIP)	Work in subject-matter expert networks, conferences or informal contacts/ad hoc problem solving. Informal meetings outside work meetings, lunches, etc.
Group work	Horizontal Persuasion or group pressure	Guidance and support from members of the work group	Responsible and responsive team members (MIP)	Co-decision making, team meetings and mutual adjustments on a daily basis
Autonomy	Horizontal Competence	Self-directed work processes	Autonomous professional (NIP)	Thinking for yourself, setting own standards, planning and evaluating your own work and performance. Reading and reflection reinforcing self-confidence and good judgement

based on influence, often of a mutual kind. You may have a colleague who is charismatic, experienced, respected and one that others tend to listen to, without having a formal superiority. That person can function as an informal leader in many situations. In several cases there is, however, also some formal recognition and support for that person, for example having a title as a senior or project leader or being responsible for a committee, etc. So the purely 'informal' leader is often not that informal, but we need to acknowledge informal leadership. (We make no strict distinction between leadership and informal leadership as leadership is always to some extent 'non-formal' – as opposed to management. Our major interest in this book is, however, leadership exercised by managers.)

We of course recognize the many ambiguous cases where the six positions are mixed, but in order to make our point clear we talk about these in terms of 'pure' versions.

The three vertical modes of organizing resemble Grint's (2005) suggestion of using the categories command, management and leadership (even if what we refer to as 'power' is not covered there), but we do not necessarily link the different variants to the nature of a specific 'problem' or to the decision-making that Grint highlights. We do not restrict leadership to only being about the solving of wicked problems. We see leadership as working with people in very different ways; including influencing morale, emotion and values.

In this discussion we could also have mentioned commonly known control mechanisms such as organizational factors, technical control, bureaucracy, input control/standardization, output control/performance measurement, client control, normative control and other similar forms (see e.g. Mintzberg, 1983). We will touch upon many of these control mechanisms later in the book, but do not highlight them for two reasons. The first is that we do not want to cover the entire field of management and organizational control, but to maintain focus on leadership and 'nearby' themes. The second is that we think that 'our' six modes of organizing come closer to what is relevant in a typical work situation in an organization, where people do not have the influence and resources of top management of large organizations. Instead, you typically work with one person or a few dozen people around or 'below' you. The average manager expected/trying to do leadership has limited ability to restructure the entire organization or decide on new performance management systems. S/he still works with adaptations within overall organizational control structures, meaning that there is an interplay or intersection between the five organizing modes mentioned plus leadership and overall 'given' forms of control. Top managers doing leadership (as defined in this book) are mainly working with and through a limited number of people, such as senior managers and people in staff positions. A CEO of a large company occasionally reaches and marginally affects the majority of subordinates through emails, letters and public speeches. On a daily basis subordinates are usually more influenced by management in terms of policies, labour processes, rules, reward systems, budgets, schedules and cost-cutting, but this is not leadership.

To repeat: based on our view of leadership as often more informal and involving a strong degree of voluntary influence, we refer not only to senior position-holders but also to other people who are resourceful, respected, admired and likely to be listened to.

The term 'high influential person' (HIP) captures both these and formal managers, where the latter has some influence, something which we cannot take as given, as many managers may have a weak impact, particular in strongly constrained organizations and situations and when subordinates have a strong position. Think of a manager in a machine-like distribution system or a highly automated factory, or a head of department at a university with many strong professors. Standardized processes and systems as well as academic culture and resourceful individuals will limit the space for leadership.

In this book we sometimes talk about leaders, sometimes managers, sometimes HIPs. In terms of verbs we use the terms leading, managing (doing managerial work), and exercising power – all three are viewed as vertical high influencing processes. Leader/ leadership refers to a person who influences through meaning and persuasion (where following and paying attention is largely voluntary) and management/managerial work is based on formal rights/obligations and refers to the planning, structure and control of work (obedience within the employment contract that is less voluntary, even if 'exit' is usually an option). Power refers to the use of force or coercion – situations where actors move outside voluntary influencing processes or the formal managerial role and the employment contract, and mobilize alternative and more coercive power resources in order to break resistance and get things done. The use of coercive power may naturally include bullying and other unethical behaviour in order to achieve results. It may also include use of resources for the social good – such as employing networks, linguistic resources, agenda setting, exaggerations of or bypassing formal rights, mobilizing group pressure – in order to deal with, for example bullying, discrimination, laziness and other problematic issues not easily dealt with through conventional management. Sometimes bullying the bully may be perceived as ethically acceptable or raising a voice to people hiding behind formal policies. Drawing upon power may also involve pressing conservative groups and people into changes assessed as necessary. Politics and power play are key parts of organizations (Cunha et al., 2013; Jackall, 1988; Morgan, 1986) and are key aspects frequently overlooked by much management and leadership literature that favours consensus, harmony and/or 'respectable' forms of power. The concept of HIP then covers a variety of vertical exercises of influence, including power. In many cases it is difficult to separate leadership, management and power. They also often work in tandem. HIP may then be a useful term, but the main purpose of our approach is to encourage thought and action based on considerations of more specific forms of leadership and alternative ways of organizing work. Following this we often draw upon and talk about leadership – our key focus – but sometimes other labels (including the broader concept HIP) are more precise and relevant.

Correspondingly, we are interested in followers – the pendant and partner to leaders – but it often makes more sense to refer to 'non-managers' or 'non-leaders'. Sometimes it is more precise to see them as subordinates (emphasizing their subordination to managers within the constraints of the employment contract and legitimate, formal authority. For a more detailed elaboration on this see Chapter 6). You follow your leader because you are convinced, but comply with your manager because of rights and responsibilities associated with the employment contract. When power in the sense previously described is at stake, the terms low-powered individuals or targets for power make more sense than the label 'follower', since people 'follow' less but are 'pushed' by more resourceful actors. A common label for all these positions or roles is 'low influence persons' ('LIPs' or people in low influencing positions). This term works in tandem with HIPs. 'Low' is relevant as all relationships involve influencing – followers/subordinates/targets of power also exercise power, but the position and influence is relatively weaker than the HIP. Not always and in all respects, but most of the time and in key respects.

While positions like middle manager or senior manager are 'fixed' positions, HIPs and LIPs are always within a relationship and more fluid. Almost no one is always a HIP. A vice-president may be a HIP in most work relations but may be a LIP in relation to the president or another more influential vice-president.

In horizontal modes of organizing, the presence of HIPs and LIPs is not that salient.[2] In group works and in networks of peers organizing means that horizontal influence dominates. People remind each other about norms, give advice and support and coordinate their work based on mutual adjustment, not followership or formal subordination or as an effect of power in use. We can talk about 'medium influencing people' (MIPs) taking care of the organizing. In a top management team where the CEO is not significantly stronger than the others, relations may be best described as MIPs, that is, most people are medium-influential. Formal positions are of course very important, but our interest is in the actual relations, which may deviate from formal ones.

In group work it is the team that is crucial. There is close-range influencing, sometimes leading to rather strong and even harsh norm-setting from which it is much more difficult to escape (concertive control, Barker & James, 1993). A united and tight group is often a much more powerful source of influence and control than a single HIP. In some cases, where a team has a common purpose and works on a project that is distinct, group work may be crucial for supervision and influencing. In many cases, groups are not that united and the impact of colleagues is fairly loose, but still people may rely on the group's resources as much or more than on the HIP.

Peer influencing may overlap with group work, but often peers can be quite distant and not belong to the team, department or other close-range directly influential work unity. Network contacts may take place within an organization but also in professional communities or private networks. Often if a person experiences a work-related problem and needs to get technical advice or to talk about conflicts or other interpersonal difficulties, s/he contacts people in the network – friends, colleagues, former managers or relatives. Many functions normally attributed to leadership, such as coaching, mentoring and providing technical advice and moral support, can be executed perfectly well by people who are not involved in work directly. People with extensive networks may be quite leader-independent as there are others who can be mobilized for help with support and direction. Listening to others may also reduce the inclination to be strongly influenced by the manager's communication of values and ideas. As a professional – teacher, physician, lawyer, academic, social worker – you may not necessarily go to your manager or nearest colleagues, but to the most competent person you know and have confidence in on a specific subject matter. Even the best of all managers/leaders may not be as excellent on certain types of issues, so going outside HIP/LIP relationships often makes sense. As with group work, this usually indicates and involves MIPs – medium influencing people and processes. In a network, there is often a process of reciprocity. Others help you and in return you try (and are expected) to help them.

Then we have the case of autonomy. Of course no person is completely autonomous, just as no person is solely a follower, subordinate, object of acts of power, group member or network contact, but a lot of work in organizations is done independently of others. A person who is responsible for planning, executing and monitoring his/her own work is referred to by some as a self-leader or self-manager due to the high degree of control and influence over that work (Manz & Sims, 1987). This represents another example where the labels leader and manager may be misleading since there are no subordinates and/or followers. We prefer the term autonomous. Here we can talk of 'no influencing people' (NIPs), in the sense that most of the work is carried out in some isolation from others, and without much direct influencing of or from others on a daily basis.

In organizations we have all these types of influence. Often they are not as clear or straightforward as presented here. In groups and networks there can be asymmetries and the presence of HIPs and LIPs, apart from the MIPs mentioned. In cases of autonomy, there may have been an earlier leader who influenced people so that they have the competence, self-confidence and 'correct' orientations to now be autonomous. The significance of the position of HIPs and LIPs is, however, much less prominent in horizontal processes compared to the vertical ones previously described. Here, MIPs and NIPs dominate.

A significant advantage of working with the six categories – three vertical (leadership, management and power) and three horizontal (group, peers/networks and autonomy) – is that they indicate alternatives and encourage less all-embracing, muddled leadership talk.

The relationship between leadership and the five other modes of organizing is, as previously said, not so clear-cut. Leadership may be involved, even central, in the creation and maintenance of 'non-leadership' modes of organizing. Good management and the exercise of power may need leadership to work as something that lubricates more rigid and impersonal modes of organizing. Also KITA (kick in the ass) acts, where power is exercised, may call for some influencing of meaning, so that the target (and others) understands why his or her butt hurts and that this is not entirely unreasonable. Managerial acts that insist on rule-following and performance control may, at least occasionally, be accompanied by efforts to make rules feel relevant and meaningful, and the delivery of results a positive experience (in addition to just fulfilling the employment contract). This may call for leadership. Also 'horizontal' modes of organizing – peer influencing, group work and autonomy – may to some extent be an outcome of or dependent on leadership support. Peers and groups as well as autonomous individuals may work because of the earlier developmental 'people-improving' or team-building work of a leader. Effective leadership may lead to a point where it is no longer needed, a bit like parenting. Leadership is also heavily influenced by the other forms of organizing. These blurred interrelationships, described above, are illustrated in Figure 2.1.

Even if leadership often overlaps and works in tandem with the other modes of organization, it does not cover all forms of organizing, as is frequently assumed in much

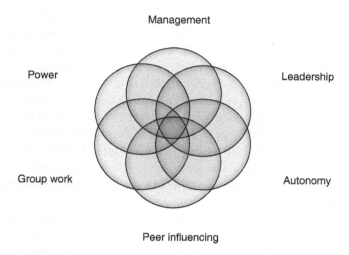

Management

Power

Leadership

Group work

Autonomy

Peer influencing

Figure 2.1   Modes of organizing as overlapping coordination mechanisms

of the contemporary leadership literature. People may be relatively autonomous based on self-confidence, education, experience, intellectual resources, intrinsic motivation or a negative view of their manager (or just a general problem with authority). Such inclinations to autonomy may prevail irrespective of (or even as a consequence of) HIPs trying to exercise leadership in the face of them. And even if leadership can play an early part in the development of people who become more independent at a later stage, this does not mean that leadership is relevant to consider when making sense of later episodes in terms of how work is organized. That a person working autonomously was positively influenced by a senior person 15 years ago is mainly of historical interest. There may be situations where management, power, peers, groups and autonomy work relatively independently of leadership. As suggested above leadership relies on persuasion and aims at meaning; management is grounded in formal authority and typically focused on behaviour, structure and/or output. The exercise of coercive power means the employment of some force and mobilization of negative feelings such as anxiety, shame and guilt. Power means moving outside formal rights and typically includes dealing with conflict and resistance.[3] A good illustration is when Lee Iacocca, former CEO and chairman at Chrysler, pressed unions to accept drastic changes in work conditions, partly using threats (Spector, 2014).

ILR – reflection upon ideas and practices of leadership

Let us now move from leadership in relation to other modes of organizing (ELR) to variations *within* leadership itself (ILR). People in leader/follower relationships, that is, frequent situations characterized by asymmetrical influencing and aiming for voluntary compliance, need to think carefully about what this really means. Process, relations and responsiveness are crucial. These elements are always important in (organizational) life, but there are more subtleties compared to management. Managerial work such as allocating tasks, controlling work performance and compliance with plans and rules are less subtle. Sometimes job descriptions reduce the need for organizing and provide clarification about what needs to be done, how, when and sometimes even why. Clarity is generally aspired to in one sense or another. But giving an instruction, measuring a result or making sure that formal requirements are fulfilled are different from trying to influence people's beliefs, understandings, identities or values, that is the key elements in leadership. Some level of ambiguity is difficult to avoid and space needs to be allowed for uncertainty and use of judgement. Leadership (and to some extent also exercise of certain forms of power) is very much about subtleties and nuances and communicating in a way that makes people connect. Key targets for leadership acts are characterized by a high level of ambiguity and meaning-sensitivity compared to most forms of behaviour and performance. We will come back to this and refer to a number of basic leadership ideas in the next chapter. These focus on overarching and long-term vision, norms, values and ideals (morality) and cognitive issues such as beliefs and reasoning (understandings), as well as dealing with relationships and feelings.

Reflexivity in terms of one's own leadership can be hard. In our many in-depth studies of managers claiming to do leadership we have not encountered many examples of people who score highly on this. Lack of reflection was for example clearly demonstrated in an interview with a seasoned and highly qualified senior manager in a global life science company. Given his experience (a PhD degree plus additional executive education) one would perhaps expect a reflective and fairly consistent view of his work in terms of leadership, but he claimed that:

> ... my view is that it is teamwork and everyone is important, everyone is needed. OK, key scientists are important. ... we must be prepared to reward them in a wholly new way as compared to what we've done. To me it is extremely important to emphasize the team, the whole team.

We note some confusion and inconsistencies in this account. Which is most important – teamwork or key scientists? It is hard to say, but the manager is dancing between two different standpoints like another Fred Astaire. If teamwork is important and one needs to 'emphasize the team, the whole team', then the significance of single members needs to be downplayed. Team emphasis typically means that the group and all its members are in focus, differences need to be de-emphasized and a shared feeling that we are all almost equally important communicated. This can be quite demanding and call for a lot of effort and creativity – people can feel more like individuals than team members and experience clear differences in terms of ability and justifiable expectations of rewards.

However, the latter view is also signalled in the manager's departure from the team focus. If there are 'key scientists' then they are presumably better and more important than others, motivating the statement that one must 'reward them in a wholly new way as compared to what we've done'. Presumably this not only means sneaking in a higher wage and hoping that nobody discovers this, but in terms of leadership giving the key people more praise, attention and certain privileges. Status and significance need to be recognized and it is important that everyone in a team has a shared understanding and acceptance that key people may not be seen in exactly the same way as others. Relations need to be carefully managed so that there is a shared meaning around this. If some feel that everybody is equally important and there should be no stars or key people while others believe that a difference between key people and non-key people is crucial for work, then there will be tensions and poor collaboration. In this case the manager seems to jump between two views without trying to find a synthesis between them, indicating a less reflective view of the subject matter.

The same senior manager continues:

> If you have an idea and you are unable to execute it, it is worthless. I've got plenty of ideas and I'm going around and spread[ing] these among people. But one thing which I think is important from a leadership point of view is that those responsible for the projects also decide upon which ideas they want to pursue. It's not me who should tell them that. I tell them what ideas I have and often they say that: 'that's no good, so we don't like it'. And that's perfectly OK for me. Sometimes they think it's good and then they appropriate it. But the important issue is that they as a group decide by themselves to carry on.

Again, there is a mismatch between the idea of leadership and letting people do what they want to. This may of course only be a matter of jargon but to be entirely liberal about whether people accept or reject the manager's ideas and proposals could be viewed as the opposite of leadership. Even if there is a strong element of voluntary following in leadership, serious efforts to influence LIPs' beliefs, understandings and priorities are key. Anyone can express ideas; HIP-work including leadership means some systematic and ambitious effort to make people buy into these. The view of the manager ('from a leadership point of view is that those responsible for the projects also decide upon which ideas they want to pursue') means that he actually refrains from doing leadership.

This can be fine, it may be much better if those responsible decide and the senior person does not care if they take his ideas seriously or not. This can be seen as encouraging group work as the key organizing principle. In this kind of work – R&D projects in a life science company – senior people often have limited knowledge or overview and there are plenty of uncertainties. The problem is rather that this is viewed as leadership. Of course, the magnitude of the problem can be debated, but it underscores the issues with a broad-brush and confusing use of leadership vocabulary to cover everything.

We cannot generalize from this example, but a large number of in-depth studies of managers indicate that having a clear idea of one's view of leadership is quite rare. The need for more reflexivity is profound – as we will show throughout this book.

SUMMARY

Our key point in this book is that we need to work with a set of ideas that facilitate reflexivity about leadership. Reflexivity means the careful scrutiny and challenging of one's ideas and lines of action and a capacity to reconsider. This can be done in a number of different ways. In this chapter we offer a framework that supports reflexivity through counteracting the widespread view that leadership is characterized as being both crucial and good. Such lazy and wishful thinking is anti-reflexive and needs to be challenged. Encouraging clear recognition of alternatives to leadership – intellectually and practically – and indicating some alternatives within leadership is helpful. We refer to this as ELR and ILR – extra-leadership reflexivity and intra-leadership reflexivity. ELR targets leadership and alternative forms of vertical or hierarchical organizing. IRL points at major alternatives within leadership: asymmetrical influencing work focusing on meanings. The latter will be the key theme developed in more detail in Chapter 8.

Vocabulary is tricky. We have moaned and groaned about the overuse of the term leader and leadership. We therefore think it is helpful to consider the terms HIPs and LIPs – they cover broad terrain when the more precise leadership (or other) language does not really work. Squeezing every version of organizing and influencing into a fluffy, all-embracing concept of leadership discourages reflexivity. In cases where horizontal organizing is salient we use the terms MIP (medium influencing person) or NIP (no influencing person, i.e. apart from 'self-influencing').

Throughout the following chapters we will work with this framework and these concepts. We are not suggesting absolute truths; rather we propose a mode of thinking that is arguably supportive of reflexivity. It is not fixed or designed to structure everything, so we will not keep strictly to the ideas and concepts in this chapter, but we will often refer to them and believe that they facilitate general thinking around leadership and its alternatives as well as practical work by managers and subordinates.

NOTES

1. http://www.kenblanchard.com/Why-Blanchard/People-Centered-Leadership
2. Of course, even in an egalitarian group working together some people might be more influential and dominant than others (by some, viewed as 'informal leaders') and this position might also change/rotate over time (sometimes referred to as 'distributed leadership' (Gronn, 2002)). The same can perhaps also be said about collaborations between peers in an extra organizational network, where a few individuals seem to dominate more than others. Here we may have issues bordering leadership or use of power.
3. There are other definitions of power, many of these quite broad (e.g. Clegg, 1989; Foucault, 1980; Lukes, 1978). We are not interested in covering the whole range here but here reserve the term for interventions with some constraint-producing intentions/effects going beyond voluntary influencing or the reliance on formal management rights, but which may involve elements of bullying, given sharp reprimands. In the book we refer to some ideas on power associated with Foucault and the Frankfurt School but restrict the term power to a rather narrow and conventional meaning, and refer to these ideas using other vocabularies, e.g. ideology and normalization.

3

Perspectives on Leadership

The literature on leadership is vast. The overview in this chapter is therefore limited to some of the more conventional and influential perspectives established during the last century. We follow these in rough chronological order while also acknowledging that they often overlap and co-exist. New ideas are sometimes little more than the re-labelling of old theories. We review the different perspectives in terms of their most important concepts but also discuss them on the basis of their assumptions about leadership. The perspectives are also related to the different modes of organizing that we discussed in Chapter 2. This provides a rationale for comparing perspectives as well as forming a basis for some critique. The latter will, of course, be developed in much more depth in the coming chapters.

Most leadership research has occupied itself with trying to find its essence: what is leadership? This has been the paramount question since the beginning of the 20th century and has consequently resulted in a variety of perspectives and views of leadership.[1] The *classic perspectives* initially discussed in this chapter consider concepts such as traits, styles and situations. This review is followed by a discussion of *symbolic forms* of leadership, more specifically targeting the cognition and emotions of people. Following on, we discuss recent trends of *supporting and recognizing forms of leadership*, including the popular notion of leadership as coaching. The chapter concludes with a section on gender and leadership.

As the purpose of this chapter is to give a concentrated overview of what is described as leadership in academic and other literature, we are less concerned about working with a precise concept of leadership, but also cover some of the theories that we believe are better represented as management or supervision than leadership

CLASSIC APPROACHES TO LEADERSHIP

It should be noted that the classic approaches to leadership are mainly interested in managers and formal superiors rather than informal influencing processes among people – HIPs and LIPs – in general. Such a formal and hierarchical view of leadership overlaps in some ways with our conceptualization of management as a mode of organizing.

The trait approach

For the last hundred years or so much leadership research has been focused on the psychology of the leader. Efforts to identify the particular traits and skills that separate a leader from a non-leader or an effective leader from an ineffective leader have been – and still are – something of the Holy Grail in leadership research. The trait approach gained momentum at the beginning of the 20th century, although some of its ideas had already emerged back in the middle of the 19th century when writings about what makes some men able to change the course of history appeared, many of which are commonly referred to as the 'great man' view of leadership.

Leadership in this sense is about relatively stable psychological dispositions that cause individuals to behave in particular ways. Some proponents of the trait approach argue that people either have these traits or they do not, and use this to determine their suitability for being a leader. Others suggest that it is more common that traits form some combination of heritage (such as temperament or intelligence) and learning (such as, for example, social needs) (Bouchard et al., 1990). Following the assumption that leaders and followers are fundamentally different in terms of traits and skills – so-called 'traits spotting' – countless studies have tried to identify these traits and skills and measure their effectiveness.

This approach typically includes lengthy lists of different kinds of psychological traits and skills that are said to constitute good (or bad) leadership. For example, Zaccaro et al. (2004, p. 104) define a leader's traits as relatively stable and coherent integrations of personal characteristics that foster a consistent pattern of leadership across a variety of group and organizational situations. These characteristics reflect a range of stable individual differences, including personality, temperament, motives, cognitive abilities and expertise. Other typical traits include a sense of responsibility, perseverance, goal orientation, persistence, boldness and originality in problem-solving, self-confidence and self-esteem. It is also suggested that traits such as being adaptable to situations, assertive, cooperative, decisive, dependable, dominant, energetic, self-confident and tolerant of stress are typically good leadership traits. Being clever, creative, diplomatic, persuasive, socially skilled, fluent in speaking and conceptually skilled are also often seen as typical leadership skills (Stogdill, 1974). It appears as if anything 'good' can be a leadership skill.

Research shows conflicting results and does not really support the idea that a person must possess particular traits in order to be a successful leader (Stogdill, 1974). Few would suggest that individual traits are irrelevant in leadership; rather the difficulty lies in identifying traits that can consistently differentiate leaders from non-leaders. For example, in some studies it is suggested that effective leaders are extroverts, in others that they are introverted and in still others this dimension is irrelevant (Wright, 1996). Sometimes one should be talkative and driven and at other times one should be able to listen and adapt.

On the basis of conflicting results from various reviews, Stogdill concluded that the possession of some traits may increase the probability of effective leadership, but that there are no guarantees. Rather than isolated traits, the specifics of the situation and

character of the followers determine whether certain traits – persistence, goal orientation, strong sense of self – are effective or ineffective (more on this under 'The situational
approach' below). It is often said that most effective leaders exhibit a variety of more or
less contradictory traits – flexible vs. consistent, pushing vs. facilitative – depending on
situational conditions, also affected by the larger social and cultural context.

Despite this, the trait approach is still very much alive and kicking in academic
writing (Antonakis, 2011; Zaccaro, 2007), focusing, for example on charismatic leadership (Colbert et al., 2012). There was a renaissance in the field with the emergence
of charisma as increasingly significant in leadership in the 1980s. We discuss this in
the symbolic approaches – charismatic and transformational leadership – later but note
here that following an interest in charisma there was a renewed focus on motivation,
honesty, integrity and cognitive ability. For example, personality traits found to typically characterize charismatic leaders overlap with some of the traits mentioned above
such as high level of self-confidence, strong moral convictions and the need to influence others (House, 1977).

In a recent review of the trait approach, general intelligence and personality are
singled out as particularly valid in predicting leadership (Antonakis, 2011). Here
general intelligence refers to the ability to learn, to process information and the capacity to abstract. Personality is normally seen as an integration of different traits that is
divided into what is understood as more specific traits, occasionally conceptualized as
the big five (Hogan et al., 1994; Smith & Canger, 2004): *surgency*, referring to extro-
version and the need for power; *conscientiousness*, referring to the need for achievement and personal integrity; *agreeableness*, referring to cheerfulness and the need for
affiliation; *adjustment*, referring to emotional stability and self-control; and *intellect-
ance*, referring to curiosity and open-mindedness. Many of the suggested traits are
similar to those found in the earlier trait approaches. Whether these are seen as stable
traits that vary among people or as orientations that vary for people in different situations can be debated. In terms of *conscientiousness*, for example, some people may be
ambitious in certain situations (sport, looks, work) and less so in others. Personal
integrity may be seen as important in some respects and less so in others. The idea of
a specific need can be debated. And that this 'need' should be comprised by achievement and personal integrity also raises some doubts. Can people not have integrity
without wanting to achieve that much and a strong achievement motive may reduce
sensitivity about personal integrity?

Leaving this issue aside, it is important to recognize that the trait approach is also
common in popular leadership and management writings and among practitioners.
For example, Level 5 leadership represents a popular trait approach (Collins, 2005).
Level 5 leadership proposes that leaders who 'build enduring greatness' for their
organizations possess seemingly contradictory characteristics, including modesty,
shyness, personal humility and timidity, on the one hand, and professional will, unwa-
vering resolve, ferociousness and fearlessness, on the other. It is not easy to see how
modesty, shyness, humility and timidity could be the secrets behind corporate excellence. The other virtues do not say that much either: whether people in very senior

positions have 'professional will' and 'fearlessness' is not easy to determine, nor is it a self-evidently good, as it may mean denial or trivialization of risks. Fearlessness may explain great disasters as much as 'enduring greatness'.

A major problem with the trait approach is the idea that a fixed psychological attribute leads to direct effects in terms of leadership effectiveness. People who are successful are probably so under certain conditions. Some people are good at innovation and expansion, but perhaps less good when effectiveness and rationalization are needed. Successful executives can display a variety of personal characteristics. Sometimes these change over time and with circumstances. It appears too simplistic and mechanistic to look for a particular combination of leadership traits.

Many admirers of leadership like to think of leaders as a special kind of people who can do extraordinary things. It is, for example, argued that people in general have a need to see leaders as gifted and the trait approach fulfils that need (Northouse, 2007). However, such illusions fuel leadership heroism fantasies and blind people to more complex interactions. This may prevent critical reflection, for example, on how organizational culture also conditions and influences leadership, rather than single leaders heroically creating organizational cultures (more on this in Chapter 5).

The style approach

Partly based on the conflicting results from the trait approach, leadership researchers in the 1950s turned their focus to the style or behaviour of leaders, primarily in relationship to subordinates. The most popular dimensions – named differently in terms of *production/concern for task* and *relationship/concern for people* – are usually seen on a continuum, along which the style of the leader can vary (Katz & Kahn, 1952). The basis for these styles is that there are two central concerns in leadership. One concern revolves around getting the task done and accomplishing results. The other is about concern for those who are supposed to get the work done.

Strong task orientation typically refers to a style that includes a leader focused upon a work schedule, delivery times, defining work roles and role expectations and the realization of expected results. Strong relationship orientation on the other hand focuses on well-being, recognition, attention, personal interests and the opportunities for personal development.

Occasionally these dimensions overlap with two alternative styles, controlling/authoritarian or participative leadership (Katz & Kahn, 1978). Authoritarian leadership refers to a leader who dictates policies and procedures and directs and controls activities without any meaningful participation by the subordinates. Participative leadership refers to a leader who facilitates subordinates' participation in decision-making. It is important to recognize however, that a task-oriented style does not necessarily imply authoritarian leadership. A task-oriented leader may employ a participative style because it is seen as the most effective way of completing the tasks. A relationship-oriented leader may also be more authoritarian, for example by enforcing procedures and HR practices intended to examine and ensure the well-being of subordinates.

A person may well be authoritarian and show concern for people, that is, the typical patriarch. A third style, laissez-faire, was occasionally drawn upon in order to characterize the absence of leadership (Lewin, 1939).

Ideas about leadership styles are popular but tend to oversimplify matters. Reality is not so one-dimensional. Early approaches often treated the various styles as discrete positions of a single dimension, which is problematic as leaders may be task oriented or more authoritarian in some situations, more relationship oriented or participative in other situations and even more passive in others. Positioning among styles may also vary over time and be contingent upon social, cultural and structural conditions as well as other situational circumstances.

A study of an R&D department showed that the correlation between the degree of autonomy and scientific productivity was strongest in departments that were neither tightly nor loosely organized. None of the leadership styles above seemed to have contributed to scientific productivity. In contrast, the study suggested that research succeeded best – in terms of productivity – under what was called controlled freedom, a situation providing freedom for researchers within a structured context rather than leaving them with total autonomy (Pelz & Andrews, 1966). Leaders were controlling in some questions and participative in others, providing researchers with a structured context that was a result of a combination of different styles.

The combination of different styles was also the key theme in the well-known leadership matrix – management grid – created by Blake and Mouton (1964). The matrix comprises two intersecting axes/dimensions of styles: concern for people (relationship) and concern for production (task). Concern for people is the degree to which a leader considers the needs of employees when deciding how tasks or jobs should be done. This can be personal or professional development or being supportive of employees' ideas and wishes. Concern for production is the degree to which a leader emphasizes objectives and productivity goals when deciding how tasks or jobs should be done. This can be rules, policies or performance standards.

Intersecting the two dimensions produces five styles. *Country club management* refers to a leadership style that shows the most concern for people and the least concern for production. The basic assumption is that happy – in terms of comfort and friendly atmosphere – subordinates will provide the best results. *Impoverished management* shows the least concern for both people and production. This is a form of management that ignores systems of work and the question of how to motivate subordinates. *Task management* corresponds to high concern for production and low concern for people. This is a form of management that emphasizes planning, directing and controlling the subordinates' work. *Middle of the road management* settles for average performance from subordinates. This leader's balanced interest results in mediocre production and employee satisfaction. *Team management* refers to an integration of human and task requirements. This is a management approach that stresses high production and high employee satisfaction in equal measure. In this style those responsible for executing a job also participate in its planning. This is supposed to form a strongly engaged organization characterized by respect, trust and work satisfaction (Blake & Mouton, 1975).

According to Blake and Mouton (1975), team management is the optimal way of creating human relations in the work context. In contrast, country club management is sometimes referred to as the 'love conquers all' style – 'if people love me they'll work well for me' – but seen as insufficient, while the pure task management style – authority and obedience – is thought to be out of place in a society that increasingly values mutual understanding about what needs to be done. Impoverished managers are those that have more or less mentally exited the organization and hence 'see no evil, speak no evil, hear no evil', while middle of the road people typically employ compromise and the accommodations of many wills in order to be pragmatic but often end up in mediocrity (see Wright, 1996).

Studies of styles have in general aimed to examine correlations between styles and work satisfaction and work performance, but results are inconclusive and contradictory (Korman, 1966). Questionnaires have been inconclusive regarding the correlation between leadership styles and performance, while experiments have suffered from the inherent unrealism of laboratory settings. A review by Stogdill (1974) suggests that both relationship- and task-orientation contribute to increased work satisfaction, even if it is more frequent in relationship-orientation. In terms of the effects of work performance there seems to be no significant difference between relationship- and task-orientation.

Based on these results it is difficult to reach certain conclusions as to which style is effective and which is ineffective in terms of influencing work satisfaction and work performance. There are no reasons to assume any universal patterns. Even what appear to be completely contradictory styles may sometimes be effective, if we are to believe a practitioner's own account on the matter, as for example stated by Richard Branson (*The Telegraph*, 2011):

> Steve Jobs' leadership style was autocratic; he had a meticulous eye for detail, and surrounded himself with like-minded people to follow his lead. … He was incredibly demanding of his people, he wasn't the best delegator – he wanted to involve himself in every detail, which is the opposite of my own approach. Personally, I have always believed in the art of delegation – finding the best possible people for Virgin and giving them the freedom and encouragement to flourish.

The universal ambitions behind the style approach also make it packed with rather broad, abstract labels that may vary in significance depending on the local work context and relations. The meaning of 'task' or 'relationship' orientations each covers very broad terrain. One can for example be interested in a 'task' in very many different ways, from Job's myopic interest in details to broader ideas on problem-solving and objectives. The abstractness also makes leadership as a mode of organizing less distinct in relation to alternative modes. For example, a high task orientation may be seen as management or imply more vertical forms of organizing than if the manager influences more indirectly by facilitating structures. Another problem with the distinction is that it masks the fact that most leadership aims for a combination or blend of task and relationship. When managers ask 'how are things going, do you face difficulties?' it is a mix of task and a person's experience at hand. The distinction and categorization into styles may therefore be misleading.

Even so, the style approach has been popular and many of its ideas – notably the concern for people style – have been reinforced by the establishment of transformational leadership and recent views of leadership concerned with recognizing and supporting followers. In transformational leadership it is typically proposed that leaders should raise the level of awareness about organizational objectives and make followers transcend their self-interest for the sake of the team or the organization (Bass, 1985). This overlaps well with team management that implies thick interaction in terms of inspiration, work morale and identification with objectives. As Blake and Mouton (1975, p. 30) argue: '… seeking for excellence through getting highest possible involvement-participation-commitment to organization purpose …'. Other more recent studies that explicitly depart from a style-perspective explore the role of various leadership styles in relation to stress (Lyons & Schneider, 2009), gender inequality (Collins et al., 2014), vision content (Sosik & Dinger, 2007) and team performance (De Hoogh et al., 2015).

Also, recent forms of leadership focusing on supporting and recognizing the followers draw to a large extent on the classic idea of relational leadership that includes ways to mobilize followers' thinking, emotions, motivation and participation in decision-making. These leadership ideas – based on overall humanism – do not view people as mere units or means of production. The relationship orientation in terms of privileging employee psychological well-being and happiness has thus become more significant lately.

The situational approach

The basic premise of the situational approach is to acknowledge the relevance the situation has for the appropriate leadership style. This requires some idea of the situations that a leader is likely to face and the appropriate leadership style to address each situation. In most cases the appropriate leadership style depends on the character – knowledge, engagement, power, task characteristics – of the relationship between the superior, as the presumed leader, and the subordinate, as the presumed follower. Two dominant and popular frameworks addressing the situation are the *situational theory of leadership* (Hersey & Blanchard, 1982) and the *contingency perspective of effective leadership* (Fiedler, 1967).

The situational theory of leadership draws on a combination of traits and styles by connecting them to the knowledge/ability and commitment/confidence – conceptualized as maturity – of subordinates (Hersey & Blanchard, 1982). The leadership style is thus contingent on the maturity of the subordinates. A high-maturity subordinate has both the ability and confidence to perform a task, whereas a low-maturity subordinate lacks both ability and self-confidence. By intersecting ability and confidence four different leadership styles are suggested, depending on the level of maturity: (1) *telling* – high task-low relationship orientation – telling subordinates what to do is likely to be most effective when people are immature because they require specific direction, while too many supportive interventions would likely be seen as lenient and rewarding poor performance; (2) *selling* – high task-high relationship orientation – selling the significance of work in order to maintain motivation is likely to be effective as subordinates become more experienced and require fewer instructions but some supportive behaviour in order to reinforce enthusiasm; (3) *participating* – low task-high relationship orientation – participative leadership is likely to be effective when subordinates are knowledgeable but still need to be motivated. This includes communication and active listening in order to support subordinates to draw upon their existing abilities: and lastly (4) *delegating* leadership – when subordinates are mostly mature and need fewer task- and relationship-orientated interventions. Subordinates know what to do and do not need a lot of additional support in order to complete work tasks.

Central here is that as subordinates (regarded as equivalent to followers) become more mature the leadership style can develop and become less commanding and more delegatory (or leadership can even be substituted by other organizational mechanisms, as suggested by Kerr and Jermier (1978)). One idea behind the model is to encourage subordinates to grow throughout by developing a higher level of independence in relation to superiors. Conversely, if followers' performance deteriorates it may motivate the leader to move backwards through the stages and draw upon an alternative leadership style.

The situational theory of leadership is popular in leadership development programmes and among practitioners, mostly because of its simplicity. This makes sense to an extent as we find that when people are new to a job or task they may need more guidance, while those that have some experience with the task are happy to be given more autonomy in order to complete it. The idea of followers maturing throughout different stages also suggests that leaders need to consider ways of nurturing and building ability and confidence among subordinates rather than assuming that those who are unskilled or inexperienced will remain a problem forever.

Situational leadership theory has a rather narrow focus on the ability and confidence of subordinates. It makes the assumption that managers have sufficient knowledge about all areas of a subordinate's job and are superior in knowledge and judgement (Wright, 1996). This is a common assumption in leadership thinking. But the HIP may not always know what is best, especially in situations characterized by complex work tasks. For example, a directive leadership style may not be appropriate if the ability and skills of the leader are equal to or below the follower's. Also, the characteristics of the follower in terms of emotional disposition and affiliation with the leader may be important and can mean that even a motivated follower still wants clear-cut instructions and direction. Based on our six modes of organizing, one could also discuss whether some of the stages – telling and delegating – are really about leadership and not better described in the vocabulary of an alternative mode. Telling could be seen as management, or power depending on the form it takes ('neutral' or with 'power'). Delegating could perhaps be seen as some horizontal form of coordination such as teamwork or autonomy, requiring less leadership. Any given success may not be the result of the leader's careful delegating, but simply of the employee working autonomously in line with professional norms or something else that does not come from the HIP's initiative to delegate.

Another situational approach is the contingency model of effective leadership (Fiedler, 1967). A basic premise of the approach is that leaders are either more task- or relations-oriented. Following this, the model suggests that effective leadership is contingent upon the degree to which the situation enables the leader to exercise influence and control over subordinates. This – called situational control – depends on the *power position* of the leader, *task complexity* and to what extent *subordinates comply* with the leader's wishes.

Based on these conditions it is suggested that task-oriented leaders are most effective in situations characterized by high and low situational control, that is, when the situation is very favourable or very unfavourable for the leader to exercise leadership. Relationship-oriented leaders are generally more effective in situations characterized by more moderate forms of influence. The reason for this is that in very favourable situations – characterized by simple work tasks and when the leader is in a strong power position and has followers' support – followers expect and are prepared to receive clear directives and instructions about what they should do, and no additional discussion or consultation is necessary. Perhaps this could be seen more as an exercise of power rather than leadership. In very unfavourable situations – involving a complex work task and a less popular leader with a weak power base – it would make sense for the leader to take charge of the situation and not engage too much with consultations and discussions, as that would not be constructive. Also this could be interpreted as a way of exercising power rather than leadership, according to our model of different modes of organizing. Here, power relies on force more than administrative/managerial systems or elaborate discussions or negotiations about the value of work. Cognition and emotions seem less salient in these forms of proposed leadership. Moderately favourable situations are characterized by a more open and tolerant climate that contributes to engagement and active participation by the followers. Leaders who are more diplomatic and open may contribute more in such situations, that is, relation-oriented leaders are more effective in moderately favourable situations (Wright, 1996).

Following this reasoning, leaders should actively search for situations in which particular traits or style seem to work well. The alternative is to alter the situation – power relations and work task characteristics – to suit the perceived traits or styles of the leader, something that is probably more difficult to achieve.

Studies of the situational model of effective leadership show conflicting results. Some experimental research has supported the model while other research has been more negative about its promise. It has also been argued that measurement techniques – of attitudes towards the least preferred colleague (LPC) – have been inadequate in order to understand the style and behaviour of leaders (Wright, 1996). A favourable attitude towards the least preferred colleague is generally seen as indicating relationship-orientation, while a relatively negative attitude towards the least preferred colleague is seen as task-orientation. However, scores on attitudes about colleagues do not necessarily overlap with how people behave in practice.

Despite critique (e.g. Graef, 1997; Thompson & Vecchio, 2009), situational theories of leadership are still around and popular in contemporary leadership discourse. Goleman (2000), for example, proposes six different leadership styles that vary in effectiveness – in terms of working atmosphere and finance – depending on the situation. The different styles are: *authoritarian* leadership – suggesting commanding and follow-up performances; *visionary* leadership – which means mobilizing minds and hearts towards the future; *relationship-oriented* leadership – which is similar to emotional leadership and involves forming bonds and harmony within the group; *democratic* leadership – referring to an interest in participation and consensus-building among subordinates; *tempo-setting* leadership – which involves expectations of excellence and self-governing subordinates; and lastly *coaching* – which focuses on developing subordinates for the future. Other recent empirical studies where a situational leadership perspective has been used include, for example, Arvidsson et al.'s (2007) study of air traffic control employees and Larsson and Vinberg's (2010) case study of leadership in 'successful' organizations.

Under situational leadership theory, the most effective leaders would be those who are able to switch between different styles depending on the situation at hand. Switching between leadership styles is likened to the situation of a golfer that switches between different golf clubs depending on the natural circumstances of the golf course. Switching styles is probably a good idea but may well prove trickier than switching golf clubs (Fiedler, 1967). Most people do not master a wide range of styles. Switching styles may also appear inconsistent and unreliable in the eyes of subordinates and cause confusion and uncertainty. Some styles, such as authoritarianism, can undermine the possibility of employing a relationship-oriented style, while a person mainly engaging in the latter may find it hard to suddenly switch into authoritarian or tempo-setting behaviour and run the risk of appearing odd or not his/her usual self in the eyes of the presumed followers. Many agree about the importance of the situation but the theories are often too broad and vague to lend themselves to specific analysis or be pragmatically helpful. A problem with the approach is that it assumes that the manager/leader (HIP) knows best and is the sole person who can decide what sort of leadership the situation requires and competently work with the appropriate style. Others may in turn assess the situation quite differently and disagree with the views of the HIP in terms of the LIPs' ability and motivation.

SYMBOLIC LEADERSHIP

Since the 1980s the symbolic dimensions of leadership have become widely popular. Symbolism moves beyond an interest in people and tasks and relates more to wider issues and lines of thinking around meaning, values and identifications. Leadership literature tends to discuss how this dimension – expressed in for example charismatic and transformational leadership – sits in contrast to the classical approaches described above in terms of an emphasis on the symbolic and higher meaning aspects of leadership. Indeed, the advocates of this approach talk of a radical break from classic ideas of leadership. Despite this, many of their ideas – recognizing individuals and their feelings for example – overlap with previous traditions. Rather than characterizing symbolic leadership forms as new approaches one could perhaps label them as continuations of certain style (relational) approaches to leadership.

Symbolic leadership focuses on the meaning and purpose of the job role, organization and accomplishments. The role of the leader is not just a job, but part of a larger whole. Like many relational forms of leadership, symbolic leadership appeals to people's emotions and morale in order to inspire identification with the organization and its mission, vision and culture, and loyalty to the leaders embodying this vision. Ideally, vision should provide direction, meaning and a common purpose as well as serve as a platform for self-esteem and identity. It is often said that the best visions are those that are straightforward and anchored in reality yet unconventional and inspirational. It is important for a leader to embody the vision and lead by example, especially in the day-to-day reality of the organization, the idea being that actions speak louder than words. This embodiment is sometimes most effective as leaders use dramatic and symbolic actions to reinforce a particular value or standard of the organization, such as when Apple's Steve Jobs physically destroyed a Windows keyboard (Isaacson, 2012). Two approaches have been particularly salient in this development: *charismatic* and *transformational leadership*. These are related in different ways, charisma is occasionally seen as central in efforts to turn people into followers. We begin with a short discussion of charisma.

Charismatic leadership

Some people seemingly influence others on the basis of charisma. Charisma usually refers to a compelling charm or appeal that can inspire devotion among other people, sometimes even regarded as a God-given talent or ability. In terms of traits it is suggested that charismatic leaders are likely to have strong willpower, high self-confidence and strong convictions about their beliefs and ideals. It is also claimed that charisma may come from great oratorical skill and emotional expressiveness (Bryman, 1992). In terms of leadership styles charisma is attributed to someone formulating a radical – but appealing – vision with the help of strong and expressive forms of communication. People taking risks and exhibiting self-sacrifice in order to attain their vision are also said to be charismatic, in addition to their acting as role models and expressing optimism and confidence in followers (Conger & Kanungo, 1987).

Charismatic leadership thus often involves strong symbolic language and rhetorical skills. This means the use of metaphors, colourful stories, sagas, value-laden narratives, cultural symbols and analogies that presumably elicit strong emotional responses and increased commitment with what the leader or the organization stands for. Future-oriented visions are perhaps the most common way to accomplish some kind of influence and organizational direction. Charisma may also partly be seen as an attributional phenomenon constructed by followers on the basis of traits, behaviour, roles, hierarchical positions and impressive titles (see also Chapter 6). Indeed, the way followers feel about charismatic leaders may be more important than what the leaders actually do, since the same words or actions can appear charismatic to some followers but seem like gibberish to others who are less enchanted and remain unconvinced.

The influencing process in charismatic leadership is typically described as being personal. Influence based on personal identification means identifying with how one perceives the leader and may occur when followers look to please and satisfy the presumed will of the leader. The leader exhibits some traits and/or behaviours that are extraordinary enough – such as a vision – to followers. Confirmation by the leader becomes an element of self-esteem. Such confirmation may be expressed by leader approval and recognition of followers' accomplishments, which then reinforce self-confidence and strong commitment to realizing the leader's expectations. Followers often take a romanticized view of leadership, become seduced and uncritical and see leaders as charismatic (Meindl, 1995). How followers identify with the leader is, of course, also a result of the followers' experience, knowledge, professional inclination, identity and self-confidence. The specific situation and social and cultural values are also important in relation to the extent to which people look for charismatic leaders to identify with and become influenced by. This may also occur in professional and knowledge-intensive contexts where people are expected to rely upon professional group work, peer support and autonomy as primary modes of organizing.

Charismatic leaders often (though not necessarily always) emerge in situations of crisis, such as economic turbulence, strong uncertainty, psychological stress and social disorder. It is occasionally also argued that it is necessary for charismatic leaders to – or at least appear to – be successful to confirm their charisma. If a charismatic leader fails or becomes associated with negative outcomes the charisma would be weakened or disappear and the person would end up as 'decharismatized', such as in the case of the previously celebrated Lee Iacocca following poor results at Chrysler (Bryman, 1992). Following the attribution approach, success and failure probably affect perceptions of charismatic leadership even when the leader has little influence over organizational outcomes. The reverse may also happen; an effective but unassuming leader may find his or her success attributed to other factors, such as growing markets. A distinction is sometimes made between 'personal' and 'office' charisma: people may also be seen as charismatic on the basis of a particular position they occupy (Etzioni, 1961). Office charisma comes from holding a particular status position such as CEO, president, bishop or king.

Although many would agree that the presence of charisma explains a lot in terms of influencing processes in organizations, there are mixed views about its value as a means of exercising leadership. Some view it as mainly positive since it leads to powerful influence that makes people committed, compliant, and ready to put in the extra effort the leader demands, which in turn benefits the organization. Charismatic leadership may create an 'achievement oriented' culture (Harrison, 1987) or a 'hands-on, value driven organization' (Peters & Waterman, 1982).

However, charisma also has its dark sides. Charisma means a strong asymmetrical relationship that is not grounded in fundamental differences in competence or ability.

Charisma means a strong dependency on and an uncritical view of the leader. Charismatic leadership tends to preclude reflections about alternative modes of organizing, and fuels tendencies of both leaders and followers to aggrandize the leader. This may reinforce the infallibility of the leader, encourage the denial of problems and failures, inhibit critical thinking and learning and create sect-like conditions involving unhealthy group thinking. Charismatic leaders may also evoke polarization in organizations to the extent that some see them as charismatic while others view them more sceptically. Rather than achieving a 'hands-on and achievement culture' charismatic leaders may contribute to organizational power games, conflicts and organizations being torn apart. In other cases, charismatic leaders may create a strong consensus, partly by sceptics exiting the organization as the charismatic leader takes over.

Another problem with charismatic leaders is their ability to divert attention away from difficult organizational problems in order to maintain their charismatic image both in their own eyes and those of others. Charismatic people are often idolized, which can feed their narcissism. Unhealthy idolization and narcissism may become objectives in their own right, detracting attention from important work (Rijsenbilt & Commandeur, 2013). Classic situations of over-dependence may be found when too many things must pass through the leader, combined with organizational members strongly positioning themselves as dependent followers. Charismatic leaders may also encourage radical change to demonstrate power and dynamics in organizations that are successful and in no obvious need of change. Interestingly but perhaps unsurprisingly, there are those who suggest that overconfident and self-centred managers tend to perform more poorly than others (Chamorro-Premuzic, 2010; Rijsenbilt & Commandeur, 2013). Even so, the concept of charisma remains popular and is also often seen as an element of transformational leadership. A somewhat lukewarm conclusion would be that 'some' degree of charisma may be a good thing, but strong charismatic leadership tends to be risky.

Transformational leadership

Transformational leadership is related to charismatic leadership but somewhat more broadly. The concept of leadership being transformational is often associated with the political scientist James Burns' (1978) idea of leadership as involving a higher purpose and inspirational commitment, and which contrasts with transactional leadership, based on a more instrumental exchange. According to several proponents of transformational leadership, the classic traditions are insufficient in terms of acknowledging the relevance of higher meaning and strong emotions (Kotter, 1982). As demonstrated by the previous discussion of the classical approaches, this may be debatable, as ideas within the relational (concern for people) leadership style often involve moral commitment and inspirational organizational objectives. Even so, at the beginning of the 1980s many of the classic approaches were regarded more as forms of management and as a key problem behind the decreased competitiveness of numerous American companies. Kotter (1990) suggested that US organizations were 'over-managed' and 'under-led', arguing that they were good at maintaining their direction in stable environments – trough management – but poor at initiating and leading transformations and change under more unpredictable and turbulent circumstances. The latter was said to require a leadership that also targeted the hearts and minds of people in terms of higher purposes, values, organizational cultures and inspirational messages (Spector, 2014).

Burns' ideas were taken up by several managerial leadership researchers, Bass (1985) in particular, and were applied in various organizations. According to Bass, in contrast to the transformational leader, the transactional leader: (1) recognizes what people want to get out of work and tries to see that people get it (given the performance requirements); (2) exchanges rewards and promises of rewards for work efforts; and (3) is responsive to people's self-interest if relevant to getting the work done. Transactional leaders also clarify work tasks and requirements in order to provide people with enough confidence to reach desired outcomes. This should provide motivation for subordinates to reach the expected level of performance.

In contrast to just aiming for an expected level of performance, transformational leaders motivate people to do more than they initially intended. A transformation is accomplished by: (1) raising awareness among followers of the value of intended outcomes and of the means of reaching them; (2) encouraging subordinates to transcend their individual interests for the sake of the work group or organization; and (3) triggering people's inner motivation – moving upwards on Maslow's Need Hierarchy – by enticing feelings of participation and self-actualization. Self-confidence is targeted as well as people's views about the possibility of reaching the outcomes (Bass, 1985). These activities are thought to provide motivation for subordinates to go the extra mile in order to do an extraordinarily good job. Transformational leadership adds something extra to the transactional leadership (transactional plus) according to Bass.[2] In a similar and later version by Bass and Avolio (2000), transformational leadership is characterized by the following:

- *Idealized influence*: Transformational leaders become role models – idealized means a good influence morally – for followers who admire, respect and trust them. They put followers' needs above their own, and their behaviour is consistent with the values and principles of the group.
- *Inspirational motivation*: Transformational leaders should motivate by providing meaning and an element of challenge in the tasks of followers. This is the charismatic aspect of transformational leadership – seen as most important – and involves rousing team spirit, enthusiasm and optimism, and helping followers develop a desirable vision of the future.
- *Intellectual stimulation*: Transformational leaders stimulate innovation and creativity by encouraging followers to question assumptions, reframe situations, and approach old problems from new perspectives.
- *Individualized consideration*: Transformational leaders treat each individual differently and act as coaches who foster personal development. Their coaching and mentoring are tailored to the individual needs and desires of each follower.

As well as overlapping with parts of the 'concern for people' style discussed above, transformational leadership embraces a broad variety of different themes and seems demanding indeed. This is seen as necessary since competitiveness and organizational development are increasingly dependent on engaged and inspired subordinates who actively participate in the creation of organizational culture (Tichy & Devanna, 1986). Ideally, transformational leadership motivates people beyond the scope of their formal work tasks to the extent that people commit and identify with the organization, its culture, vision and leaders. For example, Peters and Waterman (1982) suggested that the most successful organizations were led by people exhibiting transformative traits, including the capability to create organizational cultures inspiring people to perform beyond formal task demands. Also, Jack Welch, the renowned former chairman and CEO of General Electric, known for being tough as nails and drawing on a lot of power as a mode of organizing, suggests that leadership in terms of empowering people is central: 'You may be a great manager, but unless you can energize other people, you are of no value to General Electric as a leader' (Goldsmith et al., 2010, p. 36).

Transformational leaders are supposed to avoid or minimize formal hierarchical modes of organizing – such as management – in their influencing efforts. The idea is to reach voluntary obedience by targeting thinking, feelings, identity and generally how people look upon what is important and desirable to accomplish.

Symbolic processes and management of meaning are central. Typically 'transformational' means having high impact on individuals' thinking and emotions. These are not necessarily to be transformed all the time, but high commitment to the idealized leader and the organization are often things that need to be maintained and reproduced.

Many advocates of transformational leadership are lyrical about its potential. According to Maxwell (2001, p. 185):

> The single biggest way to impact an organization is to focus on transformational leadership. There is almost no limit to the potential of an organization that recruits good people, raises them up as leaders and continually develops them.

In-depth qualitative studies on transformational leadership are very rare, and most suggest that the celebrated type of leadership is not easy in practice. Often the leadership industry – the popular press but also practitioner-friendly academic writings – grossly misrepresents admired leadership efforts (Spector, 2014). In general, questionnaire studies are more positive about its effects – especially in terms of project leadership – but most are very limited when it comes to understanding how people are transformed in terms of cognition, inspiration and emotions (Keller, 1992). There is much research on transformational leadership, but most of it is highly questionable. There are plenty of tautological concepts blending practice and effect, for example 'intellectual stimulation' combines and muddles intention, practice and effect, neglecting the possibility that a manager may try but fail to be intellectually stimulating. Measurements are unreliable. The comparison of transformational and transactional leadership (really management) means the 'good' and 'sexy' being compared with the boring and mundane (van Knippenberg & Sitkin, 2013). In real life it is possible that most subordinates are less interested in being inspired and motivated by the leader than in having interesting job tasks and good colleagues, wages, promotion possibilities and work conditions – the latter being within the realm of transactional relations (again, management more than leadership in our terms). Interestingly, in a study of leadership researchers' views of effective/ineffective leadership in higher education organizations there were hardly any references to transformational leadership (Bryman & Lilley, 2009). Organizations are full of people with diverse interests and perceptions who are not necessarily that easily transformed into enthusiastic embracers of a vision invented and communicated by a leader (Bolden et al., 2011). Of course this is not to say that elements of what is claimed to be part of transformational leadership do not often play a role in workplaces.

Authentic leadership

In the wake of the many corporate scandals and other moral concerns in contemporary society, authentic leadership has emerged as a popular topic, especially in the US. Moral shortcomings and scandals have often been explained as the result of the wrong kind of leaders and leadership, commonly labelled non-leaders or inauthentic leadership. For example, the global financial crisis in 2008 was often labelled a leadership problem, with big headlines such as 'Failed leadership caused the financial crisis' (George, 2008). And of course what is needed to remedy these problems is not less but *more* leadership. Leadership guided by a moral compass such as authentic or real leadership can restore optimism, faith and meaning among people. Frequently referred to as a form of positive leadership, authentic leadership is proclaimed as a solution to ethical, economic and environmental challenges facing contemporary organizations and society. Influenced by positive psychology and the neo-humanistic turn in social science, ideas on authentic leadership draw on the concept of transformational leadership as a morally superior form of leadership (Avolio & Gardner, 2005).

Most writings on authenticity revolve around the importance of: (a) knowing one's true self in terms of preferences, beliefs, strengths (self-awareness); (b) representing oneself in relation to others according to how one perceives one's true self (relational transparency); (c) gathering and employing objective information that may challenge self-awareness (balanced processing); and (d) exhibiting a moral perspective in relation to self-regulation and self-determination (moral superiority). The last point also indicates that authenticity requires being oriented to higher, collective, rather than selfish, goals.

Of course this all sounds very good, but there is a wealth of problems (Ibarra, 2015). The idea of 'one true self' is rather odd. In a complex, dynamic world, most people are not cut in stone. They have many affiliations and are expected to take on different roles. Contemporary working life encourages people to be flexible, responsive and sensitive to many, often inconsistent, values and norms. There may be many selves or at least many versions of the self – it is not easy to identify and stick to the 'true one'. A senior manager who sees herself as a 'leader with integrity' may be expected to be a loyal follower to the CEO, suggesting a rather different 'self' compared to what is demanded of subordinates to promote the unit's interest. Corporate life has limited tolerance for people insisting strongly on exhibiting what they may believe to be their true self without careful concern for adaptation to senior people, subordinates, team membership, customer orientation, political correctness and other demands for smooth collaboration in complex work settings.

Another problem is the link between the various components, for example authenticity and ethics. There is a peculiar belief that knowledge about and expression of 'the true self' will lead to the exhibition of moral superiority. But people can be power hungry, narcissistic, nepotistic and greedy as much as champions of higher values. Organizations full of senior people (and junior for that matter) being authentic may not offer positive workplaces or contribute that much to the social good. For example, being authentic for one person may be sexual harassment for another. It is often more socially convenient to conceal one's motives, preferences and thoughts, since there is a strong likelihood that exaggerated openness, transparency and insensitivity to context will lead to conflict and other problems.

> Surviving work requires hypocrisy. Many thinkers have attacked this vice – and none more consistently and vehemently than Christ. But Christ never had to earn a living or endure colleagues (disciples are different). Honesty at work is a dangerous luxury. It would be foolish to reveal one's true feelings – and even more foolish to become involved in the great eruptions, the disputes and feuds and the simmering animosities. (Foley, 2010, p. 172)

Ideas on authentic leadership are yet another variant of the blessings of the right kind of leadership orientation. 'Authentic leaders' are seen as solving many problems, including the issue of a moral deficit in organizations. Nobody can object to the hope for leaders who are morally better contributing to a more ethical business world, but perhaps the idea of authentic leadership is not the way to accomplish this. The authenticity turn in leadership can be seen as a way to maintain and reinforce managers and their presumed leadership as a key force in organizations and society at large, beefed up and legitimized by the moral authority of authentic leadership. In this way, the presumed authenticity of the leader provides yet another ideologically anchored, misleading and naive characterization of the complex processes of modern organizations.

CONTEMPORARY RELATIONSHIP-ORIENTED LEADERSHIP STYLES

A central idea in contemporary relationship-oriented forms of leadership is that happy, confirmed, engaged workers will improve performance – something that was also salient in the relationship-oriented leadership style discussed above. Business magazines are happy to propagate: 'The value of happiness: how employee well-being drives profits' (*Harvard Business Review*, 2012). A core message is that: 'Employee happiness is becoming a hot topic among CEOs and in boardrooms, and it's about time'. Some of the ideas echo transformational leadership by proposing that employees are transformed into passionate advocates of their organizations, although efforts to produce well-being and make people feel good are added leadership elements. Recognition is viewed as a highly productive leadership tool for accomplishing top performance and successful organizations. For example, Barry Salzberg, Global CEO of Deloitte, says that great leaders express gratitude by never being too busy to say thank you: 'They [leaders] … stay human … and create a culture where people are recognized and valued for their contribution … I've found many small but meaningful ways to say thank you, including personal letters and company awards'.

One aspect of this is leaders as friends or '*buddies*' (Sveningsson & Blom, 2011). Intimate fraternization between HIPs and LIPs is expected to make the LIPs (and possibly also the HIPs) positive and happy and increase motivation and commitment. For example, a manager in a bank we interviewed said that: 'I always keep track of people's birthdays and similar things as part of my leadership because I know that it makes people feel good and increases commitment'.

Good leaders are not afraid of being nice and listening is seen as a key element:

> Everyone is worth a listen. Don't confuse this with the idea that everyone deserves a medal; some ideas are better than others (enough said). But pretty much all are worth a bit of a listen before moving on. (Panepinto, 2015, p. 1)

This calls for managers with plenty of time. Busy managers may feel that listening to 'pretty much all' is 'pretty much' stressful.

The ideal involves confirming employees' presence at work by talking to them in the coffee room and giving the appearance of being interested in their work and/or leisure time, letting people talk about whatever they want, work-related or not (Alvesson & Sveningsson, 2003c). By promoting an informal and friendly atmosphere, many try to support people, and maintain high spirits and motivation in their organizations (Fleming, 2005).[3]

Leadership framed as recognition and support may sound laudable, but is not unproblematic. The objective behind targeting people's inner life and identities may be to extend organizational control. Portraying managers as leaders caring for people's well-being maintains the traditional dependencies, now not only in terms of managing work but also in terms of how people feel and generally view themselves. HIPs become responsible for LIPs' happiness. A problem with happiness is that it is easiest accomplished through flattery, which can lead to an inflated self-view and the expectation that the environment should live up to it. When it does not, misery and aggression easily follow (Foley, 2010). A problem with leadership as buddy-ism is that it easily leads to nepotism. Close interaction and relationships at work make distancing difficult. It is difficult not to be extra supportive of those you have near relationships with. Furthermore, overreliance on leadership in terms of recognition may actually disempower – rather than empower – professionals and others whose work would benefit from alternative modes of organizing. One may argue that most HIPs have more important things to do than spending precious time trying to ensure others' well-being and satisfaction. There is a risk that HIPs spend more time making sure that LIPs are happy than satisfying their customers or, for example, ensuring that the students and patients get the best possible education and treatment in schools or hospitals (Zaleznik, 1997). Giving priority to results may call for sacrifices or other types of HIP intervention. It may be difficult and time consuming to have any real effect on LIPs' well-being and happiness. Simply remembering people's birthdays or engaging in friendly small talk may not lead to the miracle effects that HIPs dream about.

In addition, it may be difficult to establish a direct link between satisfaction and performance. People who are happy at work do not necessarily perform better. 'Good' leadership may influence work satisfaction but it is hard to judge the extent to which such efforts have deeper implications for the meaning of work, morale, emotions or identity. These latter elements may very well be more related to the general work atmosphere or culture, agreeable colleagues, interesting work tasks enabling professional and personal development, professional norms, relatively high salaries, speedy promotion or confirmation by satisfied customers. This is not to deny the importance of leadership, and there is every reason to minimize leadership that makes people feel bad (unless deserved). If people feel that they are being treated in a disrespectful and unfriendly way by insensitive and authoritarian HIPs this may lead to resistance and ineffective work relations (Hallett, 2007). On the whole, making people satisfied at work is positive and important, but it is not unproblematic and we need to be cautious about easy connections and over-simplified causal effects.

Coaching leadership

Coaching is yet another variety of relationship-oriented leadership and overlaps with parts of supportive and transformational leadership. Coaching has gained appeal among practitioners and leadership development programmes and is often defined as the: 'process of equipping people with the tools, knowledge, and opportunities they need to develop themselves and become more successful' (Peterson & Hicks, 1996, p. 14). Coaching leadership is different from leadership coaching. The latter involves one-on-one counseling of managers (HIPs) about work-related issues with the purpose of improving their leadership (HIP) effectiveness (Ladegard & Gjerde, 2014).

Contemporary organizations are typically seen as too complex for managers (HIPs) to know everything about or to have all the right answers. Consequently, it is suggested that they need to develop another role – the coach, someone who connects with people, inspires them to do their best and makes them 'grow' (Batista, 2015; Huzzard & Spoelstra, 2011).

Coaching is said to encourage participation and employee involvement. Leadership as coaching most often refers to having a supportive and facilitative style focusing on employees' empowerment, learning and development (Bond & Seneque, 2013). An important element in coaching is to hold back one's own opinions in favour of how others – employees – see and think about various problems and issues (McCarthy & Milner, 2013). The literature on coaching emphasizes that the leader helps the follower to identify his/her strengths and weaknesses and relate these to his/her career and aspirations in general. Coaches are expected to delegate and provide challenging tasks to their employees in order to help them grow. Often lists of guidelines or specific behaviours are provided in order to help the practising leader exercise coaching influence. This typically includes a variety of points, such as: helping people to develop by asking questions; providing constructive feedback; not providing answers in order for people to learn to solve problems on their own; expressing confidence in peoples' learning; and assisting with useful contacts within or outside the organization. The most important thing in coaching, however, seems to be to ask questions, listen and empathize with the presumed follower.

Framing leadership in terms of coaching is very popular in contemporary organizations. A bank manager we interviewed talked for example about coaching as a way to make people think:

> When I work with the personnel I am a coach. I want to lead in [a] way that makes them take personal responsibility. To make the employees think, their own thinking. In this I look upon myself as a coach. The finance services we provide are complex and I'm not the expert. But I'm the coach.

Leadership involves influencing people to take charge of their work tasks and develop independent thinking. The manager above realizes he is not an expert, but by asking questions he contributes to followers' (LIPs') confidence, knowledge and realism. Leadership involves showing openness and responsiveness and although the illustration above involves a manager, perhaps anyone with sufficient qualities can exercise coaching at any level in organizations. However, coaching typically involves managers or some other HIP with the will, mandate, resources and ability to help LIPs with their career objectives and aspirations. After all, why should you be coached/led by someone who is not superior to yourself (in key respects)?

Coaching overlaps with much relationship-oriented leadership in terms of promoting humanism, empowerment, personal growth and improved working climate. However, there are not many reliable studies of the effectiveness of coaching and in most of the studies the results are somewhat inconclusive (Wenzel, 2000). As with many of the supportive leadership styles and approaches, the coaching variety can be seen as an expression of a therapeutic managerial culture resulting from the attempt to find new means of influence, as traditional forms of leadership seem insufficient and/or unpopular. Coaching then creates a legitimate platform for managers eager to be seen as leaders. Much sounds appealing and progressive but often ends up being difficult to maintain in a reality that involves employees, unions, senior managers, clients and opinion groups. These groups perhaps expect more direct answers and guidelines, efficient administration and management, adaption and compromises rather than having their questions met with counter-questions.

In terms of leadership one could say that coaching is quite different from leadership as setting the agenda and steering meaning. Leadership in these terms would represent the opposite of coaching, providing instead clear cultural direction.

Coaching is not necessarily about this, but tends to be about the employee's concerns, ideas and ambitions. In most cases perhaps people other than one's manager are better suited to doing coaching. A senior colleague, a consultant, a mentor, a good friend or relative may offer effective coaching, and may have more of the time and distance required than a typical manager. To clarify, this is not to deny the value of coaching as part of leadership – and all HIPs do some coaching – but it is seldom a key element of what managers trying to do leadership are concerned with – nor is it specifically about leadership, as coaching is rarely based on a saliently asymmetrical relationship.

STYLES OF LEADERSHIP – WOMEN COMPARED TO MEN

Gender is important but it is also complex and difficult. The extensive research on women and leadership can be divided into two groups. One is the *no-difference camp* in which it is commonly concluded that there are few differences in the leadership style of females and males. Kovalainen (1990) found no significant differences in a study of male and female Finnish bank managers. Nor did Cliff et al. (2005) in a study of the organizational practices of Canadian entrepreneurs. Powell (1988: 165) reached the conclusion that female and male managers 'differ in some ways and at some times, but, for the most part, they do not differ'.

The other is the *gender-stereotypic camp* which believes that some crucial differences exist. Female leadership is characterized by cooperativeness, collaboration between managers and subordinates and problem-solving based on intuition and empathy (e.g. Helgesen, 1990). Often popular authors with a weak empirical grounding claim radical differences, while more systematic research gives modest and uncertain support, also stressing that it depends on circumstances (Carli & Eagly, 2011).

In a research review of gender and leadership effectiveness Eagly et al. (1995) found that on an aggregate level there were no differences in the effectiveness of female and male leaders. However, they found conditions under which men fared better than women and vice versa, 'leadership roles defined in relatively masculine terms favoured male leaders and leadership roles defined in relatively feminine terms favoured female leaders' (p. 137).

In a later contribution, Eagly and Johannesen-Schmidt (2008) emphasized the small, but important, differences in style between male and female leaders. They based this on a meta-analysis of 45 studies comparing male and female managers in the context of transactional, transformational and laissez-faire leadership. Eagly and Johannesen-Schmidt conclude that 'female managers, more than male managers, tend to adopt a transformational style, especially in their mentoring of followers and attending to them as individuals'. Their analysis showed that women were more supportive and encouraging than men and rewarded satisfactory behaviour, while men displayed more passivity, attended to problems when they became serious but attended to the mistakes and failures of followers or displayed laissez-faire leadership. Eagly and Johannesen-Schmidt also note that some of the leadership styles displayed by women overlap with gender-stereotypical expectations more than with men. They warn against simplifications, one-dimensional generalizations, and say that we need some richer understanding of the ways women and men lead.

Transformational leadership is more in line with expectations of the female role, and this style may then be an effect of pressure from the followers that women (should) act more in accordance with their gender. Therefore it is perhaps the followers' expectations – and the response to these – that one should investigate rather than the leader's or only the leader's.

The belief that women are different and have other values guiding leadership, held not just widely in society but also by many female managers, may influence their responses in interviews and questionnaires and possibly give a misleading picture. As Cliff et al. (2005) point out, some researchers focus on 'dissimilarities between men's and women's descriptions of their managerial orientations rather than their actual behaviour, as supporting the existence of sex differences in leadership behaviour' (p. 85). Female managers may believe they are different, but this may not be supported by their actual behaviour, often determined by other factors than the manager's general orientations.

Some studies indicated that when leadership or management was carried out in an autocratic way (in effect, in a more stereotypically masculine way), women were more strongly devalued. When leadership was exercised in a more gender-congruent way, women were not devalued. By contrast, men were not devalued when engaging in 'non-masculine' leadership behaviour. In terms of difficulties facing female managers, there seems to be a more restricted set of options that are more fully acceptable for female than for male managers. As Eagly et al. (1992: 18) express it: 'they "pay a price" in terms of relative negative evaluation if they intrude on traditionally male domains by adopting male-stereotypic leadership styles or occupying male-dominated leadership positions'.

Many authors claim that female managers are caught between the contradictory ideals of being feminine and being managerial, leading to great risks of negative evaluation for being unfeminine or unmanagerial (Stivers, 1993). Eagly et al.'s review indicates that this risk may be less serious than sometimes believed, i.e. if they adopt a non-autocratic style.

Gender is presumably often important for leadership relations, but it is difficult to draw any firm conclusions. Finding general patterns and differences may easily over-emphasize very small and uncertain differences – perhaps more relevant in the context of a US sample in the 1980s than for men and women in other countries today. We need to try to assess the meaning and significance in specific contexts where gender seldom plays a simple and clearcut role but is intertwined with a variety of other circumstances (see Hallett, 2007). Generally, gender is a complicated aspect that can seldom be captured by simple truths (Alvesson & Billing, 2009). Of course, gender issues change over time with large groups of well-educated women on the labour market and reduction of traditional gender roles (Carli & Eagly, 2011).

SUMMARY

Almost all dominant perspectives on leadership summarized in this chapter express a leader-centred approach to the phenomenon. The core of this argument is that leaders somehow lead followers. The followers are strongly influenced by the leadership and respond in a more or less predictable way. There is a strong reliance on leader attributes – traits, styles, priorities – that are more or less assumed to be universal and are habitually drawn upon in order to explain organizational process and outcomes. The assumption is that leaders are in control. Situational circumstances are occasionally acknowledged and sometimes even in focus – such as the maturity of subordinates or power of the superior – but it is still the leader who is expected to know the situation and act accordingly. Charismatic and in particular transformational leadership seemingly reinforce much of the classic leader-centrism – often constructing leaders as heroes or even saviours.

This overemphasis on the leader – often equivalent to managers – may reinforce leader dependency and undermine alternative modes of organizing. In most leadership studies people who are not promoted are expected to position themselves as followers in relationships with leaders. This clear-cut leader/follower divide may reinforce hierarchical relations that in turn prevent alternative modes of organizing such as autonomy, peer support and group work. If we take the creation of happiness and coaching, one could say that others may be more effective than managers (HIPs) and that it is better to avoid leader-centrism in workplaces in order to create atmosphere and facilitate good advice giving. An exaggerated dependency on leaders may also foster narrow thinking and prevent critical reflection. In addition, there is a risk that every middle manager with ambition starts – in line with the popular recipes described above – to act like/imitate/pretend/aspire to become a charismatic, transformational leader (perhaps not exactly what their subordinates need or wish for). Of course sometimes the idea that leaders lead followers in a fairly one-directional way captures reality well and may also be productive. Leadership sometimes needs to be strengthened. Strong and uncritical beliefs can also create reality, contributing to organizations where leaders lead and followers follow – but that kind of rigid division and highly unequal activity/passivity may not always lead to effective organizing. The next chapter will show the fundamental problems with too much and overly idealized leader-centricity.

NOTES

1. The well-read leadership student might miss some rather established theories and traditions here in this chapter, such as for example follower-centred perspectives, like e.g. attribution theories and ideas of shared/distributed leadership. The first is discussed in Chapter 6. We do not address the latter at length in this book, but relate to it more implicitly (for overviews, see Gronn, 2002 and Bolden, 2011).

2. A similar line of reasoning can also be found within a parallel tradition called Leader-Member Exchange (LMX): 'LMX theory is based on the premise of differential quality of relationships between leaders and subordinates[!]. High-quality relationships go beyond the contractual agreement and are characterized by mutual influence, negotiability, and trust and respect (Anand et al., 2011, p. 312).

3. A related approach is 'servant leadership'. Often characterized as a moral or ethical form of leadership, it builds on examples from the New Testament (Greenleaf, 1977). Servant leadership is seen as helping others to accomplish shared objectives by facilitating individual development and empowerment, but also that work is consistent with the well-being of the followers (Smith et al., 2004).

4

Leadership Beyond Ideology, Harmony and All-inclusiveness: The Case for a More Nuanced View

Almost all popular leadership theories are based on a view of social relations being characterized by consensus and harmony. There is at least an implicit view that leadership, if exercised reasonably competently, generally leads to shared beliefs and understanding, positive emotions, commitment and loyalty. In many organizational contexts this may be misleading. It does not take a Machiavelli to acknowledge that organizational life is full of politics, conflicts and contradictory ideals. People have different interests and orientations and not everybody is inclined to respond positively to even the best of leadership efforts. Leadership thinking often has a tendency to deny this, instead emphasizing harmony, peace, win-win and consensus. Romantic notions and wishful thinking need to be balanced with a degree of realism and acknowledgement that good things do not always go hand in hand with each other. Being authentic in situations of social conflict or competition for scarce resources, status and power may for example be politically naive and stupid.

In this chapter we will therefore discuss the relationship between leadership and ideology and why overly ideological views tend to impede good scholarship and managerial practice and foster an inability to recognize contradictions and trade-offs in organizations. We also critically address what we refer to as the all-inclusiveness problem of leadership – the tendency towards all-encompassing conceptualizations and the inability to consider alternative vocabulary outside the grand and powerful leadership discourse (ELR). We elaborate on the problems – for scholars, the leadership industry and practitioners – in terms of confusion, mystification and a loss of analytical precision. Finally, we extend the discussion from the first chapter by advocating and outlining a more restrained, nuanced view on leadership.

THE IDEOLOGICAL NATURE OF LEADERSHIP KNOWLEDGE

Ideology is a widely used concept in social science. In older traditions (e.g. Marxist writings) it often refers to 'false consciousness' that misleads the members of the lower classes, by justifying and covering up a dominant social order (e.g. Engels, 1893/1968). Ideology is here viewed as an instrumental construct used to further a particular group's interests at the expense of others, justifying the status quo or changes that benefit dominant interests. In more recent texts the element of true/false representations of social reality is downplayed, and ideology is described (in more neutral terms) as 'belief systems', describing the relevant reality, a desired state of affairs, and indicating possible ways of reaching the desired state (Czarniawska-Joerges, 1988). Ideologies order, pattern, offer and suppress meaning. They can consequently justify conservation as well as social change. They also offer avenues for making essentially contestable concepts less so. Thereby, ideologies offer clarity and comprehension, but still need to balance preciseness with vagueness in order to simultaneously attract *and* guide devotees.

In this book we refer to ideology as coherent belief systems that describe reality, point out what is desirable and show how this desirable state can be achieved. An ideology may therefore have many effects relevant to the thinking and practice of leadership, for example legitimation, portraying reality in a brighter (or darker) light, inserting hope, and offering ideals worth striving for. However, ideologies typically guide thinking into a rather selective and one-sided view of phenomena.

In a sense, all theories are to some extent ideological since they tend to privilege certain ideas, interpretations, interests or institutions by framing and labelling things in a particular way. They also reflect the ideological contexts in which they are formed (Czarniawska-Joerges, 1988, p. 8):

> [N]ot all ideologies are or can be used as science (or art or law), but all science is accumulated within specific ideological contexts and therefore can be used as ideology. New discoveries and new theories usually function as liberating devices in relation to old ideologies and as legitimating devices for new ideologies.

Science, and perhaps in particular social science, has an ideological dimension. This is certainly the case with management and organization studies (Alvesson & Willmott, 2012). This is a field that is often viewed as being *for* not *about* management and business. In business schools students are expected to be happy customers and positive messages about leadership and suggestions that the students are to become great leaders doing important things in the future are likely to feed their egos and boost satisfaction.

So rather than being a bastion free from or even against ideology, rigorous scientific methodology may actually reproduce and reinforce it. Therefore, all social scientists have good reasons to address how ideological commitments and ambitions to support certain 'good' causes may guide and sometimes counteract open inquiry and qualified understandings. But if (social) theory and knowledge are inevitably ideological, what is the problem and what can we do about it?

The first thing is that a theory can be *more or less* ideological in its nature. Feminist theories might be a good example of theories that have a strong ideological commitment and have at least to some extent been crafted in tandem with a recognizable political social movement. Bedrock geology might be an example of a theoretical field with less apparent ideological aspects.

Secondly, the ideological aspects of a theory can be more or less overt/recognized, ignored or hidden. Again, feminist theories and also post-colonial theories (eager to expose what is viewed as Western domination), for example, do not pretend or hide their ideological bias and political agenda. Traditional functionalist management theories and economic theory on the other hand often seem to ignore, repress or downplay their ideological commitments and implications. The concept of ideology is sometimes, but not that frequently used explicitly in organization studies. Surprisingly, but also perhaps tellingly, ideology is rarely directly openly explored in leadership studies (Alvesson & Kärreman, 2016, and Gemmill & Oakley, 1992 are exceptions).

Related to the first aspect above is the risk that a theory becomes 'over-ideological'. By that we mean an ideological commitment and loyalty so strong that they obstruct reflection, reflexivity and the ability to think and write ideologically in an unorthodox way (thereby making the author run the risk of being perceived as a theoretical/ideological heretic or renegade). When it comes to leadership studies – but also managerial practice by managers convinced that they do leadership – one is often struck by the unwillingness or inability to consider other alternative modes of organizing, what we refer to as ELR in this book (see Chapter 2).

Concerning the second aspect (overt/covert ideological commitment), knowledge is viewed as problematic if it is more or less openly justified by ideological arguments and ideological overtones. When it comes to leadership theories, this might for example be the case with 'critical leadership studies' where the often clearly pronounced anti-hierarchical element might turn some readers off, viewing the text more as propaganda than proper scholarly research. But as already said, a much more significant problem with many leadership studies is the inability or unwillingness to recognize its ideological bias and its (at least potential) ideological consequences.

Many leadership scholars may agree that leadership and leadership studies are inherently ideological, through supporting and strengthening dominant interests, in particular through reinforcing elitism. Managers doing leadership are portrayed as the heroes of the economy and working life, while followers are fairly insignificant and perhaps even mainly the result of leadership. The ideological aspects of this are rarely seriously considered. Instead, many leadership scholars and the entire leadership industry regularly try to conceal or ignore its ideological nature.

Ideology is neither trivial nor unproblematic. Many leadership practices are not simply justified by various leadership theories and their ideological backing. These practices in turn reinforce, reproduce and normalize various ideological elements (Schwartz, 1997). Or, as Ferraro et al. (2005, p. 12) put it, with clear relevance for leadership studies and practice:

> A theory can become true to the extent that people, acting on its ideas and under-
> lying assumptions, introduce practices, routines, and organizational arrangements
> that create conditions favoring the predictions made in the theory.

Therefore, ideology can be seen as both cause *and* effect in relation to leadership studies and leadership practice. It tends to elevate managers and other authorities into
(believed to be) leaders and turns others into followers.

Leadership can furthermore be related to the concept of 'managerial ideologies'
(Bendix, 1970, p. 529) referring to '[a]ll ideas which are espoused by or for those who
exercise authority in economic enterprises, and which seek to explain and justify that
authority'. One example of such an idea would be the legendary former CEO and
president of GE Jack Welch's famous one-liner on why one should lead: 'Control your
own destiny or someone else will.' In other words lead or be led, dominate or be
dominated. The ideological inspiration and the ideologically reproducing effects are
quite clear. Working life is a jungle. People compete over resources, positions, status
and influence. Competition, not cooperation, is the natural order of things. Influence
is a zero-sum game. The will to dominate is natural and legitimate. If you do not want
to be dominated by someone else, you had better start dominating him or her.
Freedom or autonomy *without* domination are in one way or another naive illusions.
Welch's philosophy can be debated, but this type of thinking is definitively part of the
reality of corporate and working life. In sharp contrast to the idea of 'the law of the
jungle' above, we have romantic leadership advocates who dream of everybody in
love with everyone else – if leadership with the right heart is in place. The latter
dominates contemporary leadership thinking, entering very much into relations, emotions, support, the shared and the transformational. Nevertheless, these two rather
extreme positions both provide an ideological justification for leadership, but from
very different points of departure.

Given how often leadership ideas, theories and models are used to 'explain and
justify' authority in business enterprises there almost seems to be a conceptual overlap
between many leadership theories and 'managerial ideology', at least the way Bendix
(1970) defines it. And for the sake of reflexivity, open inquiry and qualified understanding of the phenomenon, fewer ideological overtones both among scholars, leadership
mongers and practitioners seems like a good idea.

THE PASTORAL LANDSCAPE OF LEADERSHIP THEORY AND PRACTICE

Key in the problem of over-ideologizing leadership is an overly idyllic and harmonious
view of leadership (and followership). The ideologies of leadership not only emphasize the
significance and superiority of leaders over followers and reinforce and legitimize managerial privilege, power and position, they also tend to present a leadership-driven organizational life as idyllic. Leadership has often been associated with good intentions, good
outcomes, consensus and harmony. Bad outcomes are more seldom linked to leadership;

bad decisions and low morale are more often than not seen as a consequence of the *lack* of leadership, although of course 'bad leadership' is also sometimes part of the presented picture. But 'bad' is seen as a clear deviation from normal leadership.

Examples of idyllic and seductive definitions include Ospina and Sorensen (2006), who suggest 'that leadership happens when a community develops and uses, over time, shared agreements to create results that have collective value' (p. 188). The impression is that if there is no shared agreement or collective value, then 'leadership' has not happened. Uhl-Bien et al. (2007) frame 'leadership as a complex, interactive dynamic from which adaptive outcomes (e.g. learning, innovation, and adaptability) emerge' (p. 298). But perhaps an interactive dynamic may lead to outcomes that are not so 'adaptive'? George (2000) views leadership as about emotions, and refers to a range of positive outcomes following from leaders being high on 'emotional intelligence' (EI), leading to, for example, 'major improvements in their organization's functioning' (p. 1040) and the ability 'to effectively communicate with others to meet their needs and accomplish their goals and objectives' (p. 1034). Nothing is said about the problems possibly being created by leaders who are skilled at triggering the wanted emotions; this is somehow screened out as high EI is addressed in positive and functional terms. Shamir et al. (1993) also refer to charismatic leadership as leading to a wealth of (only) positive consequences (trust, confidence, self-esteem, meaningfulness, commitment, citizenship), rather than considering all the potential problems associated with charismatic leadership, for example 'followers' being mesmerized by the leader and unable or unwilling to think independently or use their judgement; this is indicated by others who suggest that leadership may be dangerously seductive (Calás & Smircich, 1991). Ideas on 'relational leadership' also tend to score high when it comes to idyllic views with their focus on creating opportunities for dialogue, the 'need to be respectful', 'having "a heart"' and 'for people to be able to "express themselves"' (Cunliffe & Eriksen, 2011, p. 1433). Leadership, at least of the right type, is by definition good. 'Relational' does not imply any other relational quality (e.g. domination-subordination, conflict, dependency, shared fixed idea or persuasion), but means a relationship that is morally and emotionally uplifting.

The tendency to describe leadership in idyllic and harmonious terms can also be found outside academic leadership books or other texts on the subject. Not only academic literature – supposedly nuanced and precise – but the leadership industry is even more active in communicating (via seminars, talks, training, PowerPoint-presentations) ideological, pastoral views of a rosy leadership reality, if managers employ the appropriate, fashionable leadership formula or have the true grit, that is Level 5 leaders, professional, hard-working, focused, modest and with high integrity (Collins, 2001).

Many practitioners describe their leadership in such a way. A CEO in Sweden we interviewed about practical examples of his leadership gave us the following example:

> It is important that people feel good and that you are responsive to people. You have to be nice to people. When Lucy felt a bit down the other day we handled

that situation well. I received an invitation to a dinner … I felt I did not have the time to attend so I sent her and her husband instead … That did not cost anything and she was very grateful and happy … Small and simple tricks that are hugely important.

Being kind and inclusive also seem to be fundamental parts of leadership according to the same CEO:

I experience myself as kind. I want everyone to be looked after. Nothing disturbs me more than when someone does not feel good. When someone ends up being outside [the group] I get pissed. Everyone has a value [referring to people at the bottom of the organizational hierarchy] and we all deserve respect …leadership to me is to make people take pleasure and feel valuable in the group.

Leadership here seems to be very much about avoiding conflicts, (perceived) injustice and a bad atmosphere in general. A one-sided emphasis on these aspects can however contribute to an overly harmonious lustre around the leader-follower relationship.

A similar view to that provided in the quotes above is also given by a middle manager we interviewed when studying leadership in a global high-tech company:

I am not the one that comes with the solution; we have many others that are better than me at doing that. I have an empathetic style – you know I do not want to dictate and overrun people. I want to have a common and shared view on what we are doing so that we feel that we are all into this together and know where we are heading – that is my leadership style.

Many of the HIPs we have studied over the last few decades – with similar ideals as expressed in the quotes above – have also indicated the need for 'toughness' when needed, for example in times of redundancies, negotiations. They are after all not that naive. But in contrast to a more Machiavellian view on leadership, they tend to see this as *deviations* from both an espoused ideal and from what they regard as 'business as usual'. The default mode is harmony, consensus and care for each other (usually in a rather paternalistic sense).

To sum up, in many influential texts leadership comes out like a pastoral landscape painting: an idyllic context, with a shepherd watching over a calm and happy flock of sheep. No rain, no drought, no wolves, no thieves and no missing sheep. But washing leadership clean of goal conflicts, opportunism, status issues, social dominance, coercion and compliance is not necessarily a wise move. To view leadership as something that goes on outside or beyond ordinary power games in organizations or as something that more or less automatically transforms potential conflicts into aligned interests and harmonic relationships seems naive. On the contrary, leadership is typically a part of organizational political realities, where narrow personal interests and agendas compete with altruism and the organizational/societal 'bigger picture'. Assuming that leadership free from struggle and conflicts will guide the organization towards a common goal may be of more use from an ideological perspective than in contributing to our understand-ing of the phenomenon in question. Instead, people – HIPs and LIPs – typically need to do some fighting to secure their voice and get the intended responses, and often other modes of organizing, for example power, formal managerial authority, networks, collective group actions, are deployed in order to reinforce – or obstruct – leadership attempts (see Chapter 2).

PUNCTUATING IDYLLIC AND IDEOLOGICAL KNOWLEDGE: RHETORICAL TRICKS, COGNITIVE DISSONANCE, TAUTOLOGIES AND DOMINANT INTERESTS

Few phenomena in organizations are well described as a matter of black and white. Even acts by well-intended and reasonably competent HIPs may have complicated and ambiguous effects. Something that is mainly functional can easily slip over into something dysfunctional.

There are many indications of the less idyllic character of managerial life and organ-izational reality. There are for example scholars that have identified very negative forms of leadership such as 'toxic' leadership (Lipman-Blumen, 2005) and 'cultish' leadership (Tourish & Pinnington, 2002). Others have shed light on the 'dark side' of transforma-tional leadership (Tourish, 2013). There are also even more critical scholars that point out the dangers of more ordinary forms of leadership, for example in terms of 'learned helplessness' (Gemmill & Oakley, 1992). But still, most texts on leadership reproduce an understanding of leadership as something both natural and rather free from conflicts and ambiguous outcomes. Often the highlighting of toxic, cultish, inauthentic and so on indicates the deviation, the really bad, from the good and the normal.

One influential example is transformational leadership as opposed to transactional leadership, as discussed in Chapter 3. The latter is described as instrumental and focused on rational exchange between leaders and followers (what we in this book rather would label managerial work). Transformational leadership on the other hand, is char-acterized by its higher moral purpose, deep engagement with followers' development and change for the better. The same pattern can for example also be seen when talking about toxic versus non-toxic leaders, when heroic leaders are contrasted with villainous leaders or when servant leaders are contrasted with selfish leaders at the top of the pyramid, uninterested in serving others. Hence, the alternative to (bad) leadership often seems to be: (good) leadership, not managerial work, power, peer relations, profession-alism/autonomy or co-working, all of which offer alternative framings and understanding than those invited by leadership language. Furthermore, 'bad' people are often exempted from the fine leadership label. Jackson and Parry (2008) for example claim that Hitler and other villains were tyrants, not leaders, thereby preserving a positive notion of the latter. Normal leadership is then safely located in a category of the idyllic.

But more relevant and interesting than clear-cut good/bad distinctions are more typical examples of leadership, which are not as easy to categorize in terms of good and bad. It is not necessarily true that there are really bad people creating bad results.

In the normal case there are complexities that make the good/bad distinction seem both trivial and naive. Most managers are neither great nor hopeless. Some studies indicate the prevalence of leaders who are not particularly effective. Bryman and Lilley (2009) found, for example, that their interviewees 'found it easier to think of ineffective leaders than effective ones' (p. 337). In a study of subordinates commenting upon their managers' leadership there were many more negative than positive opinions expressed (Cunha et al., 2006).

Also, egocentric or neurotic authorities may have positive followers who feel they benefit from their leader (Kets de Vries & Balasz, 2011). There may even be a tendency for power-hungry and aggressive people to have a strong appeal for followers (Pfeffer, 2013). Aggressiveness and evoking fear may lead to positions – or at least impressions – of power and many like to identify themselves and have positive relations with people of power. In cases of bullying, many want to avoid identifying themselves with the weaker party – the victim – and relate more positively to the bully. The case of Apple's former CEO Steve Jobs, who violated most recommendations by leadership scholars, and still accomplished quite a lot (Isaacson, 2012) is a good example of a person who exercised rather brute forms of power, for example imposing his will and being very exploitative and rude to people, but still gained many admiring followers.

By persisting in putting up overly harmonious and highly positive formulations of good leadership we run the risk of reinforcing naivety and wishful thinking, instead of developing a qualified understanding of human relations and organizing processes at work. Of course, most managers have an idea of what goes on around them. They realize that they do not work in Disneyland. But still many are to some extent victims of wishful thinking and idealizations and do not seem to be helped by the leadership industry in terms of realism and sharpness in their thinking and acting.

How can we understand the ideological bias and unhelpfulness of much, even the majority of the leadership literature (academic as well as leadership industry versions)? How come we have decades of mainstream leadership research and popular management writing that (over)emphasizes social harmony and has a tendency to ignore, downplay or suppress conflict while employing categorizations of active leaders and passive followers? One reason behind the inability to recognize the complexities of leadership is probably pure cognitive dissonance (Festinger, 1957). According to this theory, we all have an inclination to hold all our attitudes and beliefs in harmony in order to avoid dissonance and instead seek consistency. When devoted leadership practitioners and scholars experience that effects are not in line with all the expected blessings (or when good outcomes are mixed or intertwined with worse outcomes), they tend to employ various manoeuvres to reach cognitive consistency. This may include convincing themselves even more intensively of the attractiveness of the chosen alternative (doing leadership) and at the same time decreasing the attractiveness of the rejected alternatives (e.g. the other five modes of organizing described in Chapter 2). We then get good, sexy leadership, not boring management. And we get happy followership, not people insisting on being autonomous and relying on professionalism rather than leadership.

A related and important problem is that leadership is often defined based on its effects, which is highly problematic (see Chapter 1). For example, when the influential business magazine *Chief Executive* (1 May 2015) listed '9 repeatable behaviours of a great leader' the list started with 'A great leader does the right thing'. That 'good leadership' leads to 'good outcomes', where goodness in the latter is inherent in the first definition, is of course tautological. As previously described, transformational leadership research appeared to give the field an energy injection and their advocates hoped to capture the secret of effective leadership; however, much of this research is highly problematic, since many seem to tautologically measure the existence and causal force of transformational leadership through its effects (van Knippenberg & Sitkin, 2013).

But perhaps the most profound reason behind the strong ideological and idyllic nature of leadership knowledge is that it is assumed to serve the interests of managers and the leadership industry. Selling simplistic, positive and straightforward messages promising happiness for everybody is much easier than suggesting more complicated ideas. Easy, seductive vocabulary is appealing. Short quotes and one-liners on leadership flourish. For many leaders and leader-wannabees in educational settings or when reading leadership literature, boosting the ego and self-confidence is much more appealing than being seriously challenged by messages where the good and the bad do not necessarily go hand in hand.

THE ALL-INCLUSIVENESS OF LEADERSHIP

As touched upon already in the first two chapters the signifier 'leadership' tends to be used in many different ways. A vast number of more or less popular definitions flourish. Often it is not defined at all. Rost (1991) found that two-thirds of all texts on leadership did not provide a definition of the topic at hand (cited by Palmer & Hardy, 2000). Our impression is that this has not changed much. One often has to guess what authors and others mean by leadership. Of course these conditions make the relationship between leadership texts and what they are supposed to say rather uncertain and arbitrary. Not just the various definitions per se (or the lack of them), but all the implicit theories and tacit, taken-for-granted associations around the concept will make 'reality' come out quite differently.

When leadership is defined it tends to be in vague, all-inclusive ways and addressed so broadly that it becomes unavoidable. One example is Collinson (2005) who writes that 'leaders exercise considerable control through, for example, constructing corporate vision, shaping structures, influencing cultures, intensifying and monitoring work and by making key strategic and HR decisions' (p. 1426). In this case leaders seem to account for the entire management function of a firm, which moves leaders and leadership from something demarcated to something similar to management and organization as a whole. A similar inclusive view is also articulated by Hunter et al. (2007), arguing that subordinates cannot assess leaders as the latter do all sorts of things not observed by them, including much managerial work like interacting with superiors and customers. The all-inclusiveness also starts to colonize the horizontal dimension of influence (see Chapter 2). Rather than covering what HIPs may do in relation to LIPs, 'leadership' also addresses what goes on outside asymmetrical relationships (targeting MIPs and NIPs). When a manager interacts with colleagues, superiors or customers s/he is hardly best described as exercising leadership or acting like a leader – if s/he is not in an interaction where the colleague, superior or customer is clearly taking a follower position.

In some post-heroic writings leadership is viewed as a process and refers to participants 'who temporarily performed leadership in specific moments, sometimes subtle and fleeting and sometimes overt and lengthy' (Sutherland et al., 2014, p. 770). All efforts involving some influence seem to be regarded as leadership. Collaborations between peers or colleagues are referred to as shared or distributed leadership (Gronn, 2002). People being able to act independently are called 'self-leaders' (Houghton et al., 2003). Here the fundamental assumption that leadership involves followership seems to be abolished. Autonomy and freedom at work are also sometimes seen as *outcomes* of leadership (e.g. Manz & Sims, 1987), but not as an *alternative* mode of organizing work (see Chapter 2). In short; the term leadership sometimes seems to capture all forms of organizing or cooperating, meaning that there only seem to be people doing leadership in a variety of constellations and forms: only leaders or leadership, no followers or followership and no horizontal modes of organizing.

A problem is therefore that leadership often covers all six modes of organizing previously described – overlapping with management, exercise of power, horizontal collaborations in different forms as well as people acting autonomously (self-leadership) – and hence covers most social interactions in organizations. What remains as distinctly leadership is the use of the signifier: leadership is what people pay attention to when talking about leadership. This could be almost anything – resulting in total confusion. There are scholars who see a virtue in this, proposing that we should view leadership as nothing but a floating or empty signifier (e.g. Kelly, 2014). The same can however be said about many other (not to say all) concepts, for example 'management' or 'strategy'. Of course, representation is always problematic, and poststructuralists would deny its very possibility, but there should still be good reasons to use a specific term and try to indicate what it may tell us in relationship to other terms. Leadership makes sense in relationship to various forms of 'non-leadership', but it is often hard to imagine what they may be. The more alternative views within leadership discourses, the more empty and meaningless the term leadership becomes and the more confusion it creates (Blom & Alvesson, 2015). Therefore, the more texts on leadership one reads, the more confused one tends to get (Grint, 2010a).

Asking practitioners (HIPs and LIPs) how they view leadership – in general or based on their own practice – easily leads to rather wide-ranging and inexact versions. As managers and other organizational actors are typically exposed to a multitude of discourses – in education, mass media, everyday talk, corporate policy statements – about leadership being so important and accomplishing so much, personal meanings of leadership easily become all-encompassing and therefore often incoherent. For example, when asking LIPs in an R&D-department what leadership they felt they needed, the answer included activities such as influencing the hierarchy *upwards* and promoting the department's interest *outside* the unit, i.e. the HIPs should not lead their LIPs, but direct their 'leadership-efforts' elsewhere (Blom & Alvesson, 2014). Managers may claim that they dislike 'micro management' but then ten minutes later in interviews emphasize that they need to be much more operative and instructive in their relationships with their subordinates (Alvesson & Sveningsson, 2003a).

Managers are typically busy doers more than thinkers with plenty of time to spare so one cannot expect a very sophisticated and eloquent view on these matters, but still leadership is not – or should not be – a mindless activity. In everyday organizational practice, people may not need very sharp and consistent definitions, but a reasonably clear sense of meaning is important for thought and communication.

Beside the abstractions and confusion created by all the various views and recipes for success, the hope for and high expectations of what leaders and leadership can achieve create difficulties. There is a normative pressure on managers to be seen as leaders and live up to the ideal. For most people it is unrealistic to be transforma-tional, charismatic, authentic, etc. This might fuel the tendency to describe trivial, mundane activities as 'leadership' to boost one's work so that it appears in line with leadership ideals. A CEO of a mid-sized company in Sweden we interviewed described for example remembering his subordinates' birthdays, playing golf, and wining and dining as key elements of his leadership (Sveningsson & Blom, 2011). A similar beef-ing up of managerial work is described by Kelly (2008), who claims that: 'leadership is expressed through the holding of budget meetings, team meetings, through the telling of jokes, a chat over a coffee, giving speeches, dealing with complaints, send-ing e-mails, opening post and generally getting on with everyday ordinary work' (p. 770). We are not denying that small things may sometimes have important effects, but a far-reaching 'extra-ordinarization' of the mundane (Alvesson & Sveningsson, 2003c) both threatens to trivialize leadership – as practice and as a signifier – and at the same time to glorify and mystify HIPs and their everyday work. Other examples of efforts to do leadership include managers trying to encourage people in specific crea-tive leadership activities, which are not really necessary or productive but are good for impression management and self-esteem (Schaefer, 2014).

To sum up this section: the all-inclusiveness of leadership is causing confusion and ambiguity both among HIPs and LIPs supposed to relate to it and among scholars try-ing to make sense of it. Of course, it is impossible and not even desirable to agree upon one, useful conceptualization of leadership or one true essence of leadership that can be captured in one simple definition that will make sense in all possible situations (we need to also consider cultural variations between societies, industries and organ-izations). Our own 'definition' in Chapters 1 and 2 should be seen rather as a useful demarcation in relation to other potential modes of organizing than a universal truth about what leadership really 'is'. But the use of a signifier and what it is supposed to relate to can be taken too far. We claim that this is the case with leadership. Therefore, we suggest a more restrained view and careful usage of the term leadership. We believe this would benefit both academia as well as practice.

A MORE CAREFUL VIEW ON LEADERSHIP

We would therefore like to refer back to the few but vital elements we saw as characteristic of leadership in contrast to the other modes of organizing as described in the first two chapters of the book. It is important to emphasize what leadership is not, that is, what is better addressed in other ways.

Leadership needs to be understood as a set of practices, *not* as the successful outcomes of these. Leadership is not about intending or accomplishing something that is by definition good. In a messy, complicated organizational reality, doing the right thing is not easy, and it is not easy to decide what the right thing is, either beforehand or after leadership has been practised for a while. People often have different understandings of the right thing and also of the right outcome and the possible link between leadership and outcomes. Leadership is not the same as solving problems, creating community, bringing out followers' better selves, increasing customer orientation, growth or profit. These may be outcomes of leadership practices, but most of the time there is no simple one-to-one relationship between leadership as a practice and various organizational outcomes. Followers may be unaffected by leadership and respond more to other factors or they may respond in other ways than intended by the person doing the leadership.

Leadership constitutes and takes place in an asymmetrical relationship (not necessarily following the formal hierarchy) with one or several actors defining themselves as followers (on a mainly voluntary basis). Leadership calls for followership. Leadership is not a tension-free or cosy egalitarian activity. Leadership and followership mean a clear sense of superiority and inferiority. Followership is central. Leadership includes the establishment and reproduction of this. You only follow someone who is perceived to be in some way superior to yourself – more competent, intelligent, experienced, energetic, full of initiatives, better at framing issues, of a higher moral calibre. Sometimes this followership is tricky, as people are not always keen on taking a position as an underdog and being influenced about their thinking, feelings and values (in addition to what is stipulated in the formal employment contract). Of course, followership may be subtle and there is also a degree of mutual influencing. Nobody is following all the time, but still the very point of leadership is that it includes followership and an asymmetrical relationship. Doing what one is told (management and/or power) is one thing, voluntarily adopting meanings as a consequence of another person's acts of influencing (leadership) is another matter, although in many practical situations it may not be crystal clear what is what. Exactly what is voluntary and what is an outcome of strong normative pressure or a taken for granted response is not so easy to say.

SUMMARY

In this chapter we have highlighted what we see as two problematic tendencies with the current thinking in and practising of leadership: (a) ideological overtones and the wide-spread ignorance thereof, including idyllic expectations of harmony between actors, intentions and outcomes, and (b) an inclination to include more or less all organizational activities under the label of leadership. The two tendencies are interrelated. They mean that leadership often scores higher on ideology than intellectuality: there is a legitimation of managerial superiority and a naturalization of the dividing up of the world into leaders and followers.

There are some approaches that are seemingly more progressive and argue for leadership as a shared social process, but also the claim that when there is 'leadership' there is harmony and good outcomes in the interests of all involved. This often tends to be a bit too harmonious and idyllic to escape the ideology problem. It is important to have an open, nuanced view, acknowledging complexity and the mix of cooperation, competition and conflict that is common in organizations. The recognition of power, politics and irrationality (fixed ideas, big egos) thus needs to be part of the understanding.

The idyllic and harmonious view imbuing much thinking of leadership, where all good things tend to be combined needs to be questioned. HIPs and LIPs do not always share a common understanding of a common goal and how to reach it. A probably more typical situation is characterized by ambiguous effects, the struggle to further one's own interests and influence, and conflicting views of all sorts of things. Who should exercise leadership over whom, when, how and why are often open (and good) questions. Furthermore, leadership is not only about making people feel good about each other and themselves. Leadership (as well as power and to some extent management in our terms) is also about getting people to do things they do not spontaneously like or do things in a way they do not like. This might create friction, resistance and potentially intended, unintended, good *and* bad outcomes. In short, when trying to make sense of leadership we need to break free from the naive idyllic views that dominate so much of current leadership discourse. As a HIP it is therefore important to critically reflect upon potential cognitive dissonance effects when evaluating one's role as a leader.

As we have seen in this chapter, leadership seems to be all over the place and includes almost any form of influence or organizational activity, causing confusion and ambiguity among practitioners, leadership developers/consultants as well as academics. As researchers we may not always know best, but leadership practitioners may not know what they mean by leadership either. Caught in a barrage of discourses – expressed by the leadership industry – about the merits of being authentic, serving, coaching, charismatic, change-oriented, transformational, post-heroic, relational – and a variety of demands within organizations (top management, colleagues, various constellations of subordinates) and from situational contingencies (some invoked by customers, others by technical problems), navigating the leadership jungle in a systematic and coherent way is far from unproblematic.

We have advocated what we refer to as a more restrained and nuanced view of leadership. Exercising leadership means trying to influence how other people interpret and understand the reality, that is, management of meaning. Leadership occurs when someone more or less voluntarily lets him or herself become influenced by – 'following' – someone else, granting the latter the role of a leader in an asymmetrical relationship. Again, we do not want to impose yet another 'better' universal definition of leadership on the reader, but we need to demarcate it in relation to other modes of organizing. The important thing is to facilitate reflexivity: what is leadership and what is not?

5
Leadership and Organizational Culture

In this chapter we discuss leadership in relation to culture, in particular organizational culture. Culture may be seen as a system of shared meanings, understandings and values. As such it constrains and guides leadership at the same time as leadership is about influencing cultural meanings.

For some, the very essence of leadership is to form and change culture. We would not go so far, but the intimate relationship between leadership and culture is important to consider in a number of respects. What is actually supposed to be 'leadership' – and even more so 'good leadership' – is a cultural phenomenon. For some, a senior person standing in the centre and authoritatively telling people what to do may, in some contexts, be viewed as 'true leadership'. The leader creates respect and people may follow. For others, in other cultural contexts, this behaviour may be viewed as illegitimate, authoritarian and old-fashioned managerial behaviour, expressing power and *not* leadership. The latter may be seen as a matter of having dialogues, getting people involved, sharing a common understanding and agreeing upon a sense of direction. But this may in contexts in favour of 'macho leadership' be seen more as committee chairmanship than leadership. The cultural context is central to what is viewed as leadership.

In order to understand leadership we thus need to carefully consider not only the possible followers and their characteristics in terms of age, gender, experience and skills but also the broader cultural context. This may include nation, industry, region, organization and organizational subunit. These frame, constrain and guide leadership – and other modes of organizing. Cultures may be more or less hierarchical or egalitarian. In other words, they may be 'leadership-oriented' – emphasizing the HIP as the centre of the organizational universe – or emphasize horizontal relations, autonomy and professional norms and the limited or even absence of needs for leadership.

Leadership also needs to be understood in terms of its impact on culture but also vice versa. It is partly a matter of leadership influencing culture, but also of culture influencing leadership. Managers and other HIPs are thus significantly constrained and governed not only by economic, legal and structural factors, but also by culture. Organizational and occupational culture are central in the guiding and controlling of people at work. In that sense culture can be viewed as an alternative organizing principle to leadership. Given an established specific organizational culture informing people how to think, feel, value and act, there is limited need and/or space for leadership to add anything significant to what is inherent in culture. Sometimes culture marginalizes or obstructs leadership as people tend to follow the collective worldviews and values rather than the efforts of their superiors to do leadership. The HIPs' efforts to influence meaning may be weak compared to organizational culture. But of course occasionally cultural change is deemed to be necessary and here leadership is vital. Moreover, leadership is often important for the reproduction and reinforcement of culture.

From a reflexive point of view, managers and subordinates need to think through the meaning and impact of organizational culture, and its relationship to leadership and other organizing principles.

ON ORGANIZATIONAL CULTURE

Organizational culture is one of the major issues in academic research and education, in organization theory as well as in management practice. There are good reasons for this: the cultural dimension is central in all aspects of organizational life. Even in those organizations where cultural issues receive little explicit attention, how people in a company think, feel, value and act is guided by ideas, meanings and beliefs of a cultural (socially shared) nature. The significance of culture is not reduced by whether managers think that culture is too soft or too complicated to bother about or whether there is no unique corporate culture. Senior organizational members are always, in one way or another, 'managing culture' – underscoring what is important and what is less so and framing how the corporate world should be understood. Organizations practising intensive 'management by numbers' may develop and reproduce a culture celebrating performance indicators and rituals around the handling of these. The strength and significance of structure, of rules, of pressure to comply with customers and be customer oriented does not work mechanically, but how groups and individuals relate to this is a matter of cultural understandings informing interpretation.

In most contemporary organizations, corporate culture receives a lot of attention and is seen as crucial. A key concern is that 'culture management aspires to intervene in and regulate being, so that there is no distance between individuals' purposes and those of the organization for which they work' (Grey, 2005, p. 68). In other words, people are freely following the cultural ideas and meanings characterizing their organizations, voluntarily and with some (or considerable) enthusiasm doing things they see as right. Here culture takes care of steering and control.

Organizational culture is often viewed as crucial for performance. Managers frequently ascribe successes such as rapid growth to their culture. 'Companies win or lose based on the cultures they create', a CEO says (Puffer, 1999, p. 34). Many of the most influential management writers and academics agree. Kanter (2008, p. 44) recognizes that talk about values is fashionable in corporate circles, but for 'the vanguard companies we studied, values truly are a primary consideration'.

Culture is, however, a tricky concept as it is – similarly to leadership – easily used to cover everything and consequently nothing. That certain researchers, consultants or managers are interested in 'culture' – or at least use the term – does not mean that they have very much in common. Frequently 'culture' seems to refer to little more than a social pattern – for example, it refers to surface phenomena rather than exploring the meanings, implicit (not necessarily espoused) values and ideas behind them. It could therefore be advocated that in many cases the term should be abandoned in favour of something like 'informal behaviour patterns', 'norm system', or simply 'social pattern' – as distinct from formal properties (strategies, structures, procedures). Many people referring to culture seem to do so in a very vague way, and as with leadership it is important to use the concept without losing focus, direction and interpretive depth.

Culture is perhaps best understood to be a system of common symbols and meanings, at least partly implicit and taken for granted. It provides 'the shared rules governing cognitive and affective aspects of membership in an organization, and the means whereby they are shaped and expressed' (Kunda, 1992, p. 8). Culture is not primarily 'inside' people's heads, but somewhere 'between' the heads of a group of people where symbols and meanings are publicly expressed – in work group interactions, in gossip, storytelling and in board meetings, but also in material objects. It is the meaning aspect of what is being socially expressed and it is thus visible and invisible at the same time. Culture, then, is central in governing the understanding of behaviour, social events, institutions and processes. Culture is the setting in which these phenomena become comprehensible and meaningful. Culture is thus crucial for understanding leadership.

A key concept for grasping culture is *meaning*. This is also the essence of leadership, which in earlier chapters was defined in terms of the management of meaning, as Smircich and Morgan (1982) expressed it. Meaning refers to how an object or an utterance is interpreted, the specific content or understanding of an idea. It indicates what something is seen to stand for. Meaning has a subjective referent in the sense that it appeals to an expectation, a way of relating to things. Meaning makes an object relevant and meaningful. In a cultural context, it is socially shared and not personally idiosyncratic meanings that are of interest.

When thinking about culture it is important to bear in mind what culture is *not*. Making a distinction between culture and social structure is helpful. Culture is regarded as a more or less cohesive system of meanings and symbols, in terms of which social interaction takes place. Social structure is regarded as the behavioural patterns that the social interaction itself gives rise to. In the case of culture, we have a frame of reference of beliefs, expressive symbols and values, by means of which individuals define their environment, express their feelings and make judgements. At the social structural level, we have a continuous process of interaction. As Geertz (1973, p. 145) states, culture is the creation of meaning through which human beings interpret their experiences and guide their actions, while social structure is the form which action takes or the network of social relationships that actually exists.

LEADERSHIP IN THE CONTEXT OF ORGANIZATIONAL CULTURE

The relationship between leadership and culture is complex. Given the view on leadership expressed above – in which leadership deals with meanings, thinking and feelings rather than having a narrow behavioural focus – leadership may even be defined as the agent working through culture as the medium and target of action. Leadership is a culture-influencing activity, the systematic influencing of meaning. This does not necessarily mean that leadership creates or drastically changes culture, only that leadership is a cultural manifestation influencing other cultural manifestations, such as shared understandings of objectives, technologies and environment. Influencing may take place within culture, for example through reminding people about modes of relating to reality deemed natural or appropriate, on quality standards, improvements, adherence to rules and regulations, space for initiative.

Leaders forming culture

In the interplay between leadership and organizational culture different kinds of relationships and emphasis are possible. In 'pro-leadership' management circles – those including most consultants, practitioners and some popular academics – leadership is seen as having a far-reaching impact on the cultural values and orientations of organizational members. Many leadership writers emphasize the far-reaching capacity for CEOs, founders and other senior actors to produce, control and change culture. It is assumed they have the ability to 'define the parameters of the corporate culture' (Kets de Vries, 1994, p. 78), and those transformational leaders 'construct cultures that foster effective management of change. They do this by defining and inculcating in organization members the belief that they can affect, if not control, their environment, including government regulation, market competition, and technological change' (Sashkin, 2004, p. 194). We can then talk of assumptions about 'leader-driven organizational cultures', where a leader is influential in establishing or turning around certain core ideas, values and meanings. Often these ideas are attractive to managers and other HIPs as they underscore and exaggerate their significance and influence, but this can be fundamentally unreflexive and blind people to the difficulties in having a strong impact on collective ideas and meanings. As we have emphasized, leadership is difficult and often efforts only lead to modest and temporary outcomes.

The strongest case for leader-driven organizational creation or change is made by adherents of charismatic individuals in organizations, charisma being a key quality also for transformational leadership, turning self-centred people into committed organizational members positively attached to the leader and working for the good of the organization (Burns, 1978; Diaz-Saenz, 2011).

While many leadership enthusiasts of the 1990s were keen to emphasize the charismatic leader, for many the ideal leader of today is a different kind of hero; the soft-spoken, modest, yet hard-working, tenacious and skilled leader who does not crave the spotlight so much as he or she is eager to give space and recognition for the achievements of his or her colleagues (Collins, 2001). Charismatic leaders, it is now argued, rarely stimulate others to grow and make the organization heavily dependent on them by fostering followership. Instead, we are told that leaders should strive to bring longer-term corporate aspirations to fruition, by creating sustainable organizations with first-class employees (e.g. Collins, 2001). (Of course, as discussed in Chapter 3, many still emphasize the charismatic boss as an ideal, highlighting his or her positive impact on employee motivation.) The hard-working, focused, skilled person, giving credit to others, may still be important for cultural influence, but typically this will be a more long-term project, based on endurance and focus rather than mesmerizing communication.

Founders of organizations – whether seen as charismatic or not – are frequently also viewed as founders of cultures or at least significant sources of a set of values which the organizational members adapt and reproduce (e.g. Schein, 1985). Founders of organizations in a sense start from scratch, having a significant influence on the particular combination of people employed, choosing the direction of the company and thus frequently stamping their imprint on the shared ideas, beliefs and meanings that develop during the formative years of the company. High-profile people like Richard Branson, Steve Jobs and Ingvar Kamprad (founder of IKEA) are examples of founders and CEOs with such an impact.

Culture forms leadership

Although HIPs, for example founders, CEOs, chairpersons, key innovators or exceptional professionals, may be able to stamp a relatively strong imprint on an organization (or parts of it) under special circumstances – crises, changes in circumstances calling for basic reorientation, particularly favourable preconditions for strategic choice contingent upon market position and/or changes in the industry – it is debatable whether top executives can normally be seen as 'captains of culture'. Arguably, culture forms leadership rather than, or at least as much as, the other way round (Alvesson, 2011a). This is the case at least for the large majority of people designated or emerging as leaders. As Biggart and Hamilton (1987, p. 435) put it: 'All actors, but perhaps leaders especially, must embody the norms of their positions and persuade others in ways consistent with their normative obligations'.

In a sense, societal and organizational cultures set limits for the kind of managerial behaviour and arrangements that are likely to be accepted. Leadership is then often an adaptation to a cultural template for how to be. To appear to lead may be to follow a script or a set of norms: run meetings, be cheerful to people, ask how they feel, go through appraisal talks.

Organization-specific cultural ideas and meanings direct and constrain managerial behaviour and leadership in various ways. Senior managers pass on (or modify) organizational culture through being role models, using selective recruitment to managerial positions and through sanctioning or discouraging deviations. Also, subordinates have a strong impact on how leadership is shaped. If we disregard the use of management (relying on rights and obligations connected with the employment contract) and power – breaking the will of people through the use of the whip (threats of being fired or not being promoted) or more modest sanctions leading to a degree of anxiety/fear/shame – leadership means having some kind of appeal to people, to their hearts and minds. Vision, instructions, suggestions, goals and constructions of corporate reality must be perceived as legitimate and meaningful. The actions of the leader must then be fine-tuned to the frameworks and norms of those who are to be influenced. In this sense the subordinates as a collective – sharing certain cultural ideas – 'decide' what works in terms of leadership. This does not mean of course that the leader is totally subordinated to a given set of orientations or is forced to adapt to a specific style and just reproduce a given set of meanings and ideas. The leader can change these, but gradually, and must proceed from an appreciation of people holding certain ideas, values and preferences in order to do so. The leader is involved in the negotiation rather than the imposition of new or revised orientations on people. Cultural change then tends to be gradual, partial and an outcome of social processes in which a group of subordinates have as much if not more to say than the leader. Many managers try to change organizational culture, but this often involves resistance and conflict (e.g. Hallett, 2007).

It is not uncommon for managers to be located inbetween values and norms held by senior managers and those promoted by their subordinates. 'Top management' culture – sometimes seen as corporate culture – and 'functional cultures' (associated with production, R&D, HR or marketing) frequently differ and may conflict, and leadership may partly be a matter of negotiation between different kinds of normative frameworks and views on corporate reality.

The need to deal with both overall organizational requirements and the orientations of the subordinates can be illustrated by the case of a US coastguard officer who found his men – mainly college graduates whose expectations, interests and motives were at odds with the routines and lack of discretion of military life – bored and negative. Here, two cultures met and clashed: college/professional culture emphasizing freedom, stimulation and individualism and military regime based on control and obedience. Instead of trying to impose military discipline in a traditional way, the officer made a deal with his men about more discretion and certain liberties in exchange for more positive behaviour (Wilkins, referred to in Trice and Beyer, 1993). This case illustrates, among other things, how the values and orientations of a group of subordinates trigger a change in 'leadership' (if this is the right label in this case) so that it resonates better with their values and meanings.

Most people expected to exercise leadership in their jobs are much more strongly influenced by organizational culture than involved in actively producing it. Apart from structural conditions (job task, resources, position, formal rights), which are to some extent cultural manifestations and have consequences through the cultural meaning attached to them, the cultural context guides the HIP as to how leadership should be carried out. This is done, for example, by prescribing that 'leadership' goes beyond relying solely on formal authority, and involves influencing the ideas, values and orientations of subordinates on how they should interact with managers, for example in terms of the appropriate degree of subordination. This can range from marked to (almost) non-existent.

The partly 'culture-driven' nature of leadership is neglected in most of the literature and in the talk of management gurus and practitioners. Often leadership is viewed as an outcome of a manager's traits or ideas and/or is viewed as an internal affair between a HIP and the LIPs in the group. This is to some extent because the cultural dimension has traditionally been marginalized in leadership research. More significant, however, are the ideological overtones of a lot of talk on leadership (addressed in Chapter 4). As seen from the discussion in Chapter 3, there is a broad tendency, in leadership research and among practitioners, to stress the manager (the 'leader') as a superior, uni-directionally interacting with subordinates, and to neglect the fact that almost all managers are also subordinates and thus have a hierarchy above themselves (Laurent, 1978). There is a desire among many people to ascribe strong impact to leaders, reflecting a need to see somebody as responsible for different outcomes, good or bad (Meindl, 1995; Pfeffer, 1977). This fits the self-image of many managers and reinforces their status and claims for high salaries, prestige and authority in companies and society. Management writers, teachers and consultants would probably find the markets for their products and services smaller and less sympathetic if they argued for the significance of factors other than management and leaders, as well as the complexity and ambiguity of accounting for performance. Generally, the strong faith in leadership, the attribution of causal powers to it and the heroization of leaders may be seen as interesting cultural manifestations – reflecting socially invented 'truths' and worthy of investigation.

Sometimes external dependencies and structural restrictions on leadership are noticed but the phenomenon of 'cultural subordinacy' has not been treated seriously in leadership research. Leadership as the adoption, reproduction, reinforcement, creative variation and/or rejuvenation of dominant cultural orientations in organizations is a potentially fruitful line of thinking. This may appear as less impressive and appealing than cultural creation and change, but may still be important.

To sum up, culture is often seen as being affected by the leadership of the founders in particular, but to some extent and under certain conditions also of senior managers, at least if they are 'charismatic' people. Leaders are said to work *on* culture rather than to work *within* culture. We need to appreciate both. In the present book leadership is also understood as taking place within and as an outcome of the cultural context. Of course, under extraordinary circumstances leaders may transcend parts of existing cultural patterns or even contribute to the (re-)creation of culture. Also in such cases cultural context and cultural constraints must be considered. A precondition for changing culture is to connect to it. But HIPs who are reflexive, creative and eager to have a clear influence may be able to be less subordinate to cultural patterns and engage in fewer pre-formed and more 'culture-free' leadership acts. This may involve more culture-changing than the common culture-reproducing impact and possibly also influence followers more strongly.

Example 1: cultural steered leadership in CCC

The case of the IT consultancy firm CCC offers an interesting case of how founders create organizational culture and how sometimes later managers are strongly governed by organizational culture in their ways of doing their job and in particular acting towards subordinates (Alvesson, 1995). CCC had about 500 employees, was organized in the form of smaller subsidiaries with up to 50 employees, and emphasized social and communicative skills rather than technical competence as crucial for IT projects. The founders of the firm spent much time thinking about how the organization could be an attractive employer and worked intensively on culture creation: selective recruitment, emphasizing ideas and values, initiating corporate rituals like meetings with a strong emotional and symbolic content. Engaged and loyal employees who appreciated the social nature of the workplace were viewed as key. The slogan was 'fun and profit', and a strong community feeling and positive work climate was emphasized. The company tried to downplay hierarchy in favour of community and were quite successful. Only managers who were assessed as able to become friends with their subordinates were hired. The latter had a strong say in the recruitment and promotion of managers. As subsidiaries were central, the subsidiary managers had an important role. The subordinates had clear expectations of their managers in terms of the leadership to be done. Dominant values and meanings in the company were strong and clear and supported a great deal of the steering, coordination and control of work. Leadership ideals were related to the style and values of the founders. They exercised powerful, culture-creating effects that left a strong imprint on the organization as a whole:

> There is an opinion, a certain education that you get on how to be a manager in this company and that comes from the old leaders, the founders of the company. The leaders are seen as very important, to be a sort of cultural carrier and to be an ideal for the personnel. As a leader you must participate in all social arrangements. You should preferably be the funniest of all, you should be visible all the time and give a direction to the company and the personnel in the way you wish the company to function, offer nice parties and tell stories and things like that. (Subsidiary manager)

One manager expressed this as 'in CCC you only employ managers that can become buddies with their consultants' and 'the employees expect to have a beer with the CEO'. The staff more or less had the right to veto candidates for subsidiary manager positions. One externally recruited manager failed to live up to expectations to provide information. There was an impression that he tried to put up a smokescreen around a bad financial result during his first year to keep it from the subordinates. They found out, and this contributed to them successfully demanding his removal from the company.

In this company there was a rather strong and explicit cultural framing of leadership at the organizational level. Top management, but perhaps even more so the staff, had certain values and expectations on management and leadership to which the managers had to respond in order to be credible, legitimate and effective: to be active in social arrangements, to downplay status and prestige and emphasize close and informal social relationships, put staff and team building into focus. As a manager you were part of and a key player in an organizational community. All this breaks with traditional hierarchies based on differentiation and distance. For managers, this was a constraint but also a guiding framework in their leadership.

CCC was, of course, like all companies, in many ways unique. It was, at the time of the study, a young and, in terms of cultural orientations, very explicit and high-profile organization. Other companies incorporate less distinct, less espoused and more taken-for-granted ideas, beliefs and expectations. Still, there are institutionalized cultural orientations carried by superiors, colleagues and subordinates which means selectivity in terms of who is recruited to and allowed to stay in managerial positions, and cultural rules for the kind of leadership that is seen as acceptable and that people respond positively to. The case of CCC illustrates how organizational culture shapes leadership, thus reversing the opposite logic characterizing the formative years of the firm, where founders had a strong impact on organizational culture. The key point is that a 'settled' organizational culture tends to lead leadership, although the latter can be important in the reproduction of cultural values and meanings. Of course, there are also a number of issues and situations not entirely 'covered' by organizational culture, and the leadership may be more varied or bear imprints of managers' (or other HIPs') idiosyncrasies and other 'non-cultural' elements.

EVERYDAY WORK CULTURE

Culture often means a strong element of influencing in itself, that is, without and sometimes outside and even in opposition to leadership efforts. Culture means that people experience what is natural, familiar, reasonable and appropriate in terms of cognitions, values and priorities. If HIP-work is out of tune or clashes with this, the exercise of power or managerial and leadership initiatives can easily meet resistance and bounce back. This is less pronounced when it comes to management as the manager can, within formal limits, order a subordinate to follow instructions, even though it is likely that there will be hidden resistance or at least an uncommitted and poor carrying out of the instructions. Exercise of power that is viewed as out of the cultural boundaries for accepted behaviour in the particular setting will face an increased risk of resistance and/or exit among the targets/LIPs. When it comes to leadership it is mainly up to the LIP to decide if s/he is following or not, as leadership aiming for beliefs, values and meanings is very much a matter of the acceptance or buying into the aim of influencing. If feeling unconvinced, the LIP would not really follow, but may of course nod and look as if accepting the influencing efforts of the HIP – but this may be only impression management. Leadership efforts easily bounce off. Real acceptance that sticks is often not so easy to accomplish.

Everyday work activities and material conditions of the majority of employees are often 'protected' from the powerful impact of at least senior managers and centralized efforts to engineer corporate culture. The specific work context affects values, beliefs, cognitive styles, opinions about work and the company, and can represent a hard barrier for HIPs trying to exercise power, management or leadership – especially the latter.

Different types of culture are intimately related to material practices. What people actually do and interactions around that lead to shared understandings. One cannot compare a McDonald's restaurant, a call centre, a high-tech R&D unit at Apple, an infantry battalion in Afghanistan and a mental health clinic with each other in terms of 'culture' as if there are sets of free-floating values. Even if they should all be 'customer-oriented' or 'quality conscious' or give priority to caring relationships, these words are in themselves empty. Meanings will vary within local contexts, including people's work and group situations. Operations, work areas and material constraints are crucial and cannot be reduced in favour of values disconnected from the area of operation or the material work conducted. If we consider these aspects then we also realize that few organizations are so homogenous in terms of work being conducted that they can be addressed through overarching, integrative organizational cultures. At McDonald's, for example, people heating frozen meat will differ from corporate communication people creatively working with new campaigns who in their turn have little in common with top management groups mainly concerned with sales and finance issues. Cultural variation and subcultures will be profound and this will affect leadership – both in terms of cultural determinants and how HIPs will try to do leadership.

There is of course no mechanistic or one-to-one relationship between material and cultural levels. The former affects cultural manifestations, but does not simply mirror material and social conditions. The meaning given to work tasks and material conditions is also central and intermeshes with how the materiality of work content and labour processes contribute to the shaping of consciousness and interpretations of the social world.

Example 2: leadership backfiring against work experience

An example illustrating our point is the following event in a manufacturing company. A young worker was asked to report to the marketing manager who tried to persuade him to say 'business' instead of 'product' when referring to the rock drills produced by the company (Alvesson & Björkman, 1992). It was part of a corporate effort to make the firm more 'market-oriented', to make people in production recognize that there are customers buying the 'business'/product, and to create a common orientation across the different areas of the company. This is a typical example of leadership. The marketing manager did not try to order the person targeted to use a specific vocabulary for its own sake, but sought to influence meanings and understandings through the use of a term emphasizing the market and customer aspects of operations, to move thinking from production to marketing and business orientations. This attempt to adopt the term 'business' instead of 'product' encountered sustained resistance from some employees. According to the shop-floor worker:

Roland [the plant manager] has also been brainwashed with that term. I am convinced that the expression originates from the marketing manager. I have nothing whatever to do with the 'business' rock drill. It is the marketing side which has to do with the business. *There* it is a matter of business, but not *here*. I am not interested in getting closer to the market. I have enough to do as it is. [The marketing manager] tried to impress upon me that it is a matter of businesses, not of the product. He tried to find out what kind of person I am. I thought it was a damned thing to do. His job is to deal with the market. He should not come down here and mess with me, that's the task of my own boss. Roland also thought it was a bit unpleasant. [He was also there.] One wonders what kind of people they have up there. (Alvesson & Björkman, 1992, p. 147)

The worker's strongly negative reaction to the leadership effort can partly be accounted for by reference to his work situation – it is the physical product that he operates on, not a financial transaction. The term 'business' simply does not appear meaningful and relevant in a shop-floor culture. The effort to impose this kind of meaning on the employee's work experience backfires heavily and the result is the opposite of what the marketing manager wants to accomplish. Instead of a common understanding and more appreciation of customers and market considerations, the outcomes are the underscoring of differences in world-view, negative perceptions and distance between marketing and production people. One can talk about a clash not only or mainly between two individuals, but between a management and marketing oriented 'business' culture and a shop-floor culture in which material production is key. In the example, the worker also reacted strongly to the senior manager not being his own direct superior, illustrating that leadership efforts outside the managerial/ subordinate relationship may be problematic.

This kind of outcome is presumably not uncommon in efforts to manage meaning and engineer culture in organizations. Managers base their interventions on what makes sense for them and not for their subordinates, with an obvious risk of backfiring.

ORGANIZATIONAL CULTURE AS AN ALTERNATIVE TO LEADERSHIP

Based on what has been said above, leadership needs to be carefully assessed in relationship to culture. In many situations, organizational and occupational cultures do much of the framing and support work for people. Culture in the sense of a shared framework of meanings and values guides experiences and action and thus takes care of many of the functions otherwise supposed to be dealt with through leadership – and to some extent management, although the specifics of managing (planning, coordination, controlling) addressing behavioural and output issues will remain to a degree. If people in a workplace have been socialized into and carry a specific workplace or occupational culture they tend to act in line with this and there is, in principle, minimum need of leadership and modest need of management. A well-functioning organizational or occupational culture is in this sense an alternative to leadership or, to take another angle, leadership seems almost unnecessary or at least not so important if there is a collective transmission and reproduction of a web of meanings providing guidelines and a sense of purpose for individuals.

Of course, there will still be many situations that may call for managerial or other HIP interventions, including exercise of leadership or power, as assessed by managers or other people. Culture is seldom the only organizing mechanism at play, even in well-developed cultural settings – with broadly shared and 'strong' ideas, beliefs, values and meanings – there is always some need for management and/or leadership, in particular when there are conflicts, a shortage of resources or a need for change. But when shared meanings are in place and form a strong source of influencing, under normal circumstances the prospect of leadership adding a lot or being capable of accomplishing much change will be small. There is also a great risk of leadership efforts deviating from the established culture and leading to responses such as the one by the factory worker in the example above.

This is not to say that leadership is insignificant. It is vital in order to reinforce, reproduce and modify culture. Culture needs maintenance work and here leadership is key. Of course, often there is a need for cultural change. This is typically time-consuming and difficult, and leadership aiming at re-defining meanings is central (Alvesson & Sveningsson, 2015).

We need to add that many organizations are not characterized by shared meanings, values and understandings. Often organizations are socially differentiated and culturally fragmented. There are no clear common frameworks. Here leadership is important – sometimes as a source of guiding meanings and ideas, sometimes as a practice trying to deal with the misunderstandings and conflicts following from peoples' and groups' varied outlooks in relation to their work, themselves and their relationships.

SUMMARY

The chapter has treated different kinds of leadership as 'creator of' versus 'created by' organizational culture. Often leadership is viewed as a matter of creating or changing culture. The leadership industry loves to report exaggerated portraits of great leaders who create or transform culture. This easily leads to a heroic, naive understanding of high-powered leadership, although under certain conditions some HIPs may no doubt have a strong culture-shaping impact. To some extent HIPs – and to a minor degree also LIPs – do always contribute to the shaping and reproduction of culture. Everybody is doing some influencing, in particular on meanings, e.g. when exhibiting certain forms of work behaviour, taking a nap at work, using certain expressions, gossip, stories or jokes. And HIPs – then doing leadership – can be important here.

But culture also forms leadership, making the latter led by culture rather than the other way round. Managers are socialized into an organizational culture. People promoted internally are likely to already have strongly bought into dominant values, beliefs and meanings – if they have not, they are less likely to stay and be promoted.

Also, people recruited externally are often screened for cultural fit and tend to come from the same industry (and often the same industrial culture). Professional organizations typically recruit senior people within the profession, thus reproducing organizational and professional cultures. This is not to deny individual and intra-organizational variation. Few people or situations are culturally standardized.

Sometimes organizational and occupational cultures do much of the steering. In professional settings, there are strong cultural orientations produced by education and professional associations taking care of much of the basic thinking, valuing and identifying with how to do things. Professional groups have generally been seen as in no or limited need of much leadership. The latter may actually shift focus from a responsible collective, materialized in groups and networks doing supporting and guiding, to a HIP being in the centre of organizing through managing and leading. This may reduce the effectiveness and value of the former sources of organizing. As we emphasize in this book, it is seldom self-evident how to organize and do HIP work. The upgrading of leadership at the expense of other modes of organizing may sometimes be motivated, but there are often costs to the increased focus on HIPs and leadership that need to be taken seriously. Sometimes leadership could involve the paradoxical move of directing attention to cultural resources, anchored in groups and networks. 'Use your contacts, support each other, rely on the group and collegiality, ask the most professionally qualified', may be key communication from the 'leader' withdrawing from centre-staging and indirectly pointing at organizational culture as an overall organizing force, being 'operationalized' through autonomy, groups and professional networks within occupational communities and cultures.

6

Followership and its Alternatives

In many conventional understandings of leadership the follower has been more or less ignored or seen as a passive object or tool in the hands of the leader. It is usually assumed that the follower subjects to the will and ambition of the leader. The latter is seen as providing the agency in relation to which followers – as objects of influence – respond, occasionally with some variation depending on their levels of maturity for example. The leader leads, the follower follows. With the right leadership, there will be a predictable followership. The relational quality of leadership – also involving followership – is thus denied or trivialized. This is changing – perhaps less in the leadership industry than in academic work – and there is also an interest in followership in more recent literature; followers are seen as active co-producers of leadership and leadership relations.

In this chapter we discuss some contemporary views on followers and followership while also problematizing some of its traditional assumptions. In relation to this, we discuss some dilemmas with followership in terms of identity and autonomy.

LEADERSHIP CALLS FOR FOLLOWERSHIP

Leadership is attractive while followership is less so. Few people would explicitly acknowledge that they like to position themselves primarily as followers or that they search for ways to exercise followership. The unwanted nature of the follower position is illustrated by how middle managers asked to describe their work almost exclusively suggest their superiority (leading subordinates) and deny or at least bypass recognizing their position as subordinates (being led by their superiors) (Laurent, 1978; Sveningsson & Alvesson, 2016).

There are many reasons for this. An obvious one is that the role of leader is attributed to powerful and resourceful individuals, most often high-profile business executives or politicians. Typically people look at these powerful individuals in order to understand what is happening in organizations and in business life in general. As repeated frequently in previous chapters, we tend to assume that it is their vision, personality traits, convictions and ideas that to a large extent explain organizational processes and outcomes. The followers are mainly seen as an effect of the quality of leadership. As part of this the follower role appears much less attractive – who wants to be a follower when everyone is expected to take charge of his/her own work and destiny? Education or training directly focused on followership is very rare. Offering education and courses in followership would hardly pay off for institutions or participants. Even if most organizations employ people in non-managerial positions, they may not see a diploma in 'followership' as having merit, while one in leadership probably would be seen in this light. But people in contemporary society and organizations are more often followers than leaders (or neither, as discussed in Chapter 2). This includes managers at different levels who are expected to listen to and implement their superiors' visions, directives or strategies.

The over-emphasis on the leader is somewhat remedied in contemporary writings of leadership (see Chapter 3). Some recent literature takes a more critical stance towards many of the simplified views of the significance of leaders, and the follower – as well as followership – is increasingly acknowledged as a more active part in the interaction. This is hardly surprising considering that by definition leadership calls for followership.[1] Some leadership scholars, such as Grint (2010a, p. 1) even propose 'having followers' as a proper definition of leadership. Arguably, leadership relations without followers do not make sense, and the absence of the latter undermines or even precludes leadership. This does not however prevent many writers from presenting 'follower-less' ideas on leadership, This tendency – more or less explicitly expressed – can be found in supposedly progressive texts on shared and related forms of leadership and even self-leadership, with seemingly only leaders and no followers.[2] In contrast to these we agree with Shamir (2012) when he claims that: 'If it [leadership] is fully shared, I suggest that we don't call it *leadership* because the term loses any added value' (p. 487).

In more practice-oriented texts on followership (there are a few) we sometimes find checklists for what constitutes a 'good follower'. For example, Riggio (2014, quoting Robert Kelley) suggests that effective followers:

- Think for themselves
- Carry out assignments with energy and assertiveness
- Are self-motivated, self-starters
- Take calculated risks
- Receive high ratings from both superiors and peers

Besides sounding good and positive and referring to virtues, skills and assessments that are generally good in almost all areas of life, these points are problematic in the context of leadership. If people really did think for themselves, there would be little need for leadership as an act of influencing meaning. If people were self-motivated self-starters, leadership to provide cultural direction, support and motivation in various forms (key ingredients according to most understandings of leadership) would be unnecessary. To carry out one's duty with confidence and energy, taking calculated risks and then to receive positive recognition for this cannot be said to be distinctive for followers (the same is valid for non-followers, e.g. managers and independent professionals).

One could take the followership aspect more seriously and say that good followers:

- do to some extent think for themselves, in particular about operational issues, but trust the leader and heavily rely on their thinking, which is expected to be superior, in most respects at least
- enthusiastically carry out assignments, only occasionally asking critical questions or demanding justification
- are to some extent dependent on as well as highly responsive to leadership interventions to get a kick-start at work
- are cautious about deviating from their leader's ideas and wishes
- are smooth and politically sensitive in interactions and do not challenge other people at work.

This formulation would emphasize what is needed for leadership to have a strong effect and for the relationship to work without friction. It also suggests what may be less good about leadership/followership without focusing on the clearly 'bad' (toxic, inauthentic) versions. In particular, a high degree of dependence and disinclination to think for themselves (outside what is defined as the right way) can be problematic.

Key in followership is relating to people with higher status that are attributed more influence (Carsten et al., 2010). As we suggested in Chapter 2, this does not exclude followers from exerting influence, but in comparison to the HIP/leader these efforts are typically less frequent or significant. A follower is not an equal participant in this relationship. As Harter et al. (2006) write, 'it goes to the meaning of the word "leadership" for there to be some kind of inequality' (p. 290). We assume that leaders exist in tandem with followers and that the relationship between leaders and followers is asymmetric in terms of influence and status, hence the division between HIPs and LIPs. Leadership with no followers can therefore better be seen as leadership *attempts*, which vary in how well they are carried out and received. Intention and LIP response may differ considerably. Sometimes leadership attempts are viewed as embarrassing or humoristic – it can happen that HIPs come across as involuntary comedians, triggering ironic or sarcastic comments by subordinates.

Many traditional perspectives on leadership – discussed in Chapter 3 in terms of traits, styles, situational, transformational – are mostly focused on measurable effects, such as indicators of increased motivation, work satisfaction and performance among subordinates. According to some studies motivated followers exhibit 20 to 50 per cent higher productivity compared to less motivated followers (Hughes et al., 2006).

However, there are different views of followers and their role in the leadership processes. The most common is that leaders affect followers and that followers are passive outcomes of leadership. Another view emphasizes mutual influencing and followers are co-constructors of leadership, while a third view says that leaders do not matter much and followers are the ones who actually construct leadership. Next we discuss these three perspectives.

TRADITIONAL VIEWS OF FOLLOWERSHIP: LEADERS CONSTRUCT FOLLOWERS

A dominant traditional view is to regard the behaviour of the follower – the object – as a direct consequence of the traits, styles and acts of the leader – the subject. The main idea being that the leader employs some means of motivating the follower to work in specific directions and enhance performance. With the right kind of leadership most problems will be fixed. The personality, style and behaviour of the leader – such as the formulation of a vision – are assumed to have an impact on the attitude and behaviour of the employees (in terms of increased engagement and/or increased performance).

This is a key part not only in traditional ideas on leadership but also in much contemporary, seemingly progressive leadership, as discussed in Chapter 3. The literature on more 'supportive' forms of leadership suggests that the style of the leader may have a remarkable effect on the engagement and productivity of the followers. However, ignoring the work context, culture and other organizational conditions as well as individual characteristics suggests that this is an overly simplified logic that relies more on the traditional leader assumptions than on in-depth investigations of leader and follower interactions in real-life organizations. Reality is typically much more complex. Influencing processes are usually highly difficult to fully control and predict. Work morale and performance are often influenced by work environment, the complexity of the work tasks, skills, and professional and educational background. Group dynamics and norms expressed by peers in occupational communities (informally and/or in unions and other formal groups) may have a strong impact on what people see as a reasonable effort. All this reduces the impact of leadership and sometimes leads to unexpected responses or even un-responsiveness. In some cases it may also be that leadership efforts create frustration and irritation and actually hamper the possibility of concentrating on the work task. This may especially be the case if the work relies on alternative – and perhaps more appropriate – modes of organization such as peer influencing, group work or autonomy.

Not all leadership studies assume that leadership has a mechanical effect. Even if HIPs try to do, for example, transformational leadership, it is not self-evident that LIPs become transformed. Also, some traditional leadership approaches acknowledge the follower in terms of a variety of characteristics. In the situational theory of leadership the follower is acknowledged in terms of skills and maturity that moderate the characteristics and level of leadership (Hersey & Blanchard, 1982). We discussed in Chapter 3 how leaders change their styles – from more directive to delegatory – with increasingly mature and knowledgeable followers. In another approach – the path-goal theory – it is suggested that leaders (HIPs) engage in behaviours that complement subordinates' abilities and compensate for their deficiencies (House, 1996). Clarification of the paths and abolishing barriers are seen as central, where followers may occasionally need more structure and guidance, while in other cases more supportive leadership is required.

Common to these traditional – but highly influential – perspectives is that the leader is viewed as the active part and the followers are viewed as rather passive actors, dependent on and susceptible to stimuli from a leader.

FOLLOWERS AS CO-CONSTRUCTORS OF LEADERSHIP

A different approach reverses the lens and focuses on how followers as casual agents function as important antecedents to organizational outcomes. The focus is on follower role orientations, traits, schemas and characteristics, and how followers (usually as subordinates) work with leaders (usually superior managers) in ways that possibly contribute to leadership and organizational outcomes. This includes, for example, emphasizing the variety of different follower types in terms of level of activity (Kelley, 1988). Other writers suggest that followers need to be approached much more as active subjects rather than passive objects or receivers of leadership (Howell & Shamir, 2005). One may also be less categorical and imagine followers ranging from passive and deferential to active and even proactive, where the organizational context is pivotal for what roles are enacted (Carsten et al., 2010).

Followers are also seen as vital co-producers of leadership processes. This means taking a more constructionist approach by viewing followership and leadership as co-constructed in social and relational interactions between individuals.[3] Here, followership is not tied to a fixed position but to behaviour, where 'leadership and followership are enacted in asymmetrical relational interaction between people, which *might or might not* coincide with formal hierarchical roles (i.e. managers might not lead and subordinates might not follow)' (Uhl-Bien et al., 2014, p. 90, emphasis in original). This approach suggests that leadership processes are to be seen as outcomes of different people jointly producing it. Followers are seen as active participants who interpret and actively position themselves in relation to the presumed leader and thus contribute to the character of the relationship (Ospina & Sorenson, 2006). Leadership relations – and the inherent asymmetry that follows from these – are formed in the interaction between leaders' and followers' traits, personality, competencies, identity and background. Relational approaches often emphasize dialogue, mutual influence and participation. For example, it is suggested that 'leadership is a relational practice, on-going in and supportive of dialogues, emergent processes, relational responsiveness, multiplicity, and appreciation' (Hosking, 2011, p. 462). In some instances the relationship develops over different phases as those involved get to know each other better and exercise mutual influencing (Graen & Uhl-Bien, 1995). In general, good leader and follower relations are seen as based on mutual trust, win-win and a clear sense of responsibility.

A central idea in much of this is to 'upgrade' followership. This is often done by boosting its positive aspects, almost to the point of stripping the category of the conventional meanings of followership, instead constructing followers as active, skilled, participatory and in harmonious relations with leaders. We can talk of the 'de-followerization' of followers. However, some studies propose different varieties of followers, some passive and happy just to follow (Carsten et al., 2010). But also they do exercise influence by forcing the HIP to be quite active, for example asking for instructions and support, expecting attention, etc.

It is also suggested that leadership and followership are outcomes of a process in which people claim and grant identities as leaders and followers (DeRue & Ashford, 2010). Claiming occurs when an actor tries to establish an identity as leader or follower. Granting consists of the bestowment of the claimed identity by others in combination with supporting/corresponding identities (e.g. person A claims a leadership identity that is granted by person B accepting a follower identity for himself/herself). Without correspondence in the view of self and other, leadership/followership will not work. There need to be 'symmetrical meanings' about the asymmetry of the relationship and the associated identities. Although in many ways a formal managerial position is important in these relations it does not necessarily overlap with leader-follower relations. In other words, people need to agree upon the nature of the leader-follower relationship (or another type of relationship if it is not characterized by leadership, e.g. management, collegiality or team affiliation).

Important here is to consider that co-construction does not mean equality or symmetrical relations. Co-construction can mean anything from a low to a high degree of inequality. Sometimes subordinates can take a strong follower position and invite or even 'force' a superior to adopt a strong leadership position. If subordinates for example assume that the manager (or other HIP) is much wiser and superior and express strong signs of immaturity and helplessness, the manager can be pushed into a strong leader/follower relationship (or another form of asymmetrical – HIP/LIP – relation, e.g. as very superior manager/power holder and inferior subordinate/powerless person).

But again, common to all the views discussed above is that followers – together with the leader(s) – are significant co-constructors of leadership identities, relations and processes. If we generalize somewhat, the literature tends to portray followership as something rather natural, free of conflict and win-win, where the HIP and the LIP all get something out of the relationship that justifies the asymmetry. It is therefore important to both consider a counter-assumption – leadership/followership is perhaps *not* the natural order of human relations – and recognize the underlying but seemingly neglected downsides or dilemmas associated with followership. We will suggest some of these below, but first discuss leadership as a creation of the follower.

FOLLOWERS AS CONSTRUCTORS OF LEADERSHIP

Some approaches to leadership move beyond the relational aspects of co-construction to see the follower as *the* source of leadership relations. The emphasis is subsequently on the followers and attribution of leadership by the followers rather than the leader, in sharp contrast with the many leadership-centric perspectives described in Chapter 3. Leadership – as the perceived need for it – is socially constructed. A leadership position is made by the attribution of others and '*exists* only as a perception ... not a viable scientific construct ... but extremely important as naïve psychology' (Calder, 1977, p. 202, emphasis in original). This position is follower-centric. We highlight three views: psychodynamic, attribution and social identity theory.

Psychodynamic approaches aim at understanding dependency relations where followers create leaders, either by projection or by transference. Projection means that people attribute dreams, fantasies and ideals to others while transference refers to how people relate to others as though they were some other significant person met/experienced in early age. Complicated forms of psychodynamics often occur in crisis, periods of uncertainty or threatening situations, but unconscious processes may also operate and complicate reactions and relations during more average conditions (Islam, 2014). These can be unrelated to the observable behaviour and may make it impossible to see a clear relation between a HIP's actions and the emotional responses to it. People tend to fall into infantilism and subject themselves to people they experience as leaders, not on the basis of a specific trait or characteristic of these people but because they symbolize significant persons, typically a parent, that can reduce anxieties and provide security. Followers typically create leaders in order to feel safe and secure (Lipman-Blumen, 2005). This is often the case in extreme sects where people come to rely on self-proclaimed saviours. However, milder forms can also be seen in organizations that have developed strong dependencies on leaders with less reliable representations of reality (Kets de Vries & Miller, 1984). For example, in Chapter 3 we discussed the problems whereby charismatic leaders can create unhealthy dependency relations that undermine the possibility of questioning anomalous and fixed ideas/convictions among leaders. This may limit the capacity for reflection among actors, and make other modes of organizing such as peer influence, group work or autonomy hard to imagine.

According to *attribution theory*, and assuming that many people have a romantic view of leaders being remarkable people (e.g. Meindl, 1995), leadership is understood as a result of followers' exaggerated inclinations to draw upon leadership in order to understand complex and ambiguous organizational processes and results. It is notoriously difficult to unambiguously isolate the contribution individuals such as managers or leaders make to organizational results or even to subordinates' efforts. We underscored in previous chapters the complexities behind results. Even so we are still romantically attached to the idea that there is someone – usually a manager or other HIP – in charge who has control of processes and events (Pfeffer, 1977). As followers we tend to create – or attribute – leadership as a central part of the picture because we want to believe that there is someone responsible for the outcomes (Meindl, 1995). Sometimes this leads to one-sided and un-nuanced blame, at other times there is an idealization and heroization of the leader.

From a more practical viewpoint, attribution tendencies suggest that those who want to be seen as leaders should associate themselves – in talk, ceremonies and other expressive platforms – with organizations or units that perform well. Equally important is to have subordinates who take follower positions and make the 'right' attributions. Critical and autonomous people are to be avoided. The romance of leadership also suggests that rather than be seen as a cause of organizational success, charismatic leaders should be seen as an effect of good outcomes. The better the organization performs the more fantastic the leader is believed to be (although this is close to impossible to evidence with certainty). The tendency to attribute leadership is very common among academics, practitioners, management literature and media in general, and probably explains a lot of why leadership is so prevalent in contemporary society. Its status as an all-embracing explanatory device also precludes reflection on alternative modes of coordination and further reinforces its status as well as many problems – rather than solutions – in contemporary organizations.

Social identity revolves around how people understand themselves in terms of a group category. This provides additional insights into how followers attribute leadership qualities to others. Association with a group may for example correspond to a company (such as being an Apple person) or a department (such as being a marketing person). There are of course other social categories such as nationality, gender, religion and professional groups, for example journalist, physician or accountant. Identification normally implies feelings of distinctiveness and superiority in relation to other groups – us versus them – and involves certain characteristics that influence feelings, attitudes and emotions. Identifying with a particular group often involves looking at others whom one thinks express the typical characteristics of the group. People who express (what others see as) those typical group characteristics are often also those who are perceived to be most influential and leader-like. The idea is also that leaders are chosen and selected by the others in a group on the basis of being illustrative of the group's norms, attitudes and behaviour. In contrast to the dominant idea that leaders select followers for a group on the basis of the leader's aspirations, the social identity approach suggests that it is actually the followers who select who is to be seen as leader. A key point is that it is not necessarily the (formal) manager who influences others the most. A manager who is viewed as not being typical of the group will have problems, as there will be a tendency to see the manager as different from 'us'. In the case of the factory worker rejecting the intervention by the marketing manager described in the previous chapter, the former saw the latter as outside the group and clearly belonging to 'them'. More generally, there is a tendency in professional organizations that HIPs who do not belong to the professions are not fully accepted.

Someone selected as a leader in a group typically appropriates and reinforces that status by perceiving it as a personality trait – often charisma – rather than something provided by the followers. Obviously the dynamics of social identity call for reflection about the basis on which and reasons why someone is able to exercise influence and be seen as a leader. What is it that makes someone likely to be seen as charismatic? And in what ways might this preclude reflections about alternative modes of organizing?

In this section we have discussed how different forms of follower attributions actually construct leadership. This sometimes gives the impression that the leader (in making) is without agency and totally in the hands of his/her followers' ideas, preferences and conceptions. And there are cases where the leadership very much seems to be the product of pure attribution, but often an aspiring leader can influence these processes and facilitate specific attributions using his/her actions, phrasing, body language, way of dressing and ability to nurture his/her reputation. According to social identity theory, it is important for leader-wannabees to act in ways that encourage them to be perceived as similar in key respects to the group to be led. The group can of course also be influenced in terms of social identity – how to work with issues of 'how we see ourselves' is actually a key task for leadership – but it calls for the HIP being seen as part of 'we'.

There is furthermore the issue of diverging attributions among followers – often not only concerned about social category/similarity issues but inclined to see their managers/leaders in different ways (something emphasized by, for example, leadership-member theory, briefly mentioned in Chapter 3). The subordinates/followers of a sales manager – Jim – in a high-tech company we studied displayed very different attributions in relation to him as a leader (Alvesson & Wenglén, 2008).

Ralph, one of Jim's sales agents praised his importance and ability as a leader of the unit:

> He has turned the ship around. He has the best results in the [360 degree evaluation survey] and he has the best financial results in the whole EMEA [Europe, Middle East and Africa].

Another sales agent, Steve, attributes other qualities to Jim:

> When we [the sales agents] talk we all agree that these figures we could have done without James. He is totally offside! The only thing he says is: Full speed ahead!.

These two quotes illustrate how different subordinates' attributions can be, making the 'follower construction of leadership' rather ambiguous and the outcome hard to predict. But imagining leadership as a construction *primarily* by the followers may provide a useful counter-picture compared to dominant theories and prompt more critical reflection on what triggers the frequent calls for leadership, for example anxiety, lack of information, group dynamics. It potentially opens up possibilities to look for alternative modes of organizing in order to avoid falling back into infantilism and relying on simplified solutions to complex problems. This is further discussed in the section on reflexive followership at the end of the chapter but let us first look into a few important but seemingly often neglected dilemmas associated with accepting a follower position.

Some of the views mentioned can be illustrated by a quote from an HR director (Gloria) we interviewed about her work situation (Alvesson & Lundholm, 2014). When asked if she enjoyed her job she answered:

> Yes, I do that very much because I have one of the best bosses in the world [the CEO] and then it is not difficult to enjoy work. He is very open, consistent and very clear; he stands for what he says. He lives as he learns and then he is very intelligent and he is very able in various ways. He stands for everything that I think is important myself.

This can be explained by attribution, psychodynamics and social identity theory. In terms of attribution, Gloria believes that her CEO is behind all positive things. He is one of the best bosses in the world. Psychodynamically, there is an idealization of him, meeting infantile fantasies of an omnipotent parent-like figure merged in a symbiotic way with the follower. While psychodynamics tend to emphasize some differences – being the best is outside Gloria's reach in terms of self-understanding – social identity emphasizes similarities. As Gloria believes her boss stands for everything that she thinks is important the identity basis for a strong followership positioning is there. Key for Gloria is a strong identification and a 'we' feeling.

Of course, this does not mean that the CEO is not a talented person who is doing very well. This is often difficult to say – there are many ambiguities (Pfeffer, 1977). But irrespective of possible 'excellent' qualities and performance, subordinates may respond quite differently, and in the case of Gloria her responses clearly do not simply mirror the qualities of the object of her idolization.

DILEMMAS ASSOCIATED WITH FOLLOWERSHIP

To follow in terms of allowing oneself to be strongly influenced by someone else sometimes involves mixed feelings. As previously indicated, a leader can serve as a valuable source of cultural direction, meaning, moral and/or emotional support, as well as contributing to a nice work atmosphere, where a follower position might mean positive inclusion and a sense of belonging. This is often emphasized in relation to what some researchers refer to as 'in-group followers', that is, followers with a deeper and 'higher quality' relationship with their leader, that in turn also tend to lead to increased trust (between leader and follower), more discretion for the follower, and preferential treatment from the leader compared to 'out-group followers' (Harris et al., 2009). Furthermore, a followership position can provide a sense of social order (where the hierarchical element is well recognized and approved by all parties) and thereby a reduction of uncertainty and anxiety.

While recognizing that there are upsides associated with a follower position it is also important to investigate some of the challenges that might follow. We discuss the challenges associated with a follower position related to *identity* and *autonomy*. These themes are often neglected in texts on leadership and followership and perhaps also repressed in many people's experiences.

Dilemmas in terms of identity

A follower identity comes with an asymmetrical relationship, characterized by difference in social status: 'Leaders hold a position of privilege in the dualism [leader-follower] because they are considered to be superior to their followers' (Gordon, 2011, p. 196). The subordination of followers tends to make the position a less appealing source of identity work and self-esteem compared to being a leader: people seldom present themselves as 'followers'. This is partly because of the generalized expectations associated with the two positions. To be a follower is to be inferior to a leader – not in all respects or at all times, but it does not make sense if a follower feels equal or better than his/her leader. In that case a different conceptualization – downplaying the superior/inferior elements – of the relationship seems more appropriate (e.g. manager/professional, coach/athlete, agent/artist). Formal hierarchy may lead to compliance but when it comes to leadership (cultural direction, meaning, emotional and moral support), subordinates can more or less choose if they take a follower position or not.

Followership typically marks a lower social status. Being regarded, and seeing oneself, as a follower rather than a leader (or working fairly autonomously, alongside other professionals/peers/people), will typically involve a feeling of inferiority that potentially contributes to a negative self-conception (DeRue & Ashford, 2010). When accepting such an identity, the original sense of inferiority might even be reinforced and cemented, making an 'exit' out of the relationship harder to achieve.

A strong sense of inferiority might be acceptable for younger or less competent workers or people with lower self-confidence in relation to much more experienced people (especially if the inferiority is perceived as temporal). Race, gender and class might also contribute to 'acceptance' of an inferior position in relation to people belonging to what is regarded as 'superior' categories. For example, being male to a degree still signals superiority and is in many countries a source of authority, sometimes making it more difficult for females to do leadership (Alvesson & Billing, 2009). The leadership talk of today may also convince some people that their managers being leaders stands for something extraordinary compared to their own humble work and selves. Besides, it might also be acceptable, not to say attractive, to construct yourself as a follower of high-status people and/or people with exceptional talents. Indeed, to be a disciple of Christ or the Dalai Lama or a secretary of Nelson Mandela might perhaps serve as a productive resource for positive identity work, but these extreme examples are often far from the mundane reality of modern working life we are addressing in this book. The average CEO is not necessarily greatly superior to her/his senior managers, the dean of a business school is not typically much better than senior professors, the project manager may not appear to be clearly above the other project members.

In many cases people may feel ambivalent or even negative about a follower identity, making them less inclined to accept or support being part of a leadership relation. And without the willing participation of the follower, there will not be much leadership.

Dilemmas in terms of autonomy

Like leadership, autonomy is generally thought of as something good, in particular in Western cultures. Apart from young, inexperienced or dependent people, perhaps eager to attribute charismatic qualities to their leaders, most qualified individuals probably want to do the job as they see fit. Foley (2010) claims that 'autonomy is the one thing that makes professional life more fulfilling' (p. 173).

There is a possible contradiction between leadership and autonomy. One cannot argue that leadership always includes significant constraints – there may be liberating elements in leadership – but the very idea of leaders leading followers and followers following leaders involves a reduction of autonomy. Even supportive, low-control forms of leadership may be in tension with autonomy. The idea is that there is a certain dependence associated with leadership support and that this somehow matters more than support from others. The assumption of the person in need of support underlies the idea of supportive leadership, but some people may not be in need of support and those who are may get it from others instead of the HIP.

The outcome of leadership may involve a degree of pre-structured autonomy so that discretion is used in the (from the leader's point of view) 'right way': delegating may still mean that a superior manager is in control and decides the subordinates' space for discretion. This is also the idea behind the enthusiasm for working with corporate culture, and more recently, organizational identity, assuming that by identifying with and internalizing the right set of values, orientations and mind-set, people would voluntarily do the right thing without much need for alienating direct control. But still, a key ingredient of followership is to allow oneself to be influenced in an asymmetrical way.

The relationship between leadership and autonomy does not automatically represent a zero-sum game in the sense that 'more' leadership directly means 'more followership' and less autonomy. Leadership can include facilitation of some form of autonomy, in particular over time (e.g. developing followers' skills, motivation and confidence in order to be able to provide them with more responsibility and degrees of freedom in the future). But leadership simply producing or reinforcing autonomy is self-contradictory. The tensions between leadership and autonomy should be taken seriously, not glossed over by theories and claims promising superior forms of leadership that create solely positive outcomes. Rather than assuming that parallel 'good' things co-exist – e.g. leadership and autonomy – one should accept that the good and the less good often go hand in hand (as already discussed in Chapter 4). Organizational life is not free from tensions, nor are asymmetrical relations, including those based on leadership and followership.

We have outlined two important dilemmas associated with followership. The identity and autonomy dilemmas ensuing followership may cause people to try to avoid leadership relationships. Potential followers unwilling or hesitant to subject to leadership will of course undermine its effectiveness. Even a manager trying to do 'correct' leadership, that is, in line with any of the endless recipes for good leadership, may fail if people are unwilling to take a follower position. Negotiations, mutual adjustments or co-constructions of leadership may not work if (potential) followers are not interested in a leader-follower relation. This may, from a conventional leadership view, be seen as a failure, but it is not given that the result *for the organization* is negative, as followership is not always the best response and alternative modes of organizing such as management, peer support or group work may be more effective than leadership in many situations.

ALTERNATIVES TO FOLLOWERSHIP

As repeatedly emphasized, there are often alternative sources of direction, support and inspiration that might be more appropriate than the establishment of a leader-follower relationship and all employees without a managerial title are not automatically followers in the sense described in this book. 'Extra-leadership' forms of organizing include, for example, mutual adjustments within the working group, or advice and inspiration from other peers and colleagues outside the immediate working group (e.g. a community of practice or a network of experts). These 'horizontal' alternatives have already been presented in the 6M-model in Chapter 2 and will be further elaborated on in more detail in Chapter 7, but we will address them shortly from a follower/LIP perspective.

There are certainly organizational members that draw on other sources than a leader in order to obtain cultural direction, meaning and support. Most people consult co-workers and follow group norms. Sometimes other, more distant, peers are central. In an R&D department we studied, it was common to refer to the network of peers (other software engineers in other firms or other units within the organization) when pointing out influence and guidance, rather than any HIP within the organization (Blom & Alvesson, 2014, p. 349):

> I think that the ones that exercise the most significant influence on my work are as a matter of fact the other experts in the global virtual community. (Andrew, software engineer)

Also, the professional and autonomous character of the way work was organized was often emphasized in the organization (Blom & Alvesson, 2014, p. 348):

> I would put it like this: when I end up in a situation where leadership is invoked upon me it is an extraordinary thing, if you see what I mean. I have rather extensive degrees of freedom when it comes to the daily operative activities, perhaps thanks to my background within the organization. Julian [his boss] knows I am on top of things. (Magnus, head of a development team)

> My work has seldom received much leadership. Something that I appreciate (laughter)! I have had pretty much carte blanche from the beginning. Sometimes this can be tricky, but mostly I find it stimulating. I am directed by goals and dislike being told what to do. So who or should I say what is leading me? The projects' milestones and the projects' resource capacity lead my work. (Steven, software engineer)

In addition to the horizontal modes of organizing mentioned above, there are also vertical modes not necessarily best understood in terms of leadership and followership. If for example a HIP still insists on influence and compliance, a formal arms-length manager-subordinate relationship, with minimalistic compliance, or a more neutral submission to his/her will are both often alternatives to becoming that person's follower. This means that a LIP can actively seek and/or affirm a subordinate role, without being turned into a follower. One example is how subordinates might request more *management*, for example clearer objectives, well-defined targets and time frames, more efficient resource allocation, transparent performance control or better administrative processes without asking for more *leadership* (targeting meanings, ideas, values). In line with the 6M-model, LIPs can actually also request more exercise of power instead of leadership. This is perhaps especially common when thinking about what the group or organization as whole needs as opposed to oneself specifically, for example, 'this organization really needs someone who can kick people in the butt and make things happen'. An illustration of LIPs' interest in powerful HIPs comes from Steve (one of the sales agents we met earlier in this chapter) talking about his superior Jim (Alvesson & Wenglén, 2008):

> One really needs the support of the manager when you want to kick upwards. This we do not have either. Jim hangs his backbone in the wardrobe before leaving for the job. He is not though downward either. That is something John [a middle manager subordinate to Jim] has to handle. (Steve, sales agent)

In sum, LIPs have alternatives to becoming a devoted follower that do involve the dimensions associated with leadership (as conceptualized in Chapter 1). There are even alternative (mainly horizontal) modes of organizing that do not asymmetrically turn people into HIPs and LIPs. These will be further elaborated on and exemplified in Chapter 7 below. But before proceeding with these topics let us discuss the relationship between reflexivity and followership.

REFLEXIVE FOLLOWERSHIP

First of all, reflexive followership includes a careful and critical evaluation of the alternatives for people in LIP positions. If a HIP – typically a manager – is claiming leadership, it can be granted, resisted or ignored, where the potential consequences – for yourself, your colleagues, superiors, and for the organization as a whole – need to be taken into consideration. Such a reflection may lead to engagement in a leadership relation, where leadership and followership supplement each other.

Let us now assume an established leader-follower relationship between two people. As described in the literature on followership, there are many forms of followership. The degree of closeness and proactivity in relation to the leader for example can vary significantly and can to a large extent be influenced by the actions and preferences of the leaders' followers. There are several important dimensions that define the leader-follower relationship. First, the degree of *agency* and activity among followers can differ substantially, from reactive to active and even proactive behaviour in relation to their leader.[4] How marked or consistent is the HIP/LIP relationship? It may be very consistent and rigid – the leader leads, the follower follows with few exceptions – but it may also be flexible and varied, so that many interactions are equal, with some even dominated by the follower (temporarily being a MIP or even a HIP). Second is the specific focus of *attention*. What are the followers primarily paying attention and responding to? Is it the HIP's efforts to provide cultural direction/ideals, his/her attempts at sense-giving or exertions to provide emotional or moral support? Third, the *media* used for leader-follower interactions, that is, what forms, tools and objects dominate when a HIP is trying to direct or provide meaning and/or support to a LIP/ group of LIPs? Does the follower closely observe the HIP's doings and responses, engage significantly in meetings through dialogues or reinforcing the HIP's messages, seek the HIP's advice regularly, speak favourably of the HIP to other LIPs, relate to appraisal talks as significant events?

Followers significantly influence the leadership and could actually be seen as the key players. Through the followers engaging in attributions, psychodynamics and social identity categorizations, leadership becomes influential or backfires. But not only unconscious cognitive and emotional responses contribute to the formation of leadership relations, the actions and communication of LIPs do too. Their reception (embracing, resisting, ignoring) will most likely – at least over time – affect the HIP's focus and efforts when it comes to what elements to emphasize in his/her leadership attempts.

Subordinates may also more or less actively avoid involvement in and resist leadership relations and interactions, for example not go to the manager with leadership ambitions for advice or support and not appear too enthusiastic when participating in leadership-centred meetings. More actively, some scepticism can be signalled, for example raising arguments against the HIP's ideas. In the case of potential informal leadership ambitions, LIPs may downplay these by refraining from approaching the same colleague (as an emerging informal leader) too frequently and too respectfully. If different people instead are approached, one can avoid establishing a specific person as an authority and informal leader, relying more on networks of peers than informal leadership. One may favour MIP relationships and trying to bypass HIP/LIP ones. This is not uncommon in organizations (e.g. Lundholm, 2011).

It is however important to note that this situation is not free from tensions and difficulties. Resisting a manager eager to do leadership might come at a cost, for example informal degrading to what sometimes is referred to as an 'out-group'[5] (less privileged and based on formal communication and job descriptions compared to the more favoured, exclusive in-group) (Harris et al., 2009). If a follower feels that the downsides outweigh the upsides and wants to 'exit' the particular leader-follower relationship (but perhaps still keep his/her job) it might come at a price (besides the potential reprisals described above). A leader-follower relationship is often vested with loyalty and other emotions that might be hard to just put aside. If you go to a senior person with a problem it may be difficult to neglect the advice, partly because of some moral obligation, partly because of the embarrassment if a choice to not follow the advice is accompanied by a failure. Reflecting on the merits and challenges – including the issues of identity and autonomy – associated with followership is significant for learning and opens up its alternatives for consideration.

While a reflective follower carefully considers the reasons about the leadership relations and the reason for accepting and embracing being a voluntary LIP, non-reflective followership on the other hand is often characterized by quick and less thoughtful submission to a HIP claiming a leadership position. Such followership is perhaps accepted as a consequence of the HIP's title/position, his/her charisma or the LIP's relative lack of experience and/or confidence, rather than an outcome of a thorough reflective process (asking oneself critical questions such as the ones suggested above). Leadership is then an effect of follower dependence and attribution. People may of course also reject followership for bad reasons: an exaggerated view of their own ability, denial of the need for shared meanings, counter-dependence and other forms of difficulties with authority. There may be non-reflective anti-followership. This is probably quite common as many people have inflated views about themselves and their abilities (Foley, 2010).

It is important to note that HIPs can foster and cultivate more reflective LIPs, for example when approached as 'leader' and asked for direction they can instead ask questions such as 'what do *you* think' or 'what does your network of colleagues say about this'. Questions like these can trigger a more reflective approach to leadership-followership, where the alternatives are recognized and taken seriously.

SUMMARY

Leadership is not follower-free, unless leadership is defined as something positive that people do together. Leader and follower positions may (or may not) be linked to formal positions, be more or less salient or camouflaged and change over time, but are still characterized by a clear sense of asymmetry in terms of status and influence. Followership can be understood as a partly voluntary reduction of influence in favour of being influenced by a superior, seen as leader. This is what Shamir (2007) refers to as disproportionate social influence. Again, this is different from a pure manager-subordinate relationship where subordinates can accept the manager's formal superiority and rights as part of the employment contract, but do not need to become followers. An experienced teacher may respect the headmaster's formal authority, but hardly see the relationship as one of leader- and followership.

In many cases managers may find it difficult to do leadership, as for many people followership is as unattractive as leadership is attractive when closely scrutinized. The very idea of leadership-superiority to a large extent has its appeal at the expense of followership-inferiority and this creates internal tensions within the leadership-followership constellation. Sometimes there is a discrepancy between leadership ambitions and followership non-ambitions: there is surplus of the will to lead compared to willingness to follow. The precondition of leadership – that 'there is clarity in the leader-follower relationship and individuals' identities as leader and follower' (DeRue & Ashford, 2010, p. 628) – often may simply not be in place.

Followership should be seen as a *possible* position and identity, not always an attractive one free from tension and mixed feelings. Skilful leadership may mitigate experiences of inferiority, but a person who feels superior or equal to another usually does not take a follower position in relation to that person. Rather than examining how individuals socially construct their identities as followers, one may ask if (and when) individuals in Western societies really do construct their identities in this way. It is a question that we raise for reasons of reflexivity and it needs to be considered in any study of leadership/followership. The key question is: how do people actually define themselves in the context of leadership attempts?

At a time of increasingly popular discourse emphasizing the 'grandiose' nature of leadership, followership becomes increasingly negatively loaded. The more we want to become leaders, the less we want to be followers. Reinforcement of ambitions and fantasies of leader-wannabes may lead to a shortage of follower-wannabes. The ideological success of leadership is a source of its defeat in many contexts: there is much more 'leadership' (talk, fantasies, identity) than 'followership'. Leadership talk and fantasies then become decoupled from practice or relations.

As said many times before, our point is not to discourage leadership efforts and follower positions per se, nor do we suggest that people always work best if they can do whatever they want, or that vertical/hierarchical forms of organizing such as management, use of power or leadership should be abolished from organizational life. Followership positions are sometimes accepted, perceived as effective, rewarding and valuable, for example in crises or when strongly uneven capacities characterize the potential leaders and potential followers. Sometimes HIPs may improve organizations and assist LIPs in doing a better job by persuading them to take followership positions in cases where there is initial resistance. Shared meanings are important in organizations and sometimes cannot be accomplished through horizontal negotiations or other vertical mechanisms (management or power). Often leadership is needed. But the current strong emphasis on leadership in academia, society and working life – in one form or another – has a potentially colonizing impact that needs to be questioned. Particularly as followership is significantly less attractive than leadership and a problem with the latter is that it is difficult to do without the former.

NOTES

1. There is a somewhat confusing literature talking of leadership as a shared, positive practice where people find direction and alignment through participation, without any distinct leadership or followership (e.g. Raelin, 2014). We see this primarily as group work (see Chapter 2).
2. See for example Gronn (2002), Lovelace et al. (2007), Manz (1986), Manz and Sims (1980) and Pearce and Conger (2003).
3. See for example Blom and Alvesson (2014), DeRue and Ashford (2010), Fairhurst and Grant (2010) and Fairhurst and Uhl-Bien (2012).
4. See for example Carsten et al. (2010) and Blom and Alvesson (2014).
5. Close to what we in this book refer to as formal subordinates based on an employment contract (in contrast to devoted followers).

7
Modes of Organizing

As pointed out in previous chapters, managers and other HIPs need to do many things, most of these badly pressed into an obese concept of leadership. We need to be critical and sceptical both in relation to the overuse of leadership talk and to the inclination to use leadership as the solution or key ingredient to everything. A broader repertoire of lines of thinking is important. Then people can consider more options and choose the best way forward. This is key to reflexivity. It calls for access to varied vocabulary that can facilitate distinctions and clarify options. In this book we therefore address: (a) alternatives to leadership (extra-leadership reflexivity); and (b) alternatives within leadership (intra-leadership reflexivity). In this chapter we elaborate on the former and put leadership in the context of alternative ways of organizing work and social relations in organizations. We developed the ideas in Chapter 2 and in the present chapter work further with the 6M framework. We organize work within six overall modes: three 'vertical' modes – leadership, management and power – and three 'horizontal' modes – group work, peer influencing and autonomy.

Reflexive leadership calls for HIPs, MIPs, LIPs and NIPs being aware of these options, willing to reflect on them and engage in discussions about the appropriateness of the various options, either generally in the workplace or in specific action and issue contexts. The chapter elaborates on all six and briefly discusses their relationships.

MANAGEMENT

It is common to denounce management in favour of leadership. The latter sounds better and there is large industry comparing management to leadership which sets up the latter in a more positive light. A typical example is the successful Californian entrepreneur and philanthropist Paul Orfalea (2005) who claims that accountants are in the past, managers are in the present, and leaders are in the future. Who would not want to be part of the future? Statements like this lead people to easily agree to the superiority of leadership. But leadership is, as argued in previous chapters (in particular Chapter 5), most likely preached more often than actually practised. Even if many people want to spend less time and energy on management and do more leadership in terms of for example developing future-oriented visions and coaching people in line with that vision, it is hard to run modern organizations primarily based on that:

> Most managers would agree that coaching individuals yields better results than subjecting them to strict controls, especially if the company's future is crucially dependent on its employees' creativity and commitment. However, few would be willing to ease their control within a dominant form of business organization. (Magala, 2005, p. 4)

Leadership, here exemplified by coaching, sounds fine, but it is problematic for managers to let LIPs more or less do what they want. Coaching means giving advice or encouraging people to think differently about a problematic issue rather than providing specific instructions, and there are never any guarantees that LIPs will follow the given advice. This may be good for the LIP and potentially also for the organization: it is not necessarily the case that the HIP knows best and coaching can potentially lead to good results. But for management it is risky to let the subordinates decide too much. Taken too far this will be undermining and render management (as a corporate function as well as a mode of organizing) out of order.

Management is fundamental for most organizations. It can be defined as 'simply a matter of running an organisation so that the variety of people who want something out of it will go on supporting it in such a way that it is able to continue its existence into the future' (Watson, 1994, p. 10). More specifically it is about planning, coordinating and controlling organizational activities. Decision, behaviour and outcomes are in focus. When observing senior people at work, they typically do much more managerial work than 'pure' leadership (Alvesson & Sveningsson, 2003a, 2003b). Sometimes when critically scrutinizing a talk or a text on leadership it is often clear that it is really about management as understood and defined in this book. Even a celebrated 'leader' and mega-HIP such as Jack Welch used to emphasize his managerial tasks (and not some vague home-cooked leadership philosophy) when describing what is really important in his job (Welch in Garner, 2012, p. 41): 'Focus on a few key objectives ... I only have three things to do. I have to choose the right people, allocate the right number of dollars, and transmit ideas from one division to another with the speed of light'.

Management entails a broad pallet of activities. The nature of the managerial tasks differs considerably if we compare top management (such as, e.g. Jack Welch above), middle management and lower level management (e.g. supervisors, project managers). Still, most managers are responsible for some planning, staffing, coordination and controlling results. Issues around what needs to be done, when and by whom call for concrete operational planning. For organizations to function, areas such as budgeting, adhering to policies, work processes (including IT-infrastructure), dealing with work schedules and other forms of planning, resource allocation, division of labour, operational issues and handling of practical problems when they appear, financial reporting, etc. cannot just be marginalized to a matter of trivial administration. Effective administration is crucial for complex organizations to function. A visionary speech or a leader who demonstrates emotional intelligence can seldom compensate for a dysfunctional IT system or delayed payment of salaries. Management should not be mysticized and hidden under the broad label of 'leadership'. Of course, some of these tasks and functions are partly a matter of leadership; coaching may for example be relevant when (or before) deliveries are late or below expectations. In practice, there is often a combination of management and leadership. But much HIP work is hands-on and does focus on behaviour and outcomes, not only or mainly on the thinking and feeling of followers.

POWER

Power is fundamental in social life, in particular in organizations. Individuals, groups and units have different interests and perspectives. Not everybody is oriented to the general good of the organization all or most of the time. Most units and functions are inclined to believe that their work is vital and call for more resources, influence and impact. The organization can be viewed as a great mountain of resources where people – individually, in groups or in loose constellations – are fighting for material resources, power, prestige and positive work tasks.

Power and politics are thus central aspects of organizations. Making everyone feel like members of a large organizational community devoid of opportunism and self-interest sounds good and much leadership thinking promises to accomplish this, but this is not an easy task. Sometimes excellent leadership, effective management or strong centralization/concentration of power can reduce conflict or explicit political fighting; there is typically a degree of identification with and loyalty to a larger whole. But competition and clashes of wills, interests and worldviews can seldom be avoided entirely. And the will to power is an evergreen. The use of power is also an effective means of organizing. Fear is an effective driver. As Machiavelli (1993/1532, p. 130) wrote:

> ... it is much safer to be feared than loved, when, of the two, either must be dispensed with. Because this is to be asserted in general of men, that they are ungrateful, fickle, false, cowardly, covetous, and as long as you succeed they are yours entirely; they will offer their blood, property, life, and children, as is said above, when the need is far distant; but when it approaches they turn against you.

Power is a term used as widely and variedly as leadership. There are many forms and aspects of power, altogether covering everything and thus nothing. Coercive forms of power have very little in common with the discourses producing the subjectivities of people through knowledge of what is the norm for being (Foucault, 1977, 1980). In this book we are mainly addressing 'conventional' views of power: the ability to impose one's will on others and reduce or get away with opposition.

Such use of power – involving coercion to greater or lesser degrees – may be grounded in a wealth of resources. Some of these are associated with age, class, sex and ethnicity. Often a middle-aged, white, male with an upper-class background and a good education at a prestigious place has plenty of resources with which to exercise authority. Formal position and access to material resources are important. Being an owner or a senior manager and able to use staff resources, consultants and other experts to support one's will provide strong bases for the exercise of power. As do using rewards, setting wages, allocating jobs, deciding about promotion and other privileges. Much of this overlaps with management, but power draws more attention to the fact that all this can be used to build a power base overcoming the constraints of fulfilling managerial job functions in line with corporate bureaucracy. For example, vague promises of future rewards, privileges and loyalties, combined with subtle threats that all can be taken away are more related to exercise of power than typical management.

Personal style and specific acts of power are also central. Raising one's voice, appearing tough and decisive, using specific vocabulary, dominating interactions through agenda-setting, monopolizing talk and using rhetorical capacity to silence others are part of what people do when exercising power, that is, doing so in addition to the more 'disciplined' or modest forms of power involved in leadership and management. (For issues of clarity we avoid talking of leadership or management as power, although of course there is always a power aspect in this – an exercise of power is never a matter of simple brute force, but tends to be linked to some leadership or management aspects.)

Of course often power and management (and leadership) overlap but they should not be muddled: overlap is not sameness.

Two revealing examples come from two of the most famous business executives of their time. Lee Iacocca, who was CEO at Chrysler in the early 1980s at a time when the big car manufacturer was in deep trouble, was known for his tough, straightforward style. He got a strong authority base partly by frequently appearing in mass media, coming out as a hard-liner, and an honest no-nonsense speaker.

Iacocca appeared to have a strong impact and the company seemed to be transformed. At the time, ideas on transformational leadership started to become popular and some leadership researchers attributed transformational leadership and cultural change creating capacity to him (e.g. Trice & Beyer, 1993). But this was rather misleading and reflects the notorious unreliability of much leadership literature. Much of Iacocca's work was about driving through what were seen as urgent, immediate changes in order to save the company (Spector, 2014).

For example, in negotiations with unions he emphasized clear power aspects. At a vital meeting, he said: 'You've got until morning to make a decision. If you don't help me out, I am going to blow your brains out. I'll declare bankruptcy in the morning and you will all be out of work' (Iacocca & Novak, 1984, pp. 241–242).

Of course, this is extreme but putting pressure on people and invoking fear is not rare. Another well-known actor who not only relied on inspirational leadership but on much use of brute power was Apple's Steve Jobs. For example, Jobs was famous for his intense stare. If people opposed his idea, he could stare intensely into their eyes until they gave up (Isaacson, 2012). Such a tactic may in itself work for many people. But Jobs also had a very strong and broad power base. His formal position, general reputation and ability to affect people in other – more conventional management and leadership – ways all contributed to the effects of this authority figure's intense and effective staring.

But often the exercise of power is less obtrusive and more grounded in subtle control. A more mundane example is a director of a charity organization who employed a number of people from his network in the organization. They were then highly inclined to support the director, creating a basis for power and making it difficult for opposing interests and voices to have much impact (Barros, 2010). There is also the issue of manipulating agendas and work with pseudo-participation, where everybody is heard and listened to but the power-holder controls the premise and the output. This is sometimes recognized, but not without appreciation, at least not if there are some benefits.

> Of course, the person [who imposes his will the most] is the director. People already know that he imposes his preferences, which is true and it's not bad for me. Although if we take away this participation in the democratic process, when we really impose directly and brutally, the majority will leave. Now, if he imposes his view indirectly, he brings his people to vote with him, he persuades them to vote, to do what he wants … it is a better way to impose his will than to dictate it directly. (Employee, cited in Barros, 2010, p. 173)

So power has many faces. Key here is to understand that often HIPs influence not only through leadership and management but also through the skilful employment of power resources that undermines opposition. Often this is carried out somewhere in between brute force creating anxiety and subordination and manipulation through pseudo-participation, perhaps camouflaged as leadership. People may of course feel that this is negative or even horrible, but it is often an effective way of getting the work done, as highlighted by the employee cited above. Strong power players like Iacocca and Jobs were objects of much admiration by many of their followers/subordinates. Even if the latter were also exposed to more 'positive' leadership acts, creating genuine engagement, power was a central part of their work as HIPs.

LEADERSHIP

As we cover leadership in many other chapters, we only repeat some points on this mode of organizing (and do not go into the many versions described in Chapter 3 or the new framings detailed in the next chapter). A key element in leadership is an asymmetrical relationship between a HIP and a LIP, in which there is a clear degree of inequality. This is similar to management and power as defined here, although there is sometimes a 'softer' impression of the inequality (largely based on voluntary submission) in a leadership relation or context than in the other two cases. If there is an equal relationship there is no leadership. The focus of leadership is the fairly systematic influencing of the meanings, ideas, understandings, beliefs and identities of followers. The followers are then inclined to listen to and take the HIPs more or less conscious influencing efforts seriously.

Again, central here is the voluntary acceptance of a follower position, even though it may be a constrained form of voluntarism, as cultural expectations on taking a followership position in relation to managerial leadership may be strong. One chooses followership, both as a stable or permanent position (i.e. until overall conditions change) and as a temporal response. As a follower you are inclined to accept the asymmetrical nature of the relationship. The leader is seen as usually more experienced, clever, better educated, more skilled, has more local knowledge, better ideas and a general overview, so it makes sense to accept a significant degree of superiority. Typically this is partly based on formal position, but not necessarily – there is leadership based on alternative sources, calling for something more than just a formal managerial position. Sometimes there is informal leadership, that is, a person leads without a formal position. Irrespective of the degree of (in)formality, credible efforts to influence meanings, beliefs and values are important in leadership.

GROUP WORK

A powerful means of organizing is the work group. This may involve directly shared work, such as in the task force in which everyone involved is working on the same task or a project where all actions influence one another and mutual adjustment is needed. A project team may have a delimited task for which they have a shared responsibility. Careful organizing within the group is necessary.

But the work group may be less tightly coupled. People may work on individual tasks, but still be strongly influenced by surrounding colleagues. Work morality, norms and standards for working and advice-giving about how to do the work may come from people around you, not necessarily the manager. The amount of 'empty labour' (Paulsen, 2014), that is, how much time is spent at work by people not doing what they are paid for (e.g. long coffee breaks, taking a nap, surfing on the internet for fun), may be an outcome of workplace norms, set by one's colleagues. But also quality standards, the degree of service mindedness, how you deal with rules and regulations, safety precautions and so on may mainly be guided or controlled by people around you. Group norms are central steering mechanisms.

Sometimes people refer to some group work as 'leadership', typically framed as a progressive or 'post-heroic' type of leadership. Uhl-Bien et al. (2007) talk about adaptive leadership, an emergent, interactive dynamic leading to learning, innovation and adaptability. This is about 'a complex interplay from which a collective impetus for action and change emerges when heterogeneous agents interact in networks' (p. 299). Raelin (2011) sees leadership as 'a shared process focusing more on the collective capacity of people to accomplish their work together' (p. 200). We can broadly refer to this view as co-constructing or the convergence of meaning. Words like shared, intersect, responsive, dialogue and accomplish dominate in the descriptions. Contestation is sometimes mentioned, but only in passing. The impression is one of occasional conflict and friction, but generally happy and smooth work together. While most people understand that groups may not always work so well together, when people work together under the label of 'leadership' (distributed, shared, co-, adaptive) then interactions become harmonious and productive. There is not much to indicate how this is accomplished and there is little to anchor it in richer empirical work.

Complexity leadership is about 'informal interactive patterns that exist in and among organizational systems' (Uhl-Bien et al., 2007, p. 314). Interaction between people is key, there seems to be a minor role for individuals to act as 'leaders', their activity being only about enabling the dynamic. This seems very modest and it appears to be misleading to talk of leaders if they do not stand out as more significant and influential than others.

There is often an interest in 'the collaborative subtext of life, the numerous acts of enabling, supporting, facilitating, and creating conditions ...' (Fletcher & Käufer, 2003, p. 23). Such acts dominate in settings characterized by 'shared leadership'. This is about 'a dynamic, interactive influence process among individuals in groups for which the objective is to lead one another to the achievement of group or organizational goals or both' (Pearce & Conger, 2003, p. 1). In shared leadership the 'influencing process involves more than just downward influence on subordinates by an appointed or elected leader' (p. 1).

It is easy to agree that many organizational interactions involve much more than downward influencing of subordinates. But if the horizontal aspect dominates and people interact and create alignment and direction based on informal, interactive, shared, mutually influencing activities it is better not to label this as 'leadership' but to view it as group-based organizing. A typical example would be a group of engineers that has bumped into an unexpected problem with the development of a new product and meet in order to brainstorm potential solutions to overcome it. No one – not even a participating manager – is necessarily more dominant or influential than the rest and the process is based on mutual adjustments. The outcome – the chosen solution – is a collective work product, without any HIP orchestrating or monitoring (Rennstam, 2007).

The group may be a formal team or a looser constellation. A lot of the enabling, supporting, facilitating and creating conditions may actually be done on this horizontal basis. This may involve formal managers, but the formal position is not central. People influence others based on knowledge and ideas, not on their titles.

This does not mean that there may not be a combination of horizontal work and leadership. On the contrary this is rather common. But the forms of organizing need to be kept separate. When people involved in group work only do minor things to facilitate group work – making a joke, supporting statements, clarifying issues, sticking to the agenda, pushing for a decision or a conclusion, formulating compromises – without anyone having clear and systemic influence or being treated as an authority figure by others, talking of leadership adds very little apart from confusion. This characterizes much work on distributed or shared leadership.[1]

NETWORK-BASED PEER INFLUENCING

If we look at the functions that are often associated with leadership, many can be dealt with by someone other than a manager or a person in a specific superior position. Coaching and emotional support are two good examples. Many contemporary ideas on leadership emphasize what Zaleznik (1997) refers to as psychopolitics. Attending to people's psychological needs is central. But do we have to have 'leaders' or other HIPs for this? If you have a problem and need to discuss it with someone or need emotional support and care, do you necessarily go to the manager or even an informal authority figure in your workplace? Sometimes perhaps, but colleagues around you or people in your network may be equally good or better at a specific issue. They may have more time or be less sensitive to talk to about certain issues. We addressed group work organizing above and now continue with peer networks. This refers to people you know and can get help from outside your closest work context.

Often there may be people enrolled in the network: colleagues or former managers at other units within or outside the organization in which you are working, relatives, friends, people in your professional network that you have met outside workplace contexts, also consultants, psychotherapists, mentors, educators in leadership development programs may be possible resources. Some of these people may have senior positions. Former managers or appointed or informal mentors may be senior to you, but that does not mean that they exercise leadership in any specific way.

Many contacts may form part of a network associated with one's profession, for example physicians, lawyers, consultants, HR people, priests, university teachers. Professions are strong sources of frameworks and norms for thinking and acting. Professions often have strong associations, regular conferences, courses and other activities. Many professionals have a lot of contacts and good relations within the profession. In many cases, people at work are much more influenced and guided by their professional communities than their managers. This can also be true for semi-professionals such as engineers. In an R&D unit we studied, the software engineers often talked about how much direction, inspiration and support they received from their global network of colleagues, within as well as outside the particular company they worked for (Blom & Alvesson, 2014, p. 349):

> I think that the ones that exercise the most significant influence on my work are as a matter of fact the other experts in the global virtual community ... Patrick is also an experienced colleague that is useful when you need advice. Therefore, I ask Patrick for help when it comes to concrete and tangible issues. (Manager, software engineering)

There are advantages and disadvantages with using people in a network instead of one's manager for 'leadership' functions. The positive thing about centralizing functions to the HIP (manager) is her overview and coordination of organizing processes, compared to drawing upon a wide set of network resources that are only coordinated by the person in need of advice and support. When tight coordination and overview is called for, HIP or group work is needed. But if too much falls on the HIP, gaining overview and subsequently a good platform for influence will be difficult as the person becomes overloaded. As mentioned earlier, time is an important constraint and leadership is time-consuming. Very few people are good at everything so by necessity a lot of what leadership advocates like to allocate to 'the leader' is in fact done in other forms of relationship. Interactions with people listening to personal problems or discussing a technical issue are often mystified if referred to as leadership.

Many organizing problems can be solved through the systematic and careful use of network resources. Professions are sometimes strong here, providing a lot of support, direction and constraints for people within the community. Organizations can facilitate and encourage this: by resource allocation for conference attendance, education involving networking, knowledge management systems and organizational cultures emphasizing the value of knowledge sharing and support, that is, through downplaying organizational boundaries.

Leadership may actually also have a role to play – through influencing thinking on networks and encouraging people to think broadly about sources for support and advice. Management is often more significant, through the provision of resources, structures and rewards. But the basic idea is that HIPs downplay their own centrality and encourage the outsourcing of key functions (too) often and one-sidedly associated with leadership. From a non-manager's point of view, it is less a matter of turning one's attention to a HIP above oneself (manager) than of considering and making use of key resources for support and guidance in one's network, within and outside the organization. Within the profession or network, there are often collegial and symmetrical relations, and the norm of reciprocity tends to regulate relations.

AUTONOMY

A sixth possibility is autonomy, that is, people mainly being autonomous at work. For the person in love with leadership or management vocabulary, one may talk of self-leadership or self-management. But talk about how to 'leaderize' or 'managerialize' your own relationship with yourself leads to a slightly bizarre language use, reminding us of a person with a severe personality disorder. As if one part of oneself is doing the leadership or managing and then the other is following. We suggest the term autonomy, of course not indicating that a person is working entirely in splendid isolation, but in order to point out that most of the time s/he is capable of taking care of the job and organizing social relations without much need for instructions, meaning-creation, support or care from others. Of course this does not rule out communication with other relevant people such as colleagues, peers and managers, but this is not regular or significant. A person with a qualified education, some support or supervision during the initial period of working life, and credited with membership/authorization in a profession, would be able to work more or less on her or his own, with occasional support from others. A GP, an architect, or a lawyer is supposed to be able to run a practice without significant amounts of leadership or management. For many university teachers 99 per cent of all work is based on professionalism and autonomy. Also, competent people in many other occupations with some self-esteem may be mainly autonomous and able to deal with relations and collaborations necessary for the job without a HIP overseeing and guiding this. A freelancing agent (e.g. a writer, journalist or designer) is probably a good and increasingly common example as is the skilled craftsman. With autonomy there is no HIP/LIP relation. In terms of influence, a person moves out of influencing processes and becomes a NIP (no-influencing person, i.e. within the context addressed in this book).

An illustrative corporate case is 'Hill' a UK remunerations consulting firm. The firm valued individualistic and self-managing consultants who could generate large fees with minimal intervention from management. As the Managing Director explained:

> We have good people. They don't need a lot of structure and handholding. We are too busy with our clients. One of my colleagues outside this office refers to us as anarchic. I have always taken that as a compliment.

Consultants were granted considerable autonomy within the context of fairly demanding performance targets. Consultants who remained at Hill thrived within this individualistic environment. They responded to questions about their organizational values dismissively:

> I haven't seen any sign of a values statement. At Hill we are treated as adults.
> (Consultant)

Hill's very individualistic culture included nurturing the image of a tough macho loner, operating outside conventional society.

In this tough, individualistic, macho cultural environment, 'identity was for wimps' – or at least this was what the MD's rhetoric suggested. The consultants who succeeded in this environment defined themselves as people who did not need to belong to an organization in the conventional sense, but who derived their personal satisfaction and material for (individual) identity construction through tangible measures of success (i.e. fast cars, prestigious clients, and 'beating the shit out of the competition') (Alvesson & Empson, 2008).

Here the need for or indeed the possibilities of HIPs trying to do a lot of leadership would seem limited and out of place. A bit like preaching the gospel to zealous atheists.

There is often some pre-condition for autonomy to be a central part of organizing at work. Organizational or professional cultures offering a framework for meanings, beliefs and values may guide the person. These may, as in the case of Hill, reflect the work of leadership in the past. Specific recruitment and training may also be vital. HIPs may be more or less inclined to trust subordinates to be NIPs. In many cases the expertise and work situation of professionals may be such that leadership, management or exercise of power is difficult, that is, the on-paper superior person may not be able to establish a HIP/LIP relationship, as formal subordinates prefer autonomy.

PROS AND CONS OF THE SIX

All modes of organizing have their advantages and limitations. These depend on circumstances – both work and organizational contexts (tasks, resources, environment) and the resources of the people involved. You may have an excellent management structure under fairly stable conditions, where managers maintain and operate the bureaucracy leading to good results. You may have highly qualified employees doing work with limited need for coordination (e.g. dentistry or legal advice). There may be complicated, acute problems calling for rapid and coordinated action. We do not go into the myriad of possible contingencies and situational issues which mean that the advantages and problems of various modes of organizing may be more or less significant under different conditions. We only briefly suggest the major pluses and minuses of the various 6Ms.

Management is on the whole rational and creates a clear degree of order, control and predictability. It reduces uncertainty and confusion. Management is part of the employment contract as opposed to, for example, power and leadership, and is therefore easier to recognize and conceptualize from a subordinate perspective. At the same time, management is not typically inspiring and does not lead to peak performance, high motivation or creativity; it tends to be impersonal and seldom leads to much enjoyment or close work relations. With its focus on behaviour and results, it is often easier (faster, cheaper and safer) to effect organizational performance than to take the route via meaning, feelings, identity and culture.

Power means that the HIP has a strong influence. It can cut red tape and reduce lengthy discussions and resistance at work. A strong and charismatic person can reduce the plurality of wills and interests and create alignment and direction. Power may imply that laziness and egoism can be counteracted. Power may also involve the formation of alliances that mean that the majority adapt and there is a dominant orientation and a clear direction that minimizes conflict and opposition. The downside is that the risk of abuse of power is great. Objects of power often feel afraid, small and vulnerable. They are driven by excessive respect and/or anxiety and may stop thinking outside the sphere of the HIP. The use of power may create efficient action and good results, but can also lead to catastrophes. The great charismatic power player may bring about cult-like tendencies, where people are devoted but stop thinking and may do stupid things. It may also lead to resistance and severe conflicts. Of course there is an overlap between leadership and power – as is often the case, when people follow because of a combination of respect and anxiety.

Leadership has the advantage of being a mainly positive form of influence. It means that people buy into meanings, ideas, beliefs and values and are guided by these. Enthusiasm and direction follows. The downside is that it is difficult to realize, time-consuming, and often means that a lot of the specific work tasks to be accomplished are not directly addressed. Leadership is more long-term and overarching, although coaching may also focus on specific work tasks. Much depends on the leader having intellectual resources, an overview, time, energy and interpersonal skills to persuade subordinates that they are supposed to be followers and be led by the leader's ideas, which is often a difficult task.

Group work may be powerful, as agreement within a group is a strong source of influence and coordination. A team sharing certain ideas and norms is a stronger source of alignment and direction than almost any HIP; most people adapt to group norms. Group work means that everyone has a say, which can contribute to shared meanings being well grounded. In a smoothly functioning group you also save on managerial or leadership time costs. A group or team is seldom leader- or manager-free, but as the key organizing work is done through mutual adjustment, there is limited need for a HIP to spend much time or energy leading, managing or exercising power. The problem with group work is that it is not so easy to establish. People may have different ideas, values and interests and there may be conflicts or time-demanding discussions. A group may also be more interested in protecting or maximizing self-interest or avoiding stress or boring work, and may thus be less inclined to prioritize work in an overall pro-organization direction compared to a situation where a manager or other HIP is having a stronger say.

Networks are flexible, broad and usually 'free' resources to use. In principle, people with rich networks can draw upon more knowledge and insight than local relations to a manager and colleagues will allow. Using networks calls for the person in need of guidance and support to think through and actively use resources wisely, which can be beneficial compared to just going to the manager or the person next door. Network resources are also fairly neutral (not involved in the daily political games within the organization). Disadvantages include network resources being very dependent on the network user's version of the problem, which can be rather biased ('My boss is a jerk'). The network resource may have no or limited 'local knowledge'. They cannot directly be used for alignment of meanings, ideas and effort at work as they only communicate with the network user, not the entire work group or labour process, as addressed by the HIP or in group organizing. Finally, people in a network grounded in professional communities may be driven more by professional than organizational ideals; sometimes the former ideals are at the expense of organizational/commercial criteria.

Autonomy, finally, has the great advantage of being effective and is built on and reinforces self-confidence. A qualified person in no need of handholding or guidance from a HIP or some other vertical source of direction can make quick decisions and concentrate on work and results. The autonomous professional, craftsperson or other type of expert is in many ways an ideal. The amount of time spent in more or less unproductive meetings – often celebrated by advocates of 'shared leadership'/group work – can be avoided or minimized. But autonomy seldom works fully and complicated dependencies in organizational contexts mean that work in splendid or even relative isolation is rare. There is also a risk that people slack off or do bad things in a context with minimal HIP steering or control. Limited coordination with others is another problem. Knowledge sharing with other colleagues can become scanty. Sometimes people working (fairly) autonomously feel lonely and in lack of close peer or managerial support. There is of course also an anxiety and stress element in this.

ON THE RELATIONSHIP BETWEEN THE 6MS

Often leadership researchers limit the options to two: management and leadership – and then further collapse the former into an over-sized leadership term. The former is simple and straightforward, while the latter is more complicated, dynamic and sophisticated, it is said. Management is often defined as the matter of using proven solutions to well-known problems, while leadership 'refers to situations in which groups need to learn their way out of problems that could not have been predicted' (Uhl-Bien et al., 2007, p. 300).

Grint (2005) relies on a similar distinction, referring to tame and wicked problems. The former are characterized by complications but resolvable 'through unilateral acts' and with a limited degree of uncertainty. Wicked problems are tricky, complex and related to other problems – they cannot be singled out and addressed in isolation as a separate issue. Climate change and health problems in an aging population are examples. The responses to these problems are management (organizing processes addressing tame problems) respectively leadership (asking questions in order to deal with wicked problems). The former draws upon science and rationality, the latter involves 'the art of engaging a community to face up to complex collective problems' (Grint, 2014, p. 244). It could also be argued however, that according to most views of leadership, this is not just important in the face of difficult (wicked) problems. It is always important to keep up morale and engagement, deal with conflict, infuse meaning and increase identification. Dealing with exceptionally difficult problems is only a small part of what people do at work. And when there are wicked problems a group work scenario in which advanced experts discuss problems may be better than having someone doing leadership asking questions.

In addition to the tendency to bash management in favour of leadership, there is a large industry arguing against heroic leadership in favour of shared, distributed, dialogic leadership, which sees the options of organizing as between leadership and less good leadership (Blom & Alvesson, 2015). This limitation to two options reduces the spectrum of choices and constrains the horizons of people thinking about leadership and supplementary modes of organizing. We believe our six-mode framework is mind-expanding and supports reflexivity and informed choices.

As pointed out in Chapter 2, there is a degree of overlap between the six modes. They occasionally appear in purer forms but are often mixed. There is also often interplay between them. In any work group there are episodes or themes where management, leadership, power, group work, peer influencing and autonomy and/or a blend of some of these modes are exercised. Sometimes in ways in which modes complement and support, sometimes with tensions and conflict, sometimes dominated by ambiguities and confusion. We hope our framework can help clarify and deal with this.

Leadership, management or power may, over time and with occasional interventions, reinforce group work or autonomy. Leadership through a HIP working with shared meanings and a common purpose may facilitate the development of self-governing groups. Management, with the allocation of resources, creating boundaries and perhaps playing a part in the selection and exiting of people to fit the task, may also aid groupwork. Power may be used to create a positive anxiety: 'either you pull yourself together and solve the problem or I start kicking ass', may reduce opportunistic or obstructing behaviour. Leadership and power may reinforce each other, as when an authority figure is established and LIPs not only follow the employment contract as subordinates but start to take clearer follower positions, driven by a combination of respect and fear. Effective management or leadership over a period may lead to autonomy in the next stage, when carefully selected, socialized, developed and assessed employees may work based on autonomy or supported by network resources. This may mean that any notion of management or leadership becomes obsolete in relation to the work of these individuals who are no longer in need of hand-holding.

Thoughtful leadership tries to identify and support the right mode(s) of organizing, given the resources and situation. This is our key point in this book.

SUMMARY

In this chapter we have addressed six modes of organizing in terms of the 6M framework that we introduced in Chapter 2. We have emphasized the need to be selective and careful about leadership compared to other forms of organizing. Sometimes other modes make more sense, both as the major organizing principle in a unit, and as a specific mode of action in specific settings. So there are also occasions where manager/subordinate, power holder/target of power, group work, network utilization and autonomy make sense within a leader-follower relationship. When this is the case the leadership relation and associated practices are pushed into the margins, at least while other modes of organizing seem more appropriate.

NOTE

1. There is also a lot of confusion around these terms. Sometimes they refer to there being many with HIP functions – like several managers working together, i.e. a headmaster and a deputy, one or more than one standing out as doing leadership – sometimes it refers to everybody being involved in 'leadership'. These are very different phenomena, but often confused (Gronn, 2009).

8
Leadership Varieties:
The 5P Framework

As repeated in this book, we see leadership as the systematic efforts to influence followers in terms of meaning (head and heart). This may be viewed as limited and narrow by advocates of a broad and inclusive understanding of leadership with a limited interest in making distinctions. The latter is, however, crucial for sharp thinking and counteracting the foggy ideas that are all too common in the leadership field.

In this chapter we recognize that the idea of leadership as the systematic influencing of meaning within an asymmetrical relationship is still rather broad and that there are good reasons to consider some basic variations within leadership. We suggest five such varieties, framed as metaphors. Metaphors are helpful as support for memory and for the creation of imaginative gestalts and we suggest a framework based on 5Ps. Here the person doing leadership work may be *prophesying* through visions; *preaching* about morals and values; making *psychotherapeutic* interventions by targeting emotions; *party-hosting* in trying to create positive working climate; and acting *pedagogically* by trying to increase learning.

In the chapter we will mainly describe the leadership aspect of the HIP/LIP relation and interaction, although we will also briefly discuss followership in relation to the different varieties of leadership. We begin the chapter with a broad overview of the five. This is followed by a brief explanation of the motivation behind the labels. Subsequent to that follows an extensive discussion of leadership in terms of the 5P framework where we go through all the different elements (summarized in Table 8.1) and indicate possible relations. The chapter ends with a short summary.

LEADERSHIP WORK AS 5PS

The sceptical reader may view the 5Ps with their somewhat funny labels as an expression of the lightweight, popular leadership thinking emphasizing simplistic types that we are critical of. We are aware of this, but believe that the labels make sense and capture the key elements of leadership as we define it. Using the P label has some pedagogical effect. We do not emphasize fixed types, but priority work areas for people trying to do leadership.

Table 8.1 Summary of the 5P model: basic elements of leadership

Type of leadership work	Characteristics	Tools/means	Personal characteristics	Nature of relation	Common weakness	Less flattering label/risk of stigmatizing attribution
Prophesying a vision	Emphasizing the overall purpose and ambition	Rhetoric and symbolic action	Charismatic, convincing	Elevated and distant, superior insights	Limited relevance and credibility	Cliché fetishist
Preaching values and morals	Emphasizing morality and values	Moral example, rhetoric	Morally superior	Somewhat remote	Hypocrisy (in a world calling for moral compromise)	Bigot
Psychotherapeutic intervention influencing emotions	Interested in people and their inner life	Talk and more talk	Patient	Intimate, but in an asymmetrical way	Uninterested in work and performance	Shrink
Party-hosting, creating a positive work climate	Trying to create high spirits and make people happy	Social activities, jokes, being friendly	Cheerful, funny	Very close, buddy-like	Fun before profit, denial of bad news	Clown
Pedagogical work aiming to support learning and cognitive development	Trying to make people understand more/better	Training, group conferences, coaching	Lecturing	Medium to close	In need of less competent followers	School master

The 5Ps are not mutually exclusive. All HIPs do a variety of different things, but often there is some emphasis on a particular type of meaning-influencing work. If for example you see yourself as a party host – a person interested in making people happy and ensuring a pleasant working climate – this calls for skills, priorities and hard work. And this comes at the expense of other important things. It is very difficult to do a lot of prophesying, preaching values, doing psychotherapy, being very cheerful and developing people within the same working week, in particular as managers must do many other things as well.

THE 5P FRAMEWORK: BRIEF MOTIVATION

The five key work areas for leadership are informative about what is distinct about leadership as a set of practices. There are some efforts to summarize leadership through images or metaphors in the literature. Hatch et al. (2006) talk about leaders as managers, artists and priests, referring to the need for rationality (order), creativity (change and chaos) and courage (values mediating order and chaos). Western (2008) refers to the leader as controller, therapist and Messiah (transformational leader). Alvesson and Spicer (2011) use the metaphors of saint, gardener, buddy, cyborg, commander, and bully. We refrain from addressing 'the leader' (HIP) as manager, controller, cyborg and commander (these relate to management more than leadership in our terms) and address the bully under our mode of organizing called 'power'. The artist metaphor of creativity and change is seductive, but there are many ways of working with creativity. Much leadership, also of a creative nature, is not about change in any distinct sense. Often leadership addresses a variety of problems and disruptions, dealing with ongoing combinations of change and continuities as regards customers, suppliers, internal relations and labour processes, more or less continuously, and calls for a combination of managerial, leadership and other interventions. Western's idea of the Messiah illuminates a rather extreme and unhelpful notion of leadership, but has some overlap with the prophet. We draw upon Alvesson and Spicer but revise and develop their metaphors into something more distinctively leadership oriented.

As we see it, people in organizations, in particular HIPs with leadership ambitions, typically deal with:

1. the overall purpose or meaning going beyond the here and now
2. various values and morals that guide us in everyday life
3. personal problems and conflicts at the workplace, often of an emotional and less expressed nature
4. improving/maintaining good group relations and work climate
5. helping junior employees with cognitive problems and supporting their development.

These work domains are only partly captured by the metaphors for leadership (not management) suggested by Hatch et al. and Western. The five suggested here are more complete and allow for careful distinctions. They all influence cultural meanings, but on different levels: long-term ambitions, guiding 'operative' ideas, dealing with indi-vidual and collective feelings, and the need for learning and development. In many cases it is the direct, face-to-face HIP interactions that work best for dealing with most of these issues and here enters leadership. Few HIPs can do all types of leadership work, so in some cases HIPs work with combinations of leadership, management and other modes of organizing.

PROPHESYING: LEADERSHIP BY PROVIDING A VISION

Much popular leadership thinking sees the leader in a light similar to the prophet we refer to. This is about formulating and communicating a vision or an overall great cause that is aimed at accomplishing something remarkable. A vision is like a prophecy, that is, a conditional one. Sometime in the future great things will happen, given effort and everybody joining in with the fantastic project. LIPs will feel meaning and commitment.

The key element behind a prophecy is to gain strong support for what an organiza-tion can become or accomplish, suggesting that it must appeal to people's hearts and minds. A key idea is that the prophecy – cause, vision, dream – should provide work tasks and assignment with meaning and also serve as a source of self-esteem and encourage a common purpose. Ideally, prophecies should also guide the actions and decision-making of organizational members. This is perhaps especially important in organizations where employees are given a great deal of discretion and autonomy in performing their work tasks (Raelin, 1989). In this way one can say that leaders as prophets work well in tandem with alternative coordination mechanisms such as team work. But the disciples need to buy into the prophecy, that is, share the vision.

The visionary

A popular form is the idea of the visionary leader. This can be exemplified by an employment situation where people are expected to perform routine and boring work tasks such as digging holes in the ground with shovels. Performance and goal comple-tion are evaluated and controlled according to, for example, the frequency of the dig-ging and the number of holes shovelled during a given period of time, which also forms the basis for compensation. This work situation is then contrasted with a situation where a leader – usually a manager – initially explains the overall purpose behind the digging of the holes – perhaps building a recreational area for families in an underpriv-ileged community which will enable children to have a better life. The illustration points at a broader purpose or meaning to the work task, setting a wider cognitive and emotional stage for what could otherwise be seen as nothing but repetitive and boring work. The worker may then stop thinking of herself as a hole-digger and start imagining herself as being part of a child welfare project and become driven by a desire to accom-plish this worthy purpose.

A vision is an image of an ideal future and should be simple and capable of evok-ing emotions (Kouzes & Posner, 1995). It should be connected to the values and the purpose of an organization. The ability to create and form such ideal futures in a convincing manner is often – as discussed in Chapter 3 – seen as part of charismatic and occasionally transformative leadership.

Visions constitute an imaginary or visual characterization of an ideal reality that should not only be rationally understandable but also – and perhaps primarily – evoke emotional commitment. In order to make the ideological element of a vision salient it should be persuasively communicated with the help of colourful and emotional language that includes vivid imagery, stories, metaphors and sagas that engage the receivers. Narratives and stories are usually more convincing if they draw upon culturally anchored symbols such as legendary heroes, historical myths, triumphs and sacred figures that people have heard of. A dramatic and expressive display of communication contributes to the impact of visions. Included in this is also the speaker's tone, facial expressions, gestures and body movements, as well as rhythms of speech and repetition of key words.

Visions should thus reach both the hearts and minds of people and be challenging as well as realistic. The latter is seen as important in order to make the vision meaningful and credible rather than just a farfetched fantasy that people approach with ridicule and cynicism. The motivational effects of a vision may also be contingent upon the extent to which followers are confident about their ability to reach it (Senge, 1996). This connects to the classic discussion of the *Pygmalion effect* that refers to how people tend to perform better when a leader has high expectations and shows confidence in them (Eden, 1984). Highly significant is encouraging and fostering confidence and optimism when people are facing more difficult or dangerous tasks or when they seem to lack confidence. This sometimes entails reminding people of previous triumphs and victories in terms of overcoming obstacles. If such examples are lacking, leaders may use analogies about how other people overcame similar situations – often in more or less epic and/or mythical terms.

An example

The former Group CEO of the hearing aid company Oticon, Lars Kolind, may serve as an interesting embodiment of visionary leadership. Learning and development was a central part of the vision for Oticon as stated by Kolind:

> The vision was to develop a truly knowledge-based company, which could make a difference in the form of a breakthrough in user satisfaction with hearing aids. This not only requires a creative combination of technology, audiology and psychology, but also a much closer co-operation between the different professionals involved in the actual selling, fitting and fine-tuning of the hearing aid to the needs of each individual user.

Upon entering the organization Kolind redesigned the company in terms of the so-called 'spaghetti organization', claimed to be one of the first knowledge-intensive and paperless organizations in the world (Peters, 1992). Kolind was also famous for instigating a drastic reduction of the workforce – creating a 'lean team' and making all the remaining employees engaged in development activities.

The employees were encouraged to share corporate values of trust, empowerment, open communication and respect for the individual. Rather than focusing on creating a cosy culture (such as the party host would), challenging goals and individual development were more explicitly focused upon. Employees were encouraged to think the unthinkable and challenged to question the status quo. They were also asked to challenge managers' views and always eliminate activities that did not add value to customers.

In line with the vision, titles were also abolished and decisions were to be made by those influenced by them. In an effort to empower subordinates Kolind stated that: 'When in doubt – then do it. If it works it's good, if not you're forgiven' and 'It's easier to be forgiven than to get approval'. Kolind clarified this by stating that:

> The employees' hidden resources are brought out so they can play together like an efficient football team where each individual knows the objectives and the strategy and can kick the ball immediately without having to look up the rules and ask why.

Lars Kolind was not afraid to give employees responsibility, as he had seen through his many years as a boy scout that good results could be achieved through co-operation and delegating responsibility:

> No one can resist confidence. That is the greatest thing a manager can give an employee, and it most certainly activates creativity.

This sounds impressive and illustrates the prophet at work. A minor problem was that his ideas did not really work as intended. Gradually corporate reality became more conventional while Kolind continued to express his vision to an admiring business press. Also, many employees felt proud of the company, despite the mismatch between claimed ideals and actual practice (Kjaersgaard et al., 2011).

Advantages of visionary leadership

A well-formulated vision anchored in the wishes and interests of followers may be highly inspirational and motivational. If a vision is experienced as mainly managerial without any broader relevance it will hardly draw any attraction. Visions that are tied to people's values, wish for self-realization, positive self-view and relations with others tend to have more impact and provide people with extra energy and engagement to follow the vision.

Ideally, visions provide a common ground for interpretation and understanding about the 'whats' and 'whys' in terms of work tasks and accomplishments. This can facilitate communication, faster decision-making and stronger identification with the organization in question. Studies of visionary leadership suggest that training in formulating visions among managers contributes to increased work satisfaction and improved performance among employees (in comparison to managers that did not receive such training) (Hunt et al., 1999; Kirkpatrick & Locke, 1996).

Critique

Although highly popular, visionary leadership also has its limitations. For example, Nadler and Tushman (1997) point out that followers often place unrealistic demands and expectations on leaders that may lead to disappointment when things do not turn out the way they hoped. As in many of the other cases there is also the risk of strong dependency relations and infantilization of followers; the leader becomes a sort of elevated hero with close to superhuman qualities, as can be witnessed in most sects and some religious and political organizations.

Visions may also contribute to group thinking and a lack of diversity in meaning and opinions. Although this may be productive to counter fragmentation and contribute to more focused work, it also entails organizational homogeneity that may undermine development and renewal, which often build on multiplicity and dissent in terms of opinions and voices. Some degree of diversity may of course be accommodated in the visionary leadership, but strong visionary leadership may also exclude those that do not fit the specific version, perhaps expressing 'wrong' diversity.

Another problem is that it is not so easy to formulate a vision that holds water. The Oticon example illustrates the mixed blessing of a visionary message that is extremely powerful and broadly applauded. Imperfect reality strikes back, leaving the organization in a confused state. In many cases managers have problems formulating something that sounds 'vision-like'. In an interview with a manager in a support unit of a large pharmaceutical firm, she said that the biggest challenge was to make people work as a team, and see to it that work continues even if someone is temporarily absent. Vital here is a 'vision'. This was about 'a common purpose is, I believe ... that we could provide infrastructure, we do whatever is necessary to allow the scientists to produce these great projects ... which is our future' (Alvesson & Sveningsson, 2003a, p. 369). As a vision, 'to provide infrastructure' is vague and flat to say the least. And the addition of helping scientists does not make it much clearer. Sometimes a 'vision' in business life does not take off and gives an almost comical impression. However, when it does take off, metaphorically speaking, it may end up in the stratosphere, having limited contact with earth, as was the case at Oticon.

PREACHING: LEADERSHIP BY INFLUENCING VALUES AND MORALS

In contemporary society and business there is a booming interest in morality. There are debates on equal opportunities in relation to gender, ethnicity, disabilities, age, marketing methods and environmental responsibility, community involvement, greed and overpayment of executives, whistleblowing, and issues in the developing world like child labour and bad working conditions. Emphasis on individualism, consumerism and hedonism means that self-interest becomes more salient. Feelings of reduced community and increased secularization – combined with a renewed focus on religion – contribute to increased uncertainty around moral issues. It is likely that these developments form a background to a contemporary interest in morality and business ethics. This also affects leadership. Hopes and demands as well as the attractive self-identities of managers tend to breed high-moral leadership, turning the manager into a pastor-like character.

The good shepherd

Emphasizing leaders' high moral standing is hardly a new thing, but this frame and focus have become much more salient during recent decades. Integrity and high ethical standards are often viewed as characteristics of a good leader. Sometimes authors claim that when the leader is not of the right moral calibre, there is not leadership, but something less noble. For instance, some researchers claim that transformational leaders must embody morals as a core value to be assessed as authentic (Bass & Steidlmeier, 1999). The combination of authentic and immoral is not an option. Put in the crudest form, many assume that a real leader is morally irreproachable. If he or she is immoral, then he or she is not a leader. Leaders help, support, and inspire followers. They do not, push, lure, seduce or trick. The sceptic may associate this more with a fairy tale than contemporary working life.

Efforts to boost the moral qualities of leadership are common. An example of this is so-called 'Superleadership'. This involves leading followers to lead themselves through empowerment and the development of self-leadership skills. The Superleader exhibits orientations that match the pedagogue but the moral qualities are also worth highlighting – the altruism and care attributed to the Superleader being a Supermoral person. The Superleader 'focuses primarily on the empowering roles of helping, encouraging and supporting followers in the development of personal responsibility, individual initiative, self-confidence, self-goal setting, self-problem solving, opportunity thinking, self-leadership, and psychological ownership over their tasks and duties' (Houghton et al., 2003, p. 133). The Superleader does this through a range of orientations, all of which echo positive moral ideals such as encourage learning from mistakes, avoiding punishment, listening more, talking less, creating independence and interdependence, avoiding dependence, and so on.

The religious metaphor is common in leadership and invites us to consider themes such as sacredness, worship and miracles (Alvesson, 2011; Grint, 2010b). These are certainly themes in a lot of the thinking about leadership, although more emphasized among political and religious leaders and a few mass media business heroes than in many cases of mundane managerial leadership. But for some management authors, it is a mistake to emphasize the profane nature of business. Hatch et al. (2006), having studied a number of articles in the *Harvard Business Review*, claims that 'stories about the founders of business, the glory of its leaders, or its employees' extraordinary efforts reference the sacred within the business settings that are misconstrued as strictly profane' (p. 60). In the more extreme writings, the authentic leader is pure and sacred.

Bass and Steidlmeier (1999) also make a case for the existence of truly good leaders. There are some concerns that charisma may not be good all the time, leading to questions of whether transformational leadership is necessarily a blessing. These authors confidently claim that authentic transformational leadership is always on the side of the good; it 'must rest on a moral foundation of legitimate values' (p. 184). The opposite is inauthentic or pseudo-transformational leadership, where leaders act in bad faith. All sorts of good things characterize the authentic leader. For instance, some claim that authentic leaders 'call for [a] universal brotherhood' and focus 'on the best in people', whereas inauthentic leaders 'highlight fictitious "we-they" differences' and 'tend to focus on the worst in people' (pp. 187–188). The authentic transformational leader may experience a need for power, but 'channel the need in socially constructive ways into the service of others' (p. 189).

In a popular and expanding literature on 'servant leadership' moral virtues are also stressed to such an extent that the good leader is perceived to have virtues quite different from the great majority of people. Much of this literature is explicitly religious, with references to Biblical tales and the great leadership of Christ. Hatch et al. (2006) see the 'priest' as one of the faces of the leader, together with the 'manager' and the 'artist'. The priest-leader is empathic, ethical, inspiring, comforting, focused on faith, soul, transcendence and purity and embraces the saviour as the heroic ideal. There are also ideas like 'servant leadership that requires that leaders lead followers for the followers' own ultimate good' (Sendjaya et al., 2008, p. 403) and advocate putting 'followers first, organizations second, their own needs last' (p. 403). Servant leaders are authentic, altruistic, humble, and create 'an intensely personal bond marked by shared values, open-ended commitment, mutual trust, and concern for the welfare of the other party' (p. 407). Those served by the servant leaders 'are positively transformed in multiple dimensions (e.g. emotionally, intellectually, socially, and spiritually' (p. 408). The good leader then is a saintly figure capable of producing peak moral performance and avoiding the vulnerabilities that characterize the large majority of the population. These are not necessarily sinners, but it is assumed that the good leader stands out as different from the morally imperfect masses.

Some examples

This high-calibre morality is a position highly valued by many managers. Everyone we have interviewed over the last two decades has been deeply concerned with scoring highly on moral positioning. Let us give examples of managers taking a preacher-like position of high moral virtue.

Jack Welch, in his letters to shareholders, presents himself as a morally high standing person. He indicates that he leads a firm of 'saintly feats' (Amernic et al., 2007, p. 1853). According to Welch in his letters, GE is a firm of the highest standards, creating 'the spirit and soul of a small company', 'of never putting one foot outside the line of absolute integrity'. To lead a 'saintly' firm seems however to come at a cost. Welch routinely 'sacrificed' employees in order to keep the organization up to his standards, earning him the nickname 'Neutron Jack'. Even if he presented himself as a leader of the highest moral standards in the eyes of his key stakeholders and the business press, many of his employees would probably have described him as less saintly.

A more ordinary man is George, group manager of some highly skilled engineers in a high-tech firm. In his self-narrative, he comes across as a very good man. Respect, confidence, openness, being on the side of the co-workers, working for them, advocating their interests are key activities. George claims that one must:

> ... engage in the co-workers, not just what they are to produce but also to a certain level their lives, that is self-evident. And openness is then very much a matter of they should feel that I am on their side. I work for them, i.e. I bring their interests further and inform about constraints, e.g. we can't allocate all the time in the world on tool development and so on.

Interestingly, George's pastor-like self-image as a leader can be related to his difficulties in contributing significantly to technical discussions and other substantive issues. He says that:

> Earlier I had worked a lot from that I have a very good insight in the technical tasks people are working with. I have realized that it is incredibly tough here.

There is a new product segment in which people are doing 'very deep' and specialized work, which George finds 'extremely difficult to understand'. So George replaces knowledge for what goes in with walking around radiating goodness, being a 'service leader'.

High moral virtues seem to be common for many managers eager to do leadership in what they see as the right way. They find strong support in the leadership literature for this position – often echoing religious ideals (Alvesson, 2011).

Advantages of preaching-leadership

One can argue that a high moral standing could be advantageous and drive performance in at least three different ways. First, moral leadership may influence patterns of reciprocity. If a leader is viewed as having a lot of moral qualities, arguably, s/he may be at the same time perceived as doing positive things for followers. Being open, honest, and considerate are all actions that – at least when read and framed in these positive terms – call for a positive response from those presumably benefiting from these positive behaviours. This is the norm of reciprocity, a universal norm according to Gouldner (1960). You treat the HIP in the same way he or she treats you and then the relationship becomes smoother and well-functioning.

Another way moral qualities may work is through faith and trust. The less trust there is, the greater the risk of cheating, and the higher the cost of monitoring and controlling people to restrict their opportunistic tendencies. In the management literature, only subordinates are usually opportunistic and optimize their self-interest at their employer's expense. But this is of course a two-way issue. Both managers and subordinates may have well-motivated feelings of distrust, leading to the careful monitoring of the other and a preference for formal agreements. High morality means trust, goodwill and reliance on promises. People assume that their good performances will be rewarded fairly in the long run and that in a fair relationship one gets what one deserves.

A third way preacher-like leadership works is through identification. The more transformational leaders relate their vision to underlying generalities associated with positive human and/or spiritual values; it increasingly seems that 'querying any aspect of the vision becomes an illegitimate act, incompatible with continued participation in the organization's activities' (Amernic et al., 2007, p. 1854). High morality breeds trust and the general cause attracts an extra dose of identification and solidarity. This dampens the acceptance of deviating views and this promotes conformity and compliance, which may be good for business, but is probably seen as good for senior managers, if they prefer a loyal and docile work force.

Critique

There are two critiques which it is important to present. Firstly, the idea that moral leaders should exercise a strong influence over the weaker souls without integrity, moral righteousness and commitment to a noble cause expresses a specific form of elitism. It suggests that leaders are like wise parents, while followers are like savage children with a lower level of morality. Western (2008, p. 116) echoes this point when he claims that:

> The suggestion that a leader brings intelligent, adult employees to a new moral maturity is reminiscent of the Victorian paternalistic ideology which attempted to bring a new morality to the working class.

Secondly, performance pressures often put strong constraints on people living up to high ideals. Morality sometimes becomes a matter of doing what the guy above you demands (Jackall, 1988). One can question whether people with high moral standards and eager to do leadership in a preacher-like way really have made a wise career choice if embarking on a managerial career in many business and some public sector organizations? As it is sometimes joked: 'Authenticity is most important in business life, fake it and you will make it' (senior employee in an investment company).

While it would be good if leadership meant promoting good values at work and being exemplary in character and behaviour, it is important to realize that this is not so easy to accomplish. Reaching senior positions often calls more for political astuteness than high moral calibre (Jackall, 1988). Awareness of moral mazes of organizational life is probably more useful in that sense than preaching the self-evident pay-off of high morality in leadership.

PSYCHOTHERAPEUTIC WORK: LEADERSHIP TARGETING PEOPLE-IMPROVEMENT

Contemporary working life is often described as increasingly unstable, ambiguous and turbulent. Conflicting expectations and demands, ethical problems, worries, stress, a sense of lack of meaning and feelings of insufficiency form the backbone of an increased focus on how to manage the emotional well-being of employees. The idea that employees who feel well are better equipped to manage stress, anxieties, uncertainties and change has triggered a wealth of means of improving employees' well-being. We see this for example in the emergence of an organizational therapeutic culture where leaders are expected to score highly on 'emotional intelligence' (George, 2000). Leadership ideas are interwoven with this development: 'Therapeutic culture has had a huge influence on how leadership is enacted in the workplace, and how emotions and subjectivity are managed and organized' (Western, 2008, p. 94). Leadership activities should then target people's inner needs.

Contemporary ideas are partly a continuation and re-labelling of the traditional relationship-oriented, considerate and people-oriented leadership ideas which emerged in the 1950s (as discussed in Chapter 3). Leadership means privileging employees' psychological well-being and welfare. These ideas, intimately related to the Human Relations movement, suggest that more employee recognition is beneficial in order to achieve emotionally balanced employees and improved productivity. Following the Human Relations movement and Maslow's scheme on motivation, the ideas of privileging emotions, group psychodynamics and self-actualization have become conventional in respect of maintaining healthy interpersonal relations and a rewarding workplace. Following a general broadening of the definition of psychic problems and 'illness', there has been a huge increase in new age theorists/practitioners, feel-good consultants, and other people-improving groups ready to employ the right therapeutic tools for improving the emotional status of individuals and organizations (Foley, 2010). Leaders have not been immune to this development, hence we now tend to see leaders as psychotherapists.

This idea of 'the shrink' is more or less explicitly expressed in many writings on leadership in which listening, talking and recognizing people by acknowledging their presence and voice are becoming increasingly salient. Listening in particular is seen as a way to recognize people and is assumed to improve well-being and emotional status. In an article in *Forbes* (2012) titled 'Why most leaders need to shut up and listen' it is suggested that:

> One of the most often overlooked aspects of listening is thanking others for their contributions ... Even if no value is perceived, thank them for their time and input. Never forget to acknowledge those who contribute energy, ideas, actions or results. Few things go as far in building good will as recognizing others.

It is also argued that:

> As leaders, we must balance our intensity and desire to perform with compassionate attention to our employees' needs. Being more mindful of another's stress and their tension points before they impact the business requires us to boost our emotional intelligence.

This development has made leaders in organizations more involved in the management of emotions and (ill) feelings, hence we see how some leaders act as 'pseudo-shrinks' in relation to their followers.

The one there for you

The increased focus on emotionality is not only directed at the potential followers. The emotional turn also means an increased focus on the emotionality of the leader. Exercising leadership by 'heart' is regarded as requiring a particular skill referred to as 'emotional intelligence'. Examined by Mayer and Salovey (1997) emotional intelligence was more explicitly related to leadership by Goleman (1998) who lists five components of emotional intelligence at work:

- *Self-awareness* – the ability to recognize and understand your mood and emotions and their effect on others. This involves self-confidence, realistic self-assessment and a self-depreciating sense of humour.
- *Self-regulation* – the ability to control or redirect disruptive impulses and moods. This involves trustworthiness and integrity, comfort with ambiguity and openness to change.
- *Motivation* – a passion to work for reasons that go beyond money or status. This refers to having a strong drive to achieve, and showing optimism even in the face of failure and organizational commitment.
- *Empathy* – the ability to understand the emotional status of other people. This involves expertise in building and retaining talent, cross-cultural sensitivity and service to clients and customers.
- *Social skill* – proficiency in managing relationships and building networks. This revolves around effectiveness in leading change, persuasiveness and expertise in building and leading teams.

Goleman suggests that this list of 'EQ' skills is relatively more important than IQ and technical skills, characterizing the EQ skills as the 'sine qua non of leadership'. There is also the concept of cultural intelligence that narrows the scope to the ability to adjust to different contexts (Earley & Mosakowski, 2004). In addition, there are notions of contextual intelligence – a sort of 'cognitive empathy' or 'social intelligence' – that enables managers to learn about new cultural norms (Khanna et al., 1998).

Writings on emotionality in service industries – such as airline flight attendants – elaborate carefully upon how managers should aim at making employees sociable and sympathetic in order to maintain customer service (Hochschild, 1983). Emotional labour facilitates the possibility of providing what customers would experience as good service or as framed by Hochschild (1983, p. 7): 'to create a publicly observable facial and bodily display'. Emotional leadership such as listening to sense the mood among subordinates enables the manager to maintain a high level of customer service through the good feelings of the employees (Sturdy and Fleming, 2003). Leadership partly aims at creating a corporate persona or image to which employees are expected to contribute and identify with. Leaders as psychotherapists aim to influence the emotional inner life of employees and thus partly how people understand themselves, their subjectivity and identity. In different ways this idea also comes through in some well-known leadership approaches such as transformational leadership, central to which is the idea of aligning followers' emotions with the objectives of the organization.

However, the significance of emotional intelligence in relation to leadership is debated. Many of the authors above suggest that leaders' emotional skills help people bridge conflicts and build healthy relationships and subsequently a harmonious workplace. Some researchers, however, emphasize that leadership should focus on 'real work' and customers, rather than the psychological needs of employees and internal social relations (Zaleznik, 1997).

Some examples

Illustrations of the significance of the psychotherapist element are common in contemporary organizations. A manager in a public employment agency describes how she tries to see her employees:

> I have a view that if my staff feels good then both employers and job seekers will get the best service. I prioritise my staff in all respects. I always have an open door. I'm here for them. I am well aware that I see my staff so often that I see when they are not feeling good. I have my eyes and ears open for the overall atmosphere, ill-feeling, incidents and I respond accordingly.

She suggests that leadership is a matter of being able to sense how people are feeling. A similar view is expressed by a manager in an R&D department in a global telecom company, who talks about caring for subordinates by sensing moods:

> I know this thing about being responsible for people. I listen to people, I sense moods. I've had this thing about responsibility for people. I'm working to make my employees feel good. I want to back them up, but it always has to be good for the company.

The cases (more fully reported in Sveningsson and Alvesson (2016)) imply close observation of subordinates' behaviour and trying to read emotional status in order to detect any problems lurking below the surface. Like psychotherapists, who are supposed to listen attentively and occasionally intervene in order to correct a problem, managers talk of their role in detecting ill-feelings and problems. Typically, the psychotherapeutic leader should pay attention to LIPs' emotional state, alleviate pain and suffering and add meaning and encouragement to work tasks and work life.

Advantages of psychotherapeutic leadership

Maslow's (1943, p. 381) famous 'hierarchy of needs' established that on top of basic human needs, people seek 'recognition, attention, importance or appreciation' from others. Tying into this idea, contemporary leadership scholars promote emotional and social recognition to foster conditions under which workers regulate themselves in line with organizational interests (Luthans et al., 2000). Recent studies show how appreciative practices such as giving constructive feedback or assigning responsibility boost self-esteem, increase employee well-being, and reduce work stress (Semmer & Jacobshagen 2010; Stocker et al., 2015). This is argued to enhance employee loyalty and organizational performance. Additionally, over the past ten years or so, popular management accounts have been published to give managers explicit advice on 'how to' best recognize employees. Recognition is promoted as an extremely efficient leadership that 'energizes' and 'revitalizes' the workplace and creates a 'loyal, motivated, and productive workforce' (Ventrice, 2009, p. 4).

Emphasizing the importance of recognition, Chapman and White (2012) argue that 'each of us wants to know that what we are doing matters' and that 'without a sense of being valued by supervisors and colleagues, workers start to feel like a machine or a commodity' (p. 22). In order to avoid treating workers in a machine-like fashion, they promote measures of showing appreciation with the goal of securing workers' 'psychological survival' (p. 22). Leadership as focusing on people's well-being is seen as an alternative to organizational control that builds on 'coercion, fear and threats' (Nelson and Spitzer, 2003). As explained by a CEO for a large service company: 'A manager's most important task is actually to make certain that people feel good, since people that feel good also perform well' (Dagens Industri, 2: 2009, p. 17).

In sum, the psychotherapist element of leadership that focuses on followers' well-being can help counteract a bias towards viewing people as 'resources' or means that can be easily replaced if objectives and performance levels are not met. Instead, the individual is very much in the centre, and by ensuring his/her well-being performance can in turn be affected positively.

Critique

Most people agree that emotions play an important role in workplaces and are an important theme or area for leadership. A potential problem is however that an exaggerated concern for LIPs' well-being may overshadow other important organizational issues, such as productivity, external legitimacy or financial results. Time is a scarce resource and HIPs may have more important things to care about than LIPs' emotional states, especially since a lot of personal problems and sources of stress, feelings of failure, etc. can be found outside the immediate working environment. A second issue concerns the capacity of the average HIP to perform the role of listener/therapist. A trained psychotherapist has a long and formal training. There are probably fairly good reasons for this. The risk is obvious that many who embrace the sympathetic and humane idea of caring for our colleagues and subordinates enter deep water when we try to perform this role, lacking perhaps both the right skills and disposition. There are probably limited benefits to many self-appointed 'pseudo shrinks' in contemporary organizations. One could also add that the general trend towards the psychologization of society and working life is not unproblematic. This is part of a narcissistic culture, where people increasingly ask for attention and confirmation (Alvesson, 2013b; Lasch, 1978). Satisfying an increased appetite for the latter is difficult and may only fuel it, as people become increasingly focused on their emotions and expect the world to take them and their deviations from good-feelings seriously. It is probably better if workplace relations are structured so that 'the culture of narcissism' and the 'therapy society' do not penetrate too broadly and deeply into all spheres of human life.

PARTY-HOSTING: LEADERSHIP AIMING AT CREATING WORKPLACE BUDDIES

The significance of leaders as 'party hosts' has – similarly to the psychotherapists – grown exponentially as forming a social atmosphere and organizational culture that enforce the right spirit and make people happy at work are seen as increasingly important. This is an element of leadership that aims to ensure that subordinates and colleagues are having fun and that people not only appreciate but also enjoy organizational life. This is often accomplished through social activities. In the wake of a harsher, colder, more demanding and stressful working climate this variant views the social – in terms of fun – relations as most crucial in leadership.

Although ideas of having fun in the workplace and framing leaders as party hosts have received fairly scant attention in much conventional leadership literature, they are occasionally emphasized as quite significant. Seldom explicitly expressed as party hosting, many of these activities are well aligned with consideration and relationship-oriented leadership behaviour. Consideration, for example, often suggests that leaders praise and recognize followers (presence and inclusions) and relations-oriented texts usually include discussions of how leaders should encourage and support employees in order to build and maintain peoples' motivation and self-esteem (Yukl, 2006).

Writings on relational leadership occasionally focus on social recognition including awards, ceremonies and recognition events. This may include gifts and wining and dining. Also the leader as a 'country club' manager, as suggested by Blake and Mouton (1964), expresses the idea that social activities form workplace relations and affect loyalty. This also includes expressions of consideration such as small talk, common courtesy, remembering peoples' names and saying good morning. These practices are regarded as powerful managerial tools with which to achieve motivation and commitment: 'In initiated business circles, for example, it is well known that a weekend of shooting, anniversary celebrations, garden parties, a day at the races and similar social events are crucial in framing important managerial decisions' (Sjöstrand et al., 2001, p. 12).

The idea is that by promoting an informal and friendly atmosphere (off-site adventures, golfing, surprise cakes, encouraging people by using their first names, and mingling with people in the corridors) many leaders try to support people and maintain high spirits and motivation in their organizations. There are of course also cases where, for example, HIPs perform *actual* party hosting, that is, organizing social events with the explicit purpose of having fun and creating commitments (see Alvesson, 1995; Fleming, 2005). Particularly in service work, happy employees may be more positive in interactions with customers, which is a key element for customer satisfaction.

Some writings emphasize the relevance of empathizing, befriending and fraternizing with subordinates in order to reach organizational objectives, hence the view of leaders as friends or '*buddies*' (Sveningsson & Blom, 2011). This leadership approach means looking after and caring for people and ensuring that everyone feels good; conditions we routinely associate with those that buddies ideally are supposed to provide.

The funny guy

> A sense of humor is part of the art of leadership, of getting along with people, of getting things done. (Dwight D. Eisenhower)

A particular take on the party host is to look into the use of humour. It is often suggested that humour relieves stress, anxieties and boredom as well as increasing engagement and well-being, creativity, collaboration and productivity (Beard, 2014). In a recent publication dealing with leading with humour it is suggested that (McGraw & Warner, 2014):

- It's not whether or not you're funny; it's what kind of funny you are. Be honest and authentic.
- If you can't be 'ha-ha' funny, at least be 'aha!' funny. Cleverness is sometimes good enough.
- Good comedy is a conspiracy. Create an in-group.
- Don't be afraid to chuckle at yourself. It signals everything is okay.
- Laughter is disarming. Poke fun at the stuff everyone's worried about.

A leadership consultant, Michael Kerr, suggests that humour can be important for success and claims that: 'at an organizational level, some organizations are tapping into what I'd call "the humor advantage" … Companies such as Zappos and Southwest Airlines have used humour and a positive fun culture to help brand their business, attract and retain employees and to attract customers' (*Forbes*, May 2013b). The same article refers to a survey that found that 91 per cent of executives in US companies believe a sense of humour is important for career advancement; while 84 per cent feel that people with a good sense of humour do a better job. Another study by the Bell Leadership Institute found that the two most desirable traits in leaders were a strong work ethic and a good sense of humour.

However, this needs to be approached with caution. How humour and the significance of funny guys contribute more specifically to organizational processes, outcomes or competitive advantage is hard to say. Anecdotal assurances and consultancy surveys may resonate with common sense, but the significance of humour is hard to determine.

Humour is of course by definition a plus but hardly compensates for low competence. In addition, it is not always obvious what humour is: telling good jokes, laughing at other people's jokes? People that are ironic and sarcastic may be viewed as humorous or cynical. Eagerness to be funny may be tiresome. Sometimes people trying to be funny can be quite irritating and some jokes may be perceived as offensive.

Some examples

There are many versions of the party-host-like leader. Being funny and entertaining is one; being considerate and trying to make others feel good through showing concern is another.

An IT consultancy had as a general slogan 'Fun and profit', and tried to hire and encourage managers who were exceptionally good at creating a nice atmosphere, encouraging and sponsoring parties, a company chorus and other social events. Here the collective was central. The idea was to appeal to social needs and create a sense of community. This made the workplace more attractive and compensated for the loneliness of some of the work taking place outside the company (Alvesson, 1995). The emphasis on a positive workplace climate was also used to facilitate client relations and form good relationships. This made project work in collaboration with client contacts easier and generally made the clients see the IT consultancy in more positive ways.

Another emphasis is on showing appreciation and concern for people on an individual level. A manager in a bank we interviewed said that: 'I always keep track of people's birthdays and similar things as part of my leadership because I know that it makes people feel good and increases commitment'. He continues:

> When we have had a board meeting we shall have a meeting for the employees not later than ten days after that. We've had one at which I joked a little with the janitors. I think they should be part of those meetings because they tell me they feel a little left out since they are at the bottom of the hierarchy. We brief people so that they feel included and get the possibility to be part. That makes them really happy and that's important.

A good party host ensures that everyone feels a bit special and that no one is left unrecognized or forgotten.

The assumption is that mundane activities such as remembering peoples' birthdays and including people in various events (meetings, wining and dining) make them positive and happy. This is also assumed to benefit the organization in terms of increased motivation and commitment.

The party host draws on being cheerful, encouraging, creating belonging and being present, the latter in order to see, listen to and acknowledge people. It is important to recognize people in meetings and to cheer them up when they seem unhappy. Managers also point at the significance of assuring belonging, and that no one ends up alone in the corner or even outside the party. Like a good party host, as a leader you try to control the stage, settings and atmosphere as well as entertaining the experiences of the guests (followers) in a favourable direction. Who does not appreciate a good party host?

Advantages of the party host

As said above, acting as a party-host could potentially have a positive impact on followers and contribute to a variety of productive responses, perhaps mostly associated with social identity. Party hosts who manage to raise spirits among followers may contribute to increased enthusiasm, commitment and loyalty.

Increased enthusiasm may follow from more informal and buddy-like forms of interaction that support feelings of belonging and identity, increasing positive spirits. This is perhaps especially the case in more egalitarian organizational cultures. Such close interaction may also favour commitment and loyalty among people, as is the case with friend-like relations in general. People do not want to let their friends down. An important element may be trust; people who share a healthy, positive sense of humour might be viewed as more likable and trustworthy.

Party hosts may also contribute to a lower rate of staff turnover because employees look forward to coming to work. In addition to challenging and developing work tasks, people generally tend to prefer to have fun – rather than be bored – at work. It is also often the case that people who use humour are regarded as more approachable. This may also trigger more honesty and openness among other people. Humour creates an upbeat atmosphere that encourages interaction, the brainstorming of new ideas, and a feeling that there are few risks in thinking outside the box; often viewed as positive for creativity and productivity. Some also say that humour is a potential stress reducer: 'Humour offers a cognitive shift in how you view your stressors; an emotional response; and a physical response that relaxes you when you laugh' (Michael Kerr in *Forbes* 2013b May, p. 1.)

Critique

Humour is usually something good. However, there is often an element of 'see me' and 'confirm me' associated with party hosting. Leaders can easily be eager to get confirmation and win popularity contests rather than making sure that subordinates do their job in a qualified manner. It is often difficult to do the less pleasant side of HIP work after being very nice to and participating in entertaining social activities with LIPs. Assigning less funny tasks, giving people modest wage increases, or highlighting low quality of work may be more difficult for a party host than for a manager leaning towards other modes of organizing or leadership priorities. The IT consultancy with the slogan 'Fun and profit' and a very close community feeling had great difficulties in adapting to a recession, creating crises consciousness and firing people. Here the negative side of the party hosting became very salient (Alvesson, 2000).

Also, we have all attended miserable parties. Even the most eager party host can end up with disappointed guests seeking an excuse to leave early. If one 'tries too hard' or goes over the top people tend to feel awkward, and no one would use the metaphor 'clown' to describe his/her boss in a positive way. In a call centre where top management tried to emphasize fun at work many LIPs felt as if they were in a kindergarten and thought they were treated as immature and forced to have fun (Fleming, 2005).

PEDAGOGICAL WORK: LEADERSHIP AS TEACHING

Learning at work is commonly seen as important and most HIPs say that they encourage and support individual and/or organizational learning in some way. HIPs can therefore sometimes be framed and understood as pedagogues or teachers (Heifetz et al., 2009; Senge, 1996).

Leadership is then about influencing followers' understandings on how to perform work (Sandberg & Targama, 2007). An aspect of this revolves around more task-oriented issues such as clarifying role mandates and expectations as well as explaining job responsibilities and requirements. Clarification of work tasks is traditionally seen as a form of initiating structure in terms of the specifics of clarifying and communicating job responsibilities, assigning work and setting performance goals (Yukl, 2009).

Formal job responsibilities and assignments are not always sufficient to accomplish work effectively. An important idea behind the pedagogue is to facilitate – guiding, explaining and coordinating – work activities and seeing to it that people learn and understand the meaning of the job in terms of duties, responsibilities and priorities and the result/performance expected. This is particularly the case if the job is complex and requires a lot of coordination with other job activities as well as many priorities/trade-offs that may need clarification and a lot of explaining from HIPs. The exact meaning of key elements of work in the context of various ideals and dilemmas, such as following standards/being flexible, using established knowledge/innovating, being responsible/taking risks, listening to customers/using your own expertise, often calls for leadership guidance.

In highly structured and routine contexts – such as an assembly line – where standardized processes, rules and regulations prevail, or the opposite – where subordinates are skilled/experienced professionals who know how to get the job done – the need for clarification may be less significant. In the first case, management may be more relevant as a mode of organizing and in the second case more horizontal modes of organizing are likely to be more common. Still, there are many situations between those two 'extremes' where the pedagogical element of leadership might have its place in framing, developing and providing meaning to certain work tasks.

Perhaps a more pompous but still influential view of leaders as pedagogues is to emphasize their role as definers of reality of work and organization. In framing leaders as teachers Senge (1996, p. 154) suggests that leaders' primary responsibility is to define reality in order to help people develop a 'more accurate, or insightful, and more empowering views of reality'. Senge emphasizes that this does not involve leaders teaching followers about the correct view of reality in an authoritarian – supposedly as an expert – style, but rather helping people to gain a more insightful view of current reality. Work reality – technologies, rules, regulations, a variety of sometimes inconsistent demands and expectations, a wealth of social relations to deal with, many unclear tasks to be solved – call for constant interpretations, and leader-pedagogues help in making sense of phenomena. The view of leaders as teachers is generally in line with the view of leaders as coaches, guides and facilitators. Rather than suggesting that leadership is about asymmetrically influencing people's cognition, Senge argues that the pedagogue metaphor involves surfacing people's views of things and mental models that occupy their thinking. This is supposed to trigger learning and subsequently radical change. The pedagogical element of leading means uncovering and liberating people and organizations from less productive assumptions about the world of organizations, markets and competition. This calls for leaders and leadership that clearly outperform others in terms of knowledge, wisdom and insightfulness – or can at least facilitate group processes where such qualities can be put forward and lead to collective learning.

The coach

Discussing leaders as pedagogues also includes targeting the current trend of coaching aimed at facilitating learning and development. Managers are often coached themselves, often by consultants, and then sometimes try to do coaching leadership in relation to LIPs. We briefly addressed leadership as coaching in Chapter 3. The coach centres attention on other people in order to generate learning (Peterson & Hicks, 1996). It is common to make a distinction between informal coaching – a leader style anyone can express at any time in organizations – and formal coaching, the latter referring to a formal and individualized development plan, scheme or programme. In contemporary organizations it is highly popular to talk about leadership as informal coaching (Hamlin et al., 2008). Recent developments of the knowledge society and learning organizations have all contributed to new ways of looking at leadership as facilitating learning. Rather than emphasizing leadership as providing directions – such as the prophet – coaching, like many other more mundane approaches, centres on participation and employee learning. Coaches are expected to ask questions and provide people with challenging tasks in order to help them grow. Often lists of guidelines or specific behaviours are presented in order to help the practising leader to exercise coaching influence. This typically includes a variety of points such as (Yukl, 2009):

- Helping a person analyse his/her performance by asking questions or suggesting aspects to examine
- Providing constructive feedback about effective and ineffective behaviours
- Suggesting specific things that could help improve a person's performance
- Expressing confidence a person can learn a difficult task or procedure
- Providing opportunities to practise difficult procedures before they are used at work
- Helping a person learn how to solve a problem rather than just providing the answer.

There are not many robust studies of the effectiveness of coaching and the results of many of the quantitative studies are somewhat inconclusive (Wenzel, 2000). Managers who have received coaching themselves feel that they become more self-confident (Ladegard & Gjerde, 2014). Intuitively much of this sounds as if it could increase peoples' self-awareness, self-confidence, stress resistance and acceptance of the leader, but more in-depth process-oriented studies are still rare.

An example

Hale has a background as a manager and consultant. He subsequently accepted the job as a headmaster in a newly founded private school. During the start-up year, he had six teachers working with him. He described himself as 'less of a manager and decision maker' and more of a 'coach'. He said his 'goal is that the teams make decisions themselves', and his 'own role is largely giving (his) knowledge about group processes and getting round personal obstacles', that he was 'very much personnel-oriented', and if the co-workers felt at home and 'feel that they get enough of a challenge, then it will go well'. Basically Hale suggests that his work is more about facilitating the subordinates in their work than about deciding; more about setting the work potential free than about discipline; more about empowerment than holding on to authority and responsibility; and more about constructive dialogues in complex work situations than giving expert advice. These ideas about coaching sound seductive, and the idealization of what appears as morally and cognitively superior easily leads to strong identification (Wenglen & Alvesson, 2008).

Hale was convinced he could not be a more 'authoritarian' manager:

> No, I don't want that. My work builds on commitment… My leadership builds on the belief that it's about having fun and then that [being authoritarian] doesn't work. Then it's like Sara says. 'If you tell me what to do then you might as well do it yourself.' Forget that, then I'm not needed.

> … Just because I'm a headmaster I don't solve problems for others, or decide which projects we should have. We have a dialogue around this so that everybody will have to take responsibility. That is probably not the traditional view of what a headmaster does, I think.

Hale believed that coaching was an efficient and morally superior leadership style. The teachers agreed with this in the beginning, but gradually found this one-sided and restricted. They felt that Hale was indecisive and un-able to push issues upwards in the organizations, over relying on the possibility of solving everything by coaching and making others think and develop.

In Chapter 13 we will address Stella, head of a hospital clinic, being well informed and doing pedagogical leadership through informing subordinates and framing their understandings. This gives another illustration of pedagogical leadership than the coaching version illustrated above.

Advantages of the pedagogue leader

The pedagogical element of leadership can be of great importance. Organizational practices need to be both explained and justified in the eyes of the members. For example, the implementation of a new unpopular policy or time-consuming administrative routine might need to be defended so that it is understood and accepted. Here pedagogical leadership acts can have significant impact in providing meaning and convincing framing decisions.

Furthermore, leadership acts can facilitate learning – both on an individual and an organizational/collective level – in various ways. The coaching element can in best case scenarios stimulate individuals' thinking, learning and willingness to take on new responsibilities. Leaders can also stimulate organizational learning by setting a good example and encouraging more dialogue between groups of employees that do not normally exchange ideas and experiences. Leadership may be important to support knowledge-sharing in workplaces. Another example would be to stimulate and encourage more learning outside the immediate organizational environment, for example by funding and attending external conferences and seminars and in other ways supporting network organizing. Organizing and leading 'knowledge exchange seminars' where the homecoming conference/seminar participants share their insights with the rest of the organization is also a way of 'leading as a pedagogue'. The HIP talking about books s/he has read, sending articles to people, referring to knowledge from other workplaces or occupations, including good examples, inviting speakers, highlighting people who have had new ideas, solved problems or helped others may characterize leadership as pedagogical work. It is partly being pedagogical to specific LIPs, partly about trying to form a learning culture.

In sum, learning is indeed an important aspect of organizational development, renewal and long-term ability to compete. Leadership as defined in this book can play a role here, both on the individual (e.g. coaching) and collective level (organizational learning), often in combination with other modes of organizing.

Critique

Similar to the psychotherapist view of leadership, not all HIPs have the skills and dispositions to function as pedagogues. Poor teachers are something we have all experienced, and besides the frustration they tend to create among LIPs in organizations, it is potentially also a waste of the time for the non-pedagogical HIP who could (or perhaps even should?) focus on other elements of leadership (5P) or even other modes of organizing (6M). A significant challenge for many HIPs is being short on technical/functional knowledge compared to their LIPs. In technically complicated or highly specialized work, managers simply cannot help people very much. One may always try to facilitate general learning and knowledge-sharing orientations in the workplace, but without a clear understanding and link to specific work tasks and core practices this is not easy. If the HIP is not viewed as knowledgeable, leadership often tends to become peripheral compared to group or network organizing, although HIPs may support the latter and thus indirectly play some role.

Another problem with this element of leading is that the ambitious pedagogue is in need of 'pupils', that is, less competent colleagues to train. This can drive some HIPs to view (or in a more research oriented language to 'construct') and treat their LIPs as less knowledgeable than they are in order to create and conserve an asymmetrical relationship based on the idea of a more knowledgeable party (the leader) lecturing his/her less knowledgeable pupils (the followers). This can be especially problematic in the case of a professional and/or knowledge intense organization with highly skilled members, where the pedagogue leader runs the risk of being regarded as a 'head master' who is 'lecturing' (in a bad sense) to a less amenable audience, whose disinterest tends to undermine the leader-follower relationship and thereby put leadership as mode of organizing out of play. A different type of problem is associated with the coaching style, where the leader does not know (or does not use superior knowledge) and tries to help people through asking questions. This is often hard to work with in a really productive way and may not move work forward that much – as illustrated by the perception of Hale's subordinates in the example above.

Still another disadvantage of pedagogical leadership, and in particular coaching, is that it is often very time-consuming. Influencing how people understand the world is not a quick fix. Dealing with difficult tasks may also call for the leader to spend a lot of time trying to understand the problem and the reasoning of the LIP and then engaging in careful coaching or lecturing in order to increase his/her learning and competence – rather than engaging in straightforward problem-fixing.

SUMMARY

We have in this chapter discussed five common and important elements of leadership. In metaphorical terms we have labelled them the 5Ps of leadership: leaders as prophets, pastors/preachers, psychotherapists, party hosts and pedagogues. These put emphasis on different basic variants on how HIPs try to influence meanings: the overall purpose or objective, the values and morals, the emotions and psychic well-being, the workplace atmosphere, and issues around learning and development. In line with what has been said in Chapter 1, these five varieties all share in common the fact that they take place in an asymmetrical relationship involving followers. (The relationship may be formal or informal, permanent or temporal, but not merely momentary.) Leaders are trying to define meaning/reality for others (low influential persons) who are inclined to (on a largely voluntary basis) accept such meaning-making and reality-defining acts of influence.

However, the five varieties emphasize different aspects of leadership, as illustrated and summarized earlier in Table 8.1. It is important to note that no HIP/leader *is* a prophet, pedagogue, etc. not even in metaphorical terms. Most HIPs probably do most or all five types of work to varying degrees and at various times. Even a person who likes to work with visions must mainly concentrate on other things. Managers do a lot of different things, most of them not leadership. Even within leadership work there are always variations. In this book we emphasize roles, task domains and activities – not fixed leadership types.

Leadership can be described in an endless number of different ways. We delimit leadership as being about influencing meaning, that is, ideas, beliefs, interpretations, understandings, emotions and thinking. Within this conceptualization, an overall differentiation is to divide up leadership work areas/acts in these five ways, covering the different and important elements/varieties within our overall understanding of leadership. Our intention with these 5Ps of leadership is to encourage reflexivity *within* leadership discourse (ILR).

9
Constraints on Leadership in Managerial Work

We warned earlier against unrealistic expectations of leadership, neglecting the complexities of organizational reality. Being the right person who aims to do the right thing (leadership!) may not always lead to the result or impact wished for. This is partly associated with popular ideas of leadership being too general, broad and positive. They are also too individualistic and micro oriented – as if the sole leader and, at best, the group is the entire leadership universe. This is simply too naive. There are many constraints on leadership. External pressure may force organizations to act in particular ways that makes leadership irrelevant or marginal. Internal conditions such as hierarchy and bureaucracy, superiors keeping subordinate managers on tight leashes or subordinates unwilling to comply with ideas may undermine middle managers' leadership. In addition, many leadership ideals can be difficult to sort out and understand in ways that make them meaningful to act upon. In 'real' organizations, with all the constraints and forces at play, specific leadership personalities, ideals, frameworks or recipes cannot always simply be implemented. It is rarely the case, for example, that a HIP can choose freely between transformational and transactional leadership (management). Often organizations require performance management, certain remuneration policies, career planning, and other transaction-supporting elements. LIPs may also have clear expectations and demands on work conditions and rewards. The space for the transformation-oriented manager may be limited. Doing much of all the 5Ps we addressed in the previous chapter would easily fill the entire work week – only if the HIP skipped many meetings with senior managers, colleagues, customers and much of the administrative and operative work that normally takes most of their time at work would it be possible to do a full-scale 5P approach.

This is not to say that there is no space for discretion. Organizational contexts may be more or less open to leadership and its varieties (as described in the previous chapter). HIPs may be more or less resourceful and ambitious. Sometimes there are compromises between specific leadership orientations and efforts and all the forces pushing HIPs in a specific direction. But it is important to highlight not only the leadership theories and links between personalities and choices of styles and leadership practices and outcomes, but also material and other conditions that may lead to managerial work being less characterized by leadership.

In this chapter we discuss some typical constraints on leadership, including how managerial work can limit leadership. We begin with a discussion of external factors in terms of economic realities, technological forces, legal constraints, social standards and norms, customer requirements, and discursive/ideological pressures. This is followed by a discussion of the nature of relations between managers and superiors and subordinates. Lastly, we focus on how the nature of managerial work and the inevitable shortcomings and imperfections of the majority of all managers – there are no super(wo)men – more explicitly condition the possibility of exercising leadership.

EXTERNAL PRESSURES

Organizations are targeted by a variety of different wider forces making claims and demands on their operations and development. These forces may range from broader economic, legal and social constraints such as complying with business cycles, laws or ethical standards, to concrete customer requirements that organizations often need to acknowledge and recognize. Often external forces such as market pressures and internal conditions such as organizational politics are much more significant than any specific leadership (Mukunda, 2012; Pfeffer & Salancik, 1978). We discuss economic, technological, legal, social and discursive forces.

Economic forces may affect the leadership in many ways. One may imagine how an economic recession gives rise to threats of layoffs, hostile takeovers or reduction of some functions or company sites. Although these are situations that create worries and uncertainties in organizations and may call for leadership they also tend to reduce the time for leadership.

The quest for efficiency in most contemporary organizations has probably increased since the early 1990s. Increasing demands for efficiency typically follow on the basis of privatization, competitiveness, globalization, economic uncertainty and general turbulence. Following these pressures a variety of management control systems – balanced scorecards, just-in-time systems, accountability systems, process organizations, change management – have emerged to enable organizations to become more transparent and measurable. This has partly been done through consolidation, downsizing, and outsourcing but also through increased focus on traditional management. The latter has given rise to greater regulation and control of activities, tighter documentation and follow-up demands of organizational processes and outcomes, more frequent and detailed reporting of results and other statistics about production levels, disruptions, sick leave, quality problems and missed deadlines, for example. Increased coordination in terms of management – such as tighter control and regulation – takes an increasing amount of time and attention in managerial work and often conflicts with the ambition or requirement to do leadership. Leadership efforts are usually quite time-consuming and may require a lot of effort involving personal interaction, discussions and communication. This is something it may be increasingly difficult to allocate time for.

Technological forces in terms of increased pressure to use digitalized information and communication systems also frame the conditions for the leadership process significantly. For example, the reliance on these systems has in many ways reduced face-to-face interaction and created a peculiar situation where managers are expected to lead by systems – hence the creation of 'distant leadership' and 'leading by Skype' – rather than relying on social interaction. The common reliance on modern communications systems in many organizations has also facilitated the geographical dispersion of organizational premises and distribution of personnel and other resources. Organizational functions such as purchasing, production, marketing, and R&D are frequently dispersed among different countries in many global organizations. Obviously this creates dilemmas for those taking leadership seriously as a social process. Even though emails and social media do not preclude leadership, issues around the influence of meaning and feelings become much more complicated and typically much weaker in the absence of regular face-to-face contact. One might even say that leadership is, at best, marginal if HIPs and LIPs only meet a couple of times a year (acknowledging that less exposure to LIPs might actually help preserve the aura and mystique of some HIPs).

Also *material* forces, not only IT, such as physical operations, equipment and working processes are often central and to a lesser or greater degree heavily influence leadership (Hawkins, 2015).

Legal forces affect managerial work because of a variety of laws related to safety, health, environmental policies, governance issues, contracts, labour relations and unions, tax, and regulations on leave and working hours, etc. Organizational policies and regulations constrain leadership. These may for example include laws on priority rules in situations of layoffs or on having pre-structured, standardized appraisal talks, etc.

Leadership is also constrained by *social standards* dealing with work environment, safety, health issues and broader social norms, the latter occasionally formulated as ethical standards or codes of conduct. Ethics, value grounds and codes of conducts – CSR, social accounting, global reporting initiatives etc. – typically involve values such as trust, good behaviour, fairness, environmentalism, respect and equality in terms of gender, sexuality and religion, etc. These policies are often similar across organizations within the same industry and/or sector as a result of social trends that gain broader attention in popular management texts, mass media, and governmental agencies and among opinion groups.

These social and legal trends often increase the administrative burden on managers and may conflict with time allocated to leadership. It is popular to emphasize the dynamic, non-bureaucratic nature of contemporary organizations, which are full of networks, teams, visions, projects, innovation and leadership – reducing rules, regulations and hierarchies to the margin. This is misleading – most organizations over a specific size are in key respects still based on a hierarchical and vertical division of labour, standards, work procedures, formal rules and regulations (Alvesson & Thompson, 2005; McSweeney, 2006). Also, innovative companies, such as are found in the pharmaceutical industry, are heavily reliant on these modes of organization (Kärreman et al., 2002). Organizations can increasingly be characterized as glass cages, where employees are monitored by various IT systems as well as by colleagues and customers (Gabriel, 2005).

Legal forces and social standards in some areas might lead to organizational work being regulated in detail and HIPs carefully following and monitoring compliance, leaving little room for initiative and creativity and thus for leadership:

> We have an elderly care that is so characterized by the fear of doing wrong, which we know is devastating for any sector that wants to develop. I have been a councillor in Westby [pseudonym] for six years with special responsibility for elderly care and LSS and can strongly certify that what you describe is true. There are valiant efforts taking place to highlight 'good examples' and in other ways focus on the positive, but the shape of the formal demands with associated regulatory [systems] makes 'error searching' and fear dominant.
>
> This spring [I have worked with] a new living concept for elders, where they are offered attractive residences where we intend to be able to meet the changing needs of community, service and care which can occur during the second part of life. What we focus on the most now is trying to find wise ways of meeting all the surprisingly detailed demands that are set – and we realize it makes it difficult/impossible to find new ways of accomplishing elderly care. (Vice President, elderly care company)

One may still say that leadership is important to make organizations comply with legal requirements, and of course there are still many issues not covered by these. But the acts of HIPs become less an outcome of personality or leadership style proposed by a textbook or management development programme than the outcome of a massive set of demands. In a sense it is rather the latter that exercises 'HIP work' and the HIP doing leadership is a minor element in all this.

The market and ideas of *customer orientation* are other forces that increasingly constrain the leadership process. Commonly, customer orientation restricts the scope of action in organizations and may conflict with the possibility of exercising leadership. LIPs are expected to follow the demands of their customers rather then their HIPs, in some cases this is framed as client control. In some consultancy work, it is mainly the client that stands for the management of projects and consultants, and we can say that management/leadership is outsourced (Alvesson, 2004). The manager of the consultancy firm may mainly do housekeeping work. Still there may be leadership, in particular project management, but this is complicated, partly because the client manager is often not interested in the long-term development of the consultant's thinking and competence. The pressure to deliver in time may not facilitate leadership processes involving pedagogical discussions and interaction of the meaning of time schedules and delivery dates. A similar issue is the case when there is an internal division between departmental managers and project leaders, where the latter may be focused on efficient delivery, and characterized by time pressure (Holmberg & Tyrstrup, 2010).

Ideological forces are represented by the many management and leadership ideals that are constantly developed and made fashionable by academics, consultants, leadership educators, the business press and popular management publications. Popular leader ideals during the last two decades include many different directions, such as visionary leadership, leadership emphasizing leaders of a heroic character that take charge and provide clear direction, leaders that listen to and accommodate subordinates' voices and opinions – being more post-heroic and coaching – leaders that are engaged in daily work and exhibit knowledge about the substance of work, leaders that are authentic. In one sense the bombardment of managers with messages pushing them to identify themselves as 'leaders' is encouraging and helpful. But it also pushes managers to fit into a specific formula, in accordance with what is fashionable at the time. This may mystify and restrict the possibility of doing leadership as a more reflective practice. Leadership ideals represent pure notions of how to think and act, and much of it can be difficult to apply in real-life organizations as well as combining these with alternative and competing ideals.

In general, external pressure gives rise to material and symbolic constraints such as organizational routines, policies, rules and regulations that contribute to increased standardization of organizational practices and subsequently in many cases administrative demands. As some of this administration replaces leadership, it also reinforces the administrative burden of managerial work and may restrict leadership, which often demands resources such as time and energy.

We will come back to whether all this necessarily means the exclusion or reduction of leadership. For the moment we will only say that HIPs aiming to do leadership need to consider and deal with these forces or constraints.

SUPERIORS AND SUBORDINATES

According to many popular management and leadership writings, it would seem that the managerial world only consists of admirals and generals rather than the lieutenants and sergeants who are supposed to more or less execute what others have decided within quite tight frameworks (Laurent, 1978). Although people typically associate management with privileges such as power, influence and social status and the exercise of leadership, almost all managers are under the influence of some *superior* whose wish, command and interests they mostly have to accommodate. Having loyalty upwards and being seen as reliable by superiors are important for managers (Jackall, 1988). Rather than being generals on their own with the ability to act without regard to superiors (or subordinates) most managers should perhaps be seen as sergeants who need to recognize others' thoughts and opinions. Very few people in medium and large organizations are sovereigns in their own kingdoms. Also, CEOs and owners of small firms may be very dependent on customers and suppliers and have to dance to their tune rather than doing very much independent leadership.

A board of directors or owners that decide important matters such as investments over a certain level, more significant recruitment matters, important projects and growth strategies can hold senior corporate managers on a tight leash. The pressure to conform to capital markets and the presumed wishes of shareholders also seem to be increasing. Rather than routinely viewing senior executives as strategic leaders, it may often be more realistic to view company management as followers – securing the overall objectives with alternative modes of coordination – of a direction decided by their superiors.

As suggested in the discussion of different forces above, managers live in an increasingly regulated world of plans, policies and regulations that need to be implemented smoothly in order to keep the organizational machinery running. Implementation means enforcing plans and strategies in a prescribed and increasingly standardized manner together with reviewing and reporting frequent follow-ups to superior managerial or executive levels. Considering the increasingly frequent implementation of management control systems, this work entails additional management and occasionally some power as coordinating mechanisms.

This indicates that much of the present-day talk about doing leadership – especially perhaps more aggrandized versions including strategy and vision – among managers may reflect wishful thinking or fantasies rather than actual managerial practice.

When it comes to *subordinates*, it is important to recognize that although under certain circumstances a formal managerial position may facilitate the exercise of leadership it would be naive to assume that having subordinates automatically implies having followers.

Subordinates are not always easily influenced by leadership efforts. Some subordinates may strive for strong independence or counter-dependence and even rebel in order to avoid or fight managers' leadership tendencies. Professionals and knowledge-workers who mainly rely on their professional knowledge often prefer to work mostly autonomously or using networks (Hallett, 2007, 2010). Some may even consider that managerial leadership efforts interrupt work and see them mostly as disturbing professional autonomy. Sometimes people are not happy about too many meetings spent listening to senior managers. People working with highly regulated, standardized and routinized processes might see limited value in managerial leadership efforts given that their key source for direction and support can be found in the standards and guidelines for how work should be conducted.

We can also note signs of increased cynicism in the workforce in many Western countries (Naus et al., 2007), making workers less inclined to engage in idyllic leadership/follower relationships, where they for example are 'transformed' by transformational (authentic, servant) leadership into being more committed to the leader and the organization than to their own work benefits in terms of pay, tasks, career and other instrumental factors. Bryman and Lilley (2009) found that lack of trust or integrity stood out in terms of frequency of the number of mentions in a study of leadership in higher education. People may comply but this undermines the prospect of voluntarily following leadership initiatives.

Besides subordinates unwilling to comply with or being sceptical of managerial leadership because of task characteristics, politics or other reasons, they are also targeted by a swarm of other actors trying to influence them in different directions. Trying to embody the dictum that the customer is always right – perhaps formulated by managers trying to be leaders – subordinates may feel obliged to live up to customers' wishes that conflict with organizational and/or professional practices, such as safety concerns or quality inspections. Others – colleagues, peers, suppliers and union representatives – try to influence subordinates in order to promote their interests and wishes. Subordinates are also targeted by administrative rules and regulations as well as by material and technical conditions that may constrain the leadership activities of superiors. Sometimes subordinates draw on these conditions in order to avoid or obstruct leadership efforts or other forms of managerial intervention, for example through working pedantically and following rules, something that naturally creates a lot of interruptions and delays in production.

Of course, all this does not mean that leadership is impossible or just a marginal phenomenon. If senior people or external forces have clear demands, leadership within limits may still make a difference. Even subordinates who are disinclined to want or be easily seduced by leadership may be persuaded to modify their orientations and become more leadership-responsive. Our key point is that organizational reality often offers a high degree of complexity that sometimes makes the life of the ambitious and hopeful HIP wanting to do a lot of leadership confusing and disappointing when the idyllic picture provided by the leadership industry is at odds with the messy and imperfect organizational reality. The latter does not always offer a fertile ground for leadership, at least not for the rather clean versions that the leadership industry offers (visions, coaching, authenticity). In cases where people actually yearn for more and/or different leadership from their superiors, they might be unaware of the many constraints that make this hard to live up to. Being aware of all this may make it easier for managers to develop more realistic ideas about leadership and then make it function better.

THE MANAGERS THEMSELVES: CAPABLE OF DOING LEADERSHIP OR NOT?

The external pressure, variety of actors and organizational conditions that occasionally conflict with, restrict and undermine managerial leadership make it more difficult to accomplish than is often assumed in the leadership literature. But what about the manager (or other resourceful person/HIP in the organization) him- or herself? Has not the person with leadership skills the ability to do leadership as intended and counter all the external constraints? Is not true leadership a matter of the leader putting his or her mark on the environment rather than the other way around? For some people, with extraordinary resources and fortunate circumstances, this is the case. Most of the time, however, the environment probably makes a stronger imprint on the HIP, even those in very senior positions (like the CEO, chairperson or director of a museum or other institution), making him/her likely to follow institutionalized conditions and external pressures. For most HIPs there may be obstacles in the work situation and in many cases also limitations in terms of ability. Far from everyone in senior positions has the time and resources to make subordinates look up to them as inspiring leaders.

Time pressure and limited time for reflection and leadership

The pressures discussed in the initial section suggest that the demands and expectations on managerial work are becoming increasingly administratively formalized – although still fragmented and complex – and of a very time-consuming character. This leaves relatively little room for leadership, which often demands time for influencing people. Communicating a quick slogan ('the customer is king', 'be creative') may not accomplish much.

Mobilizing time dedicated to thinking about and exercising leadership may be tricky considering that managerial work is varied and fragmented. Managers typically engage in a multitude of different activities each day, promoting an 'action mind set' – possibly a mindless set – where quick, instrumental, pragmatic and routine-following behaviour counteracts reflection. Managerial work – including when trying to do leadership – is frequently interrupted by all kinds of requests and discussions, ranging from the type of coffee to purchase for the canteen to long-term budgeting issues involving millions of euros (Yukl, 2009). The constant blend of trivial and more important questions demands frequent shifts in intellectual ability. In Mintzberg's (1973, p. 33) study 'half of the activities were completed in less than 9 minutes'.

Managerial work is also typically reactive. The fragmented nature of disconnected interactions and the frequent variety of requests reflect that many interactions are initiated by others, making the work more reactive than proactive. Managers often need to react to immediate and pressing requests, such as sanctioning a certain course of action or decision, keeping to deadlines for customers or superiors, or trying to control crisis situations such as a conflict among subordinates (Yukl, 2009). Also, considering the digitalization of the workplace managers receive continuous requests for information and assistance from superiors, subordinates, peers and people outside the organization such as customers and media. In general, managerial work involves a substantial amount of interaction with colleagues and people outside the organization, not least the customers, as indicated above. But there are also suppliers, people in the financial markets, industry, government and community people that are important to exchange information with and keep happy (Kotter, 1982). Naturally, networking also involves a lot of gatherings such as ceremonies, social events, trade shows and professional associations, partly in order to try to manage the right impressions – of oneself as well as the organization one represents – and catch up with the latest gossip (Yukl, 2009).

Obviously a key dilemma in much managerial work is time. Short-term and close at hand issues often dominate the working day and are difficult to ignore. It is common to talk of 'time famine', where people feel that there are never enough hours in the workday. Time – or the lack of it – is crucial for the exercise of leadership, the latter involving communication and interaction that people experience as meaningful in terms of how tasks should be accomplished or how they view themselves. As suggested by a recent article in a management journal: 'Administration has taken over the leadership'. The article states that: '... many [managers] put more time than ever on administration.

This at the expense of ... time for reflection and the daily leadership' (*Chef*, 2015). Another study indicated that most managers feel they have little or no time for doing leadership (Kairos Futures, 2006).

Of course sometimes very efficient managers use limited time very well. And sometimes unnecessary administration can be minimized and time for leadership created. But basic issues like having offices, IT, wage administration, schedule settings can seldom be substituted by the slogans of top management and the leadership industry about the need for leaders, not managers, leadership, not management. This sounds really good and the person who likes to hear populist slogans will immediately nod in agreement, but such statements often simply reflect thoughtlessness, ignorance or hypocrisy.

The political nature of managerial relations

Managerial work is also often political in terms of conflicting interests, priorities, demands and pressures. This partly results from people having varied assumptions, frames of references, values, backgrounds and identities. Rather than being a rational and systematic process, decision-making is often characterized by conflicting interests and priorities and in many cases managers must comply with superiors' interests.

As suggested above, managers typically interact with superiors, subordinates, peers and others when making decisions, especially if required actions are not immediate. It is also the case that people disagree about the nature of problems and what solution to choose. Political processes – especially the case in more important decisions – can be lengthy and prolonged and quite exhaustive, requiring a lot of mobilization of resources, networks and alliances (Yukl, 2009).

The nature of the relationship with superiors typically affects the possibilities for managers to exercise leadership. Less demanding or distant superiors with less opportunity to or interest in monitoring managers typically provide more autonomy than active and present superiors who employ explicitly vertical modes of organizing – management and power – in order to control managers.

A manager in a bank with quite an autonomous position with regards to his superiors, located at a regional office far away from the headquarters, had built a solid reputation among subordinates for being an accommodating, reliable and trustworthy leader. The large scope for manoeuvre contributed to this position and subordinates spoke of him as a leader who respected subordinates and someone you could count on; he was their leader. Appropriating this favourable image and attributing it to his personality the manager was subsequently appointed CEO, that is, a hierarchically superior position, in a smaller firm where he expected to leverage this perceived personality and create a similar leader position. However, the superiors in the new organization kept the manager on a very tight leash, expecting him to implement their commands and leaving little room for managerial autonomy or independence in relation to subordinates. Here was a clear use of both management and power, sometimes also sidestepping the manager in the chain of command. In conflicts of interests between superior management and subordinates the manager frequently sided with the superiors or remained neutral. Rather than emerging as a reliable and trustworthy leader, the manager was seen as a yes-man, someone who was in the hands of superiors and unreliable in relation to subordinates. Many of the attempts to do leadership, including appearing 'authentic', were thus not seen as credible (Sveningsson & Alvesson, 2016).

The case above suggests that the opportunity to mobilize followers depends on the nature of relations with superiors. As discussed previously, it is common that senior managers – in turn pressured by various external demands on performance, accountability, etc. – pull rank or draw on power in relation to subordinate managers. This may constrain the leadership potential for managers in general. This is something that contrasts with the contemporary ideal of developing every manager into a leader, an ideal that is perhaps just a way of trying to compensate for the fact that most managers are expected to implement what others have decided.

Limited intellectual and emotional abilities

The general limits of classic rationality also put the cognitive and emotional abilities of the manager in focus. Rather than assuming that managers are some kind of super(wo)men, it can be seen that they manoeuvre based on their own limited abilities and preferences. A manager may have good practice-knowledge and problem-solving ability but lack an overall view and understanding of long-term requirements. Another manager may be a good people person but fail to understand technical operations very well. As said before, contemporary discourses on leadership involve many different and often contrasting ideals that call for different abilities and skills which may be difficult to combine and which perhaps do not always provide a good guide for how to think and act when it comes to leadership in real organizational practice.

If we take the ideas of transformational leadership, it is in the first instance not so clear what this actually means, but it is even more problematic for many managers to be able to live up to the requirements. Individual consideration is perhaps not so difficult, time permitting, but idealized influence, charisma and intellectual stimulation are not easy to accomplish. Few people are (seen as) charismatic or can simply improve the way they are. Intellectual stimulation calls for scoring significantly higher than people around you in terms of knowledge, intelligence and pedagogical qualities. Not all managers outscore all their subordinates. The leadership literature often seems to assume that leaders are giants surrounded by dwarfs, but often managers are not that different from their immediate subordinates in terms of qualities.

Our general impression, based on many years of close studies, is that the majority of managers cannot do the leadership they claim they do particularly well.[1] They often know leadership talk, but practical applications are at best uneven. Let us give an example of how managers may have difficulties mastering leadership ideas and situations. A manager in a high-tech organization embarking upon an organizational cultural change programme was expected to implement it with his working group of engineers.

The manager in question was widely renowned for his good technical problem-solving ability. He had also attended a lengthy leader development programme and claimed he was good at working with general strategic issues as well as with the team. Despite this the culture change workshop went quite badly. Rather than providing guidelines for the future and clarity of vision and mission, the workshop ended in confusion as to the relevance and meaning of most of the new values and ideas that the group was supposed to clarify and work with, including the idea of a cultural change as such (Alvesson & Sveningsson, 2015).

This situation is typical. Managers participate in leader development programmes and acquire popular concepts and ideas according to a variety of leadership ideals. But the ideals and concepts presented are often abstract and cleansed of real-life complexities and complications and difficult to translate into concrete work situations. In the case above even the manager had difficulties in understanding the concepts as such, as well as their relevance to the situation at hand.

IDEALS AND MANAGERIAL WORK

The wide circulation of management and leadership ideals may provide inspiration and widen managers' intellectual repertoires. However, they are abstract and difficult to work with in practice. Leadership ideals often produce wishful thinking and unrealistic ideas about the nature of managerial work, such as typically working with broad strategies and visions or being authentic. Seductive and popular as they are, they also create intellectual traps that lead managers to follow the map rather than reality, with the consequence that real problems and alternative modes of organizing are overlooked or framed too narrowly, so that they fit the leadership idea in vogue. In this way many leadership ideals actually counteract more realistic and nuanced views of HIP work or alternative modes of organizing.

Leadership ideals may sound intuitively good and self-evident, not least because they are often contrasted against something that sounds morally bad. For example, as suggested in Chapter 3, a highly popular ideal in contemporary leadership is to be an authentic leader. Authenticity is typically understood as morally good and often contrasted to being immoral, fake and corrupt. Authenticity is typically seen as enabling subordinates to be recognized and acknowledged: 'Authentic leaders are experts at identifying the unique skill sets that lie within every person – because they place an emphasis on individuality, one's unique strengths, and they allow employees to have a voice that matters and is heard' (Llopis, 2014). Who then does not want to – or claim to – be an 'authentic leader'. Those eager to present or view themselves as inauthentic managers, please raise their hands. In reality, the latter may often be easier, but less appealing for one's self-image.

Talk of authenticity in managerial work may, however, easily backfire as the meaning of being authentic may vary between people and contexts. For example, being genuine and straight with people – such as taking charge and doing most of the talking – may be experienced as hurting and insulting, that is, in contradicting the ideal of recognizing subordinates by letting them do the talking. Also, if authenticity comes with disregard of social and cultural conventions it may be quite offensive. Or as suggested by Gruenfeld and Zander (2011, p. 1): 'In practice, we've observed that placing value on being authentic has become an excuse for bad behaviour among executives ... For people, what comes naturally can also get pretty nasty'.

Managers in a construction company said they exercised authentic leadership in terms of being driven, determinate and talkative and suggested they provided guidance and direction for subordinates. This view resonated well with leader-centrism, where the role of the leader is to be in control and express superior insights – being truly superior in relation to subordinates. One manager said that: 'I want to be active in meetings. A person who really wants to talk, it is stupid if that one is quiet, because you are expected to act in line with who you are by nature ...'.

Although acting in a way he believed to be authentic he received strong criticism from his subordinates who viewed him as bossy: '... the criticisms I got is that I'm too direct, I forcefully instruct'. Also other managers stated that subordinates looked upon their leadership as 'destroying others', 'awful' or 'forceful' referring to how the determinate and talkative style silenced subordinates. Authentic leadership in these cases contradicted the subordinates' wish to be acknowledged and recognized. The natural behaviour appeared bossy, dogmatic and perhaps seen more as a power mode of organizing, according to subordinates. Acknowledging this situation, the managers in question expressed problems with deciding which leg to stand upon: should they be authentic and express their natural orientations or should they be 'good' and meet the expectations of the LIPs (Sveningsson & Alvesson, 2016)? The ideal of authentic leadership is not a simple recipe for success. More on how to approach this dilemma will follow in Chapter 11.

The case suggests that authenticity as reinforcing leadership-centrism and classic heroism as understood by the managers above, may conflict with post-heroic leader ideals – shared and relational – such as recognizing subordinates' views and allowing them considerable space.

As the meanings of different leadership ideals are stretched in different directions – in practice and conceptually – they come to refer to many different and contradictory elements. Many ideals are also unrealistic and distract managers from approaching real organizational problems. A key element in transformational leadership suggests that managers should practice individualized consideration of subordinates by listening and acknowledging their wishes and opinions. This sounds good and self-evident – being progressive and humanistic – but may turn out to trap managers in wishful thinking and prevent them from approaching real problems such as low working morale, complaints over workload or subordinates blaming others for all kind of problems, faults or insufficiencies. Talking about his considerate style of leadership, one manager we studied said that:

It is challenging with colleagues that are negative and always see problems and feel sorry for themselves. People that experience that all evil always strikes them. The problem is that I fall in the trap of trying to help them instead of being damned straight with them and say that 'this is what should be done'. It is a trap that makes you feel damned bad. You try to do something good but ends up fooled.

Here is a manager who tries to influence subordinates to see work favourably through coaching leadership but frequently ends up feeling ignored and ultimately fooled by subordinates. Although the manager sees the leadership ideal as a constraint to approaching the real problem, he frequently falls back on the same style. The self-evident and good leadership ideal ends up being a trap preventing the manager from taking alternative modes of organizing, including using power (confrontation), seriously. Maybe this tells us something about the strength of certain leadership ideas and the conviction with which people subject to them. But considering the increased pressure to deliver – documents, accounts, results, products, services – in contemporary organizations, it is probably difficult to maintain a consistent supporting leadership in terms of acknowledging subordinates to the extent that everyone feels recognized and cared for. But even if people cannot be consistent, they may still have problems in acting thoughtfully in flexible and varied ways.

Abstract concepts and ideals are difficult to combine in practical managerial work and may be seen as constraints to substantive managerial practice as they often obstruct reflection of how to approach substantial problems in terms of alternative modes of organizing. Abstract ideals and good principles – formulated in fashionable terms – are inherently difficult to work with in concrete and tricky organizational situations. The prevalence of nice-sounding but vague values and ideals also results in decoupling and fragmentation between thinking, preferences and action. Many leadership ideals could probably be seen as the problem rather than the solution in many contemporary organizations, as managers are caught in confusions and contradictions.

Most leadership thinking proceeds from abstract ideals and is based on the notion of managers having a set of traits, a style, adopting a leadership framework, and/or forming a happy union with followers, creating a shared leadership practice. Here the idea is that the leadership can be seen as a special thing, forming the workplace and the followers and their actions. But often leadership efforts – and their absence – are more strongly formed by the situation.

Here is a CEO of a private school company expressing some experiences from the organizational reality that are not necessarily so salient in leadership studies.

I am a courageous bastard so I have told them to go the whole hog to a maximum, I will take the beating. But my six principals and the teachers constantly object and say that the Education Act says so and the curriculum says so. If we make any wrongdoing the School Inspection will beat us. Not a single new idea pops up. I have to create all the solutions and persuade them to work smarter (it's not going very well). They say yes, but often continue in the same old tracks. I won't bore you with more details, but I can assure you I could have continued for at least a whole page … We have as you said created a monster (the public sector but also detail-driven organizations like independent schools) with only one means to solve the problems – 'We need more resources', never ever 'smarter solutions, lateral thinking and courage'.

At least as the CEO sees the situation, there are heavy external public sector regulation forces that matter much more than leadership interventions for organizational practices and outcomes. Of course, much 'leadership' is oriented to making people understand and follow rules and regulations – many of these are well intended and provide some assurance for quality and patients' and students' rights. So, detailed regulation does not entirely marginalize leadership, but this appears more like an adjunct to structural and legal forces having much stronger imprints on people's thinking and behaviour.

This is not to suggest the impossibility of leadership. Our point is that one needs to carefully pay attention to context, think about different obstacles and realize that attractive leadership recipes often do not function particularly well. It may even be the case that the more appealing a recipe is, the more difficult it is to make it work. Leadership calls for actors with resources and drive, but also reasonably favourable conditions. Often some of the preconditions for effective leadership are not there, and then it is counterproductive to insist on working based on leadership recipes one feels attached to.

SUMMARY

The huge popularity of leadership in contemporary society puts a lot of pressure on people in organizations to talk about how they exercise leadership and generally to think that leadership is important and necessary to tackle key organizational problems. Given all the leadership talk and leadership development one may assume that contemporary organizations and managerial work are full of leadership in one sense or another.

However, leadership development milieus and other contributions by the leadership industry constitute artificial settings rich in ideological overtones. Programmes, texts and general talk about the virtues and powers of leadership are mostly cleansed of real-life complexities and ambiguities. Indeed, leadership programmes often aim at presenting leadership as a necessary solution to a wide variety of different organizational problems, while marginalizing or avoiding reflections upon alternative options. Real-life organizations present a contrasting environment – filled with external pressures and demands, contradictions, complexities, uncertainties, and with people sometimes less inclined to conform to any specific leadership effort.

Many of the external forces make managers increasingly entangled in administrative work that they feel occupies them, leaving less room for leadership. A manager in a pharmaceutical company felt unable to exercise leadership because of the administrative burdens, and in order to characterize her impossible situation she said that: 'Soon they probably want me to document the quantity of hair of the employees'. This sounds ridiculous but studies suggest that much of the increased administrative burden seems less justified and not really thought through: '... seven out of ten managers say that each day or week they put time into administration that someone else should do. Half of them suggest that the administration done shouldn't be done at all' (*Chef*, 2015). A vice-chancellor of a major European university was asked about 'leadership' in her work and responded that 'there is nothing to lead'. Laws and regulations, union agreements and a very autonomous senior faculty meant that it was very difficult to find clear targets for influence.

These may be unusual cases, but it is likely that the HIP with full freedom and agency, deciding upon leadership and forming social relations, practices and outcomes at work mainly based on leadership, may be even more unusual. But again, this does not mean that leadership is entirely marginal or irrelevant. Often it does play a role, to a greater extent at some times than others. With careful thinking and reflexivity it may be even more significant.

NOTE

1. See Alvesson and Sveningsson (2003a) and Sveningsson and Alvesson (2016). Support for our impressions are provided by, e.g. Bryman and Lilley (2009) and Cunha et al. (2009).

10

Alignment or Misfit in Leadership Constructions?

When trying to make sense of leadership and followership there are often taken-for-granted assumptions about the existence of leaders (leadership), who the leader is, what form of leadership he/she is (or should be) doing and its effects. In the literature, in management education and organizational practice it is often assumed that there is an agreement on the type of leadership carried out, for example, that this is task orientation, this is coaching, this is delegation, etc. In other words that all involved agree what takes place and how to label this. However, this *alignment of meaning* – shared understanding of what goes on – cannot be taken for granted. Often people in a relationship view things differently. Leadership is no exception. The manager may see herself as a leader, the subordinates may think of her as an administrator.

The purpose of this chapter is therefore to facilitate a more qualified understanding of the significance of the alignment and misfits of meanings of HIPs and LIPs in constructions of leadership. Misfits may be about disagreements and conflicts, but also ambiguities and confusions. Forms and sources of misfit are discussed and a case is made for well-functioning leadership that involves creating shared meanings and alternatively clarifying divergence in meanings, in terms of key areas of the leadership relation. Here, the views of the LIPs are often crucial and HIPs doing leadership may be more or less in tune with these.

ACKNOWLEDGING DIVERGENT MEANINGS

As touched upon in several of the chapters, most traditional understandings of leadership include leaders doing something and followers responding to that, thereby shaping some form of influencing process. According to, for example, Antonakis et al. (2004):

> Most leadership scholars would agree, in principle, that leadership can be defined as the nature of the influencing process – and its resultant outcomes – that occurs between a leader and followers and how this influencing process is explained by the leaders' dispositional characteristics and behaviours, follower perceptions and attributions of the leader, and the context in which the influencing process occurs. (p. 5)

This would imply a strong interest in both what the leader brings in and does *and* how followers perceive and attribute meaning to (reason about) these inputs and acts. But these two elements are often conflated in leadership texts and seldom the targets of careful scrutiny. When the concept of leadership includes both the influencing process and the resultant outcome (as in the definition just cited) there is a common, cardinal error. The act and the outcome should not be seen as by definition the same. An effort to influence does not necessarily lead to the targeted outcome. So when leadership is in focus, the intention, the act and the outcome are often coupled and placed in the same box. As Sandelands and Drazin (1989) pointed out, this kind of reasoning is common in organization studies. Combining intention, act and outcome in leadership encourages a tendency to produce built-in results and insensitivity to process and relational issues. The elements in Antonakis et al.'s (2004) definition above – the leader's dispositional characteristics and behaviours, follower perceptions and attributions of the leader, and the context – should be considered separately, if taken seriously, and relations investigated. The leader's behaviours may not be a direct offspring of dispositional characteristics; followers' perceptions of behaviour may deviate from the leader's intention and meaning of behaviour, and attribution processes may go beyond and differ from perceptions of specific behaviours, but may reflect 'background constructions' full of discourses and ideologies – as emphasized by attribution theory (Meindl, 1995). Even where HIPs and LIPs both think they have fairly good relations this does not necessarily mean that they understand their social realities – including leadership – in similar ways. People may think they agree, but this does not exclude the possibility of diverse meanings perhaps creating problems that are not understood and not attributed to variation of meaning. The slipperiness and multiple, context-dependent meanings of language mean that shared and stable understandings are difficult to establish.[1] Of course, completely different worldviews are perhaps uncommon and would undermine positive relations, but there is still the possibility of considerable variations in meanings, sometimes leading to ambiguities and misunderstandings rather than direct clash or conflict.

Key dimensions in alignment-misfit

One central dimension concerns the *degree of alignment* (convergence of meaning) between HIPs' and LIPs' views of the leadership, that is, what it is and should be about. Alignment refers to the existence of shared meanings, that is, similar views of the issues of relevance for and ways of relating to the leadership relation. This dimension may involve high alignment (coherence between people) or misfit (diverse, conflicting or confused meanings) or something in between, for example ambiguity and vague (dis-)agreement. For example, if a manager maintains close contact with a subordinate and often asks questions and comments on work, is this viewed as a matter of control and micro management or consideration and relationship building? Both meanings are possible, from the managers' and the subordinate's sides, and they may thus give the same behaviour different meanings. The manager may think that she is considerate while the subordinate may feel that she is checking work quality. Another dimension is the degree of *overlap or diversity in the assessment* of quality/value influencing efforts (leadership). This may concern the value/relevance and/or the quality/effectiveness of these efforts. For example, the people involved may agree that the manager should try to do team building, but diverge in their view of whether or not this is important. Or both parties may agree that active and supportive leadership is needed, but have different views about whether this is accomplished or not.

Our point is *not* mainly about a general feeling of positivity or lack thereof, but more about how people see and assess the situation in terms of shared or differing meanings. One may imagine situations where the assessment is positive, although the perceived meanings of the situation differ. The manager may be close to a subordinate and believe this is necessary and important because monitoring and control is called for, while the subordinate may think that the manager is supportive and considerate and consider it appropriate and appreciate it.

In Figure 10.1 we suggest a broad framework for understanding the two key dimensions discussed above.

High-alignment leadership means that there are shared meanings between leader and followers about the leadership carried out and how to assess the value of the leadership (efforts). Such high-alignment is typically an advantage but this does not necessarily mean that it is always 'good'. A Hitler, a Mao or a sect leader and their devoted followers may have a shared but crazy understanding of the nature and superiority of the leadership. Lack of dissent is often harmful. Still, it is normally an advantage if people are working on the same cognitive planet.

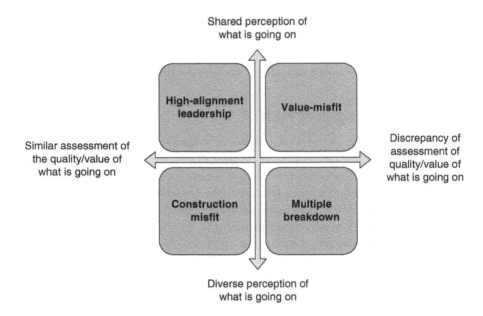

Figure 10.1   Key dimensions in leadership alignment – misfit

Value-misfit indicates that the parties have a broadly similar understanding of the leadership conducted, but vary in their assessment of its quality or relevance. Leader and followers may see the leadership as dominant and authoritative, but assess this quite differently as either good ('powerful leadership') or bad ('old-fashioned and demotivating') respectively. Or both see the leadership as about coaching, but the follower may want this while the HIP may feel that it takes too much time with an insecure and high-maintenance LIP and would have preferred less time-consuming pedagogical work.

Construction misfit would indicate that the parties have different views about what goes on, but are still similar in their assessment of the quality and value of the leadership. The HIP may feel she is very inspirational and persuasive, a visionary. The LIPs may not share this view but appreciate other qualities and contributions and like the person or be happy with the HIP focusing on talk (and not interfering with the work), so on the whole the relationship may be good, despite the variation in their constructions of the relationship and world views of those involved. Or the HIP may feel that s/he has trust in the LIPs but still wants to stay close to them and be involved, while the LIPs may appreciate hands-on contact and a control that prevents mistakes and reduces uncertainty.

Multiple breakdown means that there is a discrepancy in both respects – what is done and how it is evaluated. There is thus a high degree of ambiguity and confusion around the leadership. This may appear alarming, but one could say that the ambiguities of leadership are hard to avoid and most HIP/LIP relations have some degree of multiple breakdowns at least in certain respects.

Of course, there is always variation within a relationship. There are some areas or aspects where there is high-alignment, others where there is value misfit, construction misfit or multiple breakdowns. There are always misunderstandings, disagreements, general confusion, idiosyncratic interpretations, etc. Our interest is in key elements in a relationship, in central aspects where leadership (and other modes of organizing) thinking and practice can be clarified and addressed in cleverer ways than usual. Given that so many in academia, the leadership industry and in organizational practice believe that 'leadership' is an objective fact upon which all agree, opportunities for more thoughtful thinking seem significant.

Although high-alignment may be seen as the best and multiple breakdown the worst it is not necessarily so. It is important to try to avoid the conventional trap of conflating the various inputs or practice components in leadership with a positive outcome. The two dimensions addressed are not exhaustive for how leadership works. One can imagine situations of high-alignment and mediocre leadership and breakdowns in cognition and assessment that still work reasonably well despite the diversities of meaning involved. It is also possible that sometimes productive conflict between HIPs and LIPs about type or degree of leadership can be a good thing – different views may encourage critical reflection and awareness of different possibilities. Productive dissensus may be positive (Deetz, 1992; Tourish, 2014), although creative dissent may also be possible if leader and follower agree that leadership is about initiating and supporting debate. In that case high-alignment may not necessarily prevent dissensus and debate. High-alignment also facilitates smooth leadership. So in most cases striving for alignment (reducing misfit, clarifying divergent views and assessments) by revising views of leadership and followership in order to create more shared meaning would be beneficial (more on this in the next chapter).

Is misfit a significant issue in leadership?

One could argue that good or effective leadership means that alignment on meanings of the intentions, acts and responses has been accomplished and that only bad or failed leadership includes misfits. Of course, there are plenty of examples of converging views within a firm. A medium-sized IT consultancy firm with a corporate culture emphasizing 'fun and profit' and with a very good social climate, tight social relations, a downplaying of hierarchy and formality, an expectation that managers would be liked and appreciated by co-workers, had a distinct leadership model embraced by the founders-owners, executives, managers and co-workers. The latter had a strong say in the appointment of new managers who were expected to fit into the culture. As a consequence, there was a high degree of shared understanding and assessment of leadership within the firm (Alvesson, 1995).

But to assume that this is always or even normally the case may reflect an ideological and romanticized view of the subject, underestimating ambiguity, divergence and fragmentation of meanings. Also, in the absence of conflict people may vary in their understanding of leadership relations, producing divergent or even fragmented and contradictory forms of relationality. The views HIPs have of themselves and their leadership are often not fully in line with, and even clearly different from, how others see them and their leadership acts. Research on leader-member exchanges shows a modest correlation between leaders' and followers' perceptions of the relationship quality (Cogliser et al., 2009; Erdogan & Bauer, 2014). When asked about effective and positive leadership by their superiors many respondents find it easier to come up with examples of ineffective or negative leadership, presumably indicating a gap between their views and the understandings of their superiors (Bryman & Lilley, 2009; Cunha et al., 2009).

FOUR CASE ILLUSTRATIONS

Below we will present four case studies[2] that together illustrate the four positions in Figure 10.1. The cases are presented because they provide some useful 'flesh and blood' in terms of how HIPs and LIPs relate to the leadership taking (or not taking) place.

Case 1: Justin Johnson – high alignment

Justin Johnson is a senior middle manager in a very large high-tech firm where work is highly specialized and the managers typically only master parts of what their subordinates are doing. Justin's subordinates are very qualified engineers who generally do not expect or want much leadership. Justin expresses the view that he is not very active as a manager doing leadership and that his subordinates neither need nor want interference from their boss. He has a view of himself as reactive, responding to the initiatives of the others. A lot of the literature promoting leadership would probably condemn this as 'laissez-faire' and predict dissatisfied subordinates, but in this case it is clear that the subordinates do not want too much interference and that all involved agree that this is rational.

Well, mostly it is them [the subordinates] that contact me when they need help with some issue ... They need a manager that is sufficiently technically skilled in order to be able to give them support, but generally I do not think they need or want any interference from the boss. I have received a lot of feedback that confirms this. (Justin)

Interviews with subordinates confirm this. As one of them says, a high level of autonomy is optimal:

My work has seldom received much leadership. Something that I appreciate (laughter)! I have had pretty much carte blanche from the beginning. Sometimes this can be hard, but mostly I find it stimulating. I am directed by goals and dislike being told what to do. So who or should I say what is leading me? The projects' milestones and the projects' resource capacity lead my work. This is what my group and I primarily have to adapt our work to. (Stanley)

Another subordinate says that he frequently uses another colleague when he needs to discuss something or get advice, contacting Justin only if there is something that he is specifically competent about. Here we find 'the surrogates for leadership' that are perhaps significant in many contemporary organizations, downplaying the need for or appreciation of leadership in the sense of a superior exercising great influence through close contact and interference with the subordinate (Jermier & Kerr, 1997). The subordinates express a nuanced view, acknowledging that occasionally this level of discretion can be stressful, but they mainly find it stimulating.

The alignment of meaning about the relationship is striking. Both the manager and his subordinates agree upon the latter having a lot of discretion and that the former becomes engaged in his capacity mainly on the initiative of the others. Overall, there is a high degree of shared meaning around how the relationship works.

Case 2: George Green – a case of value-misfit

George Green, who we referred to in Chapter 8, is a new manager of a group of eight development engineers doing advanced programming of micro processors, which are a key component of the technologically advanced products developed and sold by the firm. George is eager to work as a manager, doing leadership. He has moved away from seeing himself as an engineer and strongly identifies himself with leadership. This means working with the group and its internal relations, clarifying boundaries, increasing job satisfaction, facilitating collaboration and development, etc. George clearly expects that being open, honest and considerate – an authentic leader – shines through in how others view him as a leader.

I'm quite sure that they think that I am open and that I am very inviting. I'm like, I tell them about my private situation and I say what I can and cannot do, and so on. And I hope they have caught that. [...] But then, I think, like, my group has no potential project leaders, so to speak. They are really deep technically, want to be deep technically. And there, it's not to be prejudiced, but it is a fact that this category does not reflect as much over their manager as others do.

The subordinates seem to be less interested in what George is doing and are not particularly impressed by George's style and actions. When asked about George's leadership specifically, a subordinate says:

> Hmm ... what do we do really? We go to his meetings and answer his questions, and beyond that ...

The rest of the sentence is left unsaid and indicates that not much comes out of this. Later, when asked about what functions George has in the group the same employee remarks:

> It should be someone who makes ... parties and such. Well, what functions does he really fill, apart from being an administrator? Well ... if we are now expected to work in a different way he has something to do with defining that. And that he has been getting involved in, enthusiastically. A bit too much, because I mean, we have been able to work before and suddenly it has to be defined and structured, it feels a bit overambitious, to say the least.

It is quite clear that the interference is not welcome. A good manager, it seems, refrains from leadership and management. Another of the workers reinforces the impression by arguing for the importance of:

> trusting the people in the group to do what they should and not intervene and decide everything.

The need for personal development, feelings of commitment and joy are attributed to the work content – the very things it is preferable that George stays away from, as he is not an expert. A third worker summarizes his view in a rather lukewarm comment:

> So far there haven't been any problems [with George].

To the workers, George's leadership efforts do not evoke much interest, which makes him somewhat frustrated. It is quite clear that they care more about the work than about leadership. George is still seen in mildly positive terms, though. He is viewed as someone who can maintain relations between the group and the rest of the organization. To the group, he is less a servant leader than a gatekeeper. From a leadership point of view, he seems to be in a desperate need of followers, but there are no volunteers. But as long as he does not interfere, cause problems or bother the workers too much, he may just as well continue with his 'leadership'.

Here we have a misfit in terms of the *amount* of leadership called for and the relevance of this kind of work. George thinks that leadership is good and wants to do a lot of things for or targeted at the co-workers. They on the other hand are not interested, see leadership as marginal and prefer to concentrate on their work. The leader-wannabe in search of followers meets professional engineers wanting autonomy, preferring a manager who does some administration, arranges parties, deals with external relations and leaves subordinates alone. All involved have a broadly shared view of this, for example there is some common awareness that George likes and wants to do leadership and the co-workers are not so fond of it and want it minimized. There is not so much a cognitive discrepancy as a value-misfit. Alignment would mean a reconstruction of the engineers into followers and group members (rather than autonomous professionals) or for George to channel his managerial ambitions into other tasks than doing leadership as he views it.

Case 3: Benjamin Book – a case of construction misfit

Benjamin Book is a former newspaper director who was recently appointed CEO for a publishing company. In this new context he aims to establish his leadership as he developed it in the newspaper industry. In the latter context Benjamin had a reputation for being an excellent and convincing, relationship-oriented leader, indeed even loved. Many of Benjamin's former subordinates – as followers – talked about him as very trustworthy and honest, especially emphasizing his ability to understand people and genuinely create mutually respectful relations. Something that Book himself emphasizes in describing his leadership:

> When you recognize others it must be genuine, you have to be authentic because people will see through you otherwise. If you're not authentic people look upon you as you are just playing, pretending, and then the leadership becomes wrong.

Benjamin also describes part of his leadership as trying to recognize people's ceremonial days such as birthdays, something that constituted a substantial source of admiration among his followers in the newspaper organization. Benjamin links genuine care and authenticity:

> You have to be genuine, that's absolutely the most important thing, that you're honest.

According to Benjamin, his excellent leadership based on his authenticity and altruistic care is confirmed and celebrated by his subordinates:

> We had a development day with the personnel and it was great. You get confirmation: 'We've got a CEO we can trust, he knows what he's doing. He's strong and gets things done, so we've got him to fall back on.' It feels great to know that they've got confidence in you. They know that I'm there for them – that's what I want to be known for. The most important thing for me is to feel this positive

attitude from the staff. When it comes down to it, you want them to say: 'He's someone you can respect, because he's honest, direct and you know where you are with him', that kind of feedback.

Book emphasizes the reciprocity of confirmation – the leadership supports the well-being of subordinates – and suggests that there is a strong alignment between his leadership and subordinates' view of this.

How then is he regarded by his present subordinates? Some very much appreciate Book, in particular those who do not know him so well. But people in his team have a different impression. One of his closest managers suggests that:

I think that Book exaggerates. All this recognition of others, it's just a routine. It is just a way of expression and there's no thought behind it, just shallow. Take Lisa for example, Book was furious at her the other day when she was away from work. But then when she is back Book just says 'Hi Lisa, how are you?' It is not straight or honest as he said that she was stupid just the day before. When he says nice and recognizing things to me I don't know how to interpret them.

Benjamin Book's leadership is seen as false and dishonest rather than trustworthy and reliable. This misfit is reinforced by subordinates' view of Book as a weak manager in relation to the owners of the organization, said to be 'running the company without being seen, as they intervene all the time in the management committee and we are just junior managers' (manager). Rather than understanding Book's leadership as strong and reliable they see him as a 'yes-man'. A manager in the management committee says that: 'He can't do as he likes, the owners are keeping him on a tight leash. He is clipped by his wings'.

This contrasts to Book's ambitions to exercise authentic leadership in terms of the overall and strategic questions and directions of the organization. We also see a construction misfit between Book and his subordinates in terms of how they understand what is going on in terms of determining the overall orientation of the business.

We label the diverging views as a construction misfit rather than a typical case of multiple breakdowns, since there is some alignment about the value of a leadership that is authentic and trustworthy in relation to the owners as well as the subordinates. Both parties would consider such a leadership to be valuable and effective. But according to the subordinates, Book far from lives up to this ideal, while he, although acknowledging problems with owners intervening, thinks that he is exemplary in terms of authenticity. To a certain degree those involved seem to be living on different cognitive planets.

Case 4: Milt Masterson – meaning breakdown

Milt is a manager of a sales unit in the national subsidiary of Compland, a large international firm selling advanced office equipment. He describes himself in quite varied ways, but mainly as a man with many leadership styles and an ability to adapt to the situation. He also claims to be extremely successful and can point to excellent results after he took over the job as a manager. This is accepted by some – one subordinate describes Milt as a star leader – but not confirmed by most of the people around him. According to one subordinate, Steve, Milt is more or less a redundant floater. Improved results were only a coincidence and a matter of the timing of Milt starting his new job. Top management decided to focus on this particular customer segment, structured the work process and accordingly approved of hiring people for this. Steve continues:

> By that it was not more difficult than to recruit people and start calling. Basically, to start taking care of the customers ... The structure was there before, but not the heads.

According to Steve Milt had no part in the success:

> When we [group of employees] talk we all agree upon that these figures we could've done without Milt. He's totally offside. The only thing he says is: Full speed forward!

There is, however, variation amongst the subordinates. Some feel that Milt is okay, if somewhat insufficient. One of them, Milt's deputy manager John, claims to be 'pleased with Milt' but also expresses ambivalence. On the one hand he appreciates being given the opportunity to take on responsibility and through that being able to learn and show what he is capable of. On the other hand this leads to blurriness and too much work:

> It's a tense matter ... The salesmen cannot tell the difference between Milt's and my work ... They find Milt anonymous ... He doesn't do much. He delegates the most to me ... Milt wants me to join the meetings [with superiors] because I'm the one who knows the figures and what is happening with the different custom-ers. This is also why I'm running the weekly meetings with the salesmen ... Then I have to support and drive the internals ... Now I sound critical, but at heart I am very pleased with Milt. We work well together ... On the one hand, to be able to participate in the meetings takes a lot of time. On the other hand I want to progress.

A superior financial controller (Carl) is also rather sceptical towards Milt, saying that how Milt can deliver such good results is a 'mystery' to him:

> Off the record, I don't see Milt as an analytically strong person or a strong communicator ... He can jump between subjects and then we are all lost. He doesn't follow a structure ... and has a personality that I have problems to get to know. At the same time I cannot belittle the fact of his results and how his team feels. But it's a mystery how he does it ... Milt is in some way the buddy type. He can run his team members' errands ... I haven't seen him being a manager in his relations to his team members. The internal American managerial model that is about delivering, structuring, organizing, following up, he has nothing at all of

that. But maybe he knows this. That's why he needs John. So that's why I don't think one should belittle his performance ... He's not doing management by numbers and if he hadn't delivered it would have been very easy to say: obviously it's the wrong guy at the wrong place.

This is an interesting case as there are a lot of different views about Milt's seemingly excellent results – Milt emphasizes how performance and employee satisfaction were boosted after he became manager of the unit and claims that 'nobody can take the [excellent] figures from me', while others either are uncertain about how things hang together or doubt his significance in relation to the results. There are also discrepancies in the views about what Milt does and how important it is. Some people see him as a 'buddy type' or highly laissez-faire, while he views himself as a complete manager, in particular good at leading and developing other managers, in line for promotion to a more senior job. We see here considerable variation, confusion and clashing of meanings both in terms of what the manager does and its possible impact.

Comparison of the four cases

In the high alignment case of Justin all involved define good 'leadership' in terms of minimalism, perhaps close to laissez-faire, allowing subordinates autonomy and to take the initiative in involving the manager. The subordinates primarily use peer network resources for support and advice, but can also be said to use broad parts of the spectrum of modes of organizing suggested by our 6M framework, with occasional references to leadership and management (Blom & Alvesson, 2014). The case of the leadership of George is an interesting contrast. George's ideas of a partly leader-driven unit, where the manager has a strong impact outside core work processes and actively addresses group-building and climate-improvement, differ significantly from the ideas of his co-workers. They, like Justin's workers, see themselves as self-propelling, that work itself is the central source of satisfaction and that managers should not interfere or disturb people too much. There is a degree of misfit regarding the meaning of leadership (improvement vs. interference) and the assumptions about how the work should be done – through managerial and team support or autonomously.

The case of Benjamin signals a high degree of construction misfit in relation to what is happening, although the manager and his subordinates broadly agree about the ideal. While Benjamin regards his leadership as authentic and as providing recognition and direction, the subordinates see inauthentic actions expressing conformity to social conventions and subjection to owners. This contrasts radically to the high-alignment construction of Justin and also somewhat to the value misfit of George. In contrast to the case of George – where people disagreed on the value of leadership – Book and his subordinates seem to value the idea of a leadership that is authentic and trustworthy in terms of setting the overall direction. In contrast to the situation of George, Benjamin's subordinates would welcome such a leadership. Benjamin seems to believe he is exercising this, but this belief – unfortunately – is not shared by many of his subordinates.

The case of Milt signals a diversity of misfits and a higher degree of ambiguity than in the other cases. Milt sees himself as a primary source of good results, while most people around him are confused about what he does or see him as insignificant. Milt views himself as a developer of people, while at least some tend to see him as a 'buddy type' (errand runner) and as rather invisible at work. There are also other, more moderate understandings of his (possible) leadership or lack thereof. Listening to different representations of Milt gives the impression that people are talking about almost completely different people. Still, the unit's results are good and some attribute this to Milt, while others deny any such connection. Diversity of meaning in terms of skills and impact is thus strong.

SUMMARY

One of our key points in this book is that leadership is a relationship. It is a combination of leadership and followership. For it to work the people involved need to perceive and value the relationship and practices in broadly similar ways. That is not necessarily the case in efforts to do leadership. Actually, it is an open question whether or not 'leadership' normally works like this. The theme of shared/diverse meanings is thus fundamental.

We have in this chapter outlined four 'types' (or tendencies) of shared/diverse meanings. *High-alignment* leadership means that there is a shared understanding between leader and followers of the meaning of the leadership carried out and their assessment of this. *Value-misfit* indicates that the parties have a broadly similar understanding of the leadership (or other vertical mode of organizing) conducted, but vary in their assessment of its quality or relevance. *Construction misfit* would indicate that the parties have different views of what goes on, but are still similar in their assessment of the quality and value of what the manager does. *Multiple breakdown* means that there is a discrepancy in both respects – what is done and how this is evaluated.

A high degree of alignment between the meanings of and responses to leadership is an accomplishment, not something that is part of business as usual. Apart from managing meaning and instilling/negotiating values and visions, any manager wanting to have an impact needs to pay careful attention to the meanings, cognitions and emotions attached to the relationships and interactions. This applies to specific conversations and for specific issues, but also in terms of the more aggregated view of what the leadership is about and what the leader is supposed to do (and not do). How this can be facilitated in practice will be further discussed in the next chapter.

NOTES

1. See various language theories on organizations and social life (e.g. Alvesson & Kärreman, 2000; Cooper & Burrell, 1988; Potter & Wetherell, 1987).
2. These cases have been presented as empirical material in previous publications. Case 1 and 2 in Blom and Alvesson (2014), case 3 in Sveningsson and Alvesson (2016) and case 4 in Alvesson and Wenglén (2008).

11
Reflexive Group Work on Leadership and its Alternatives

A key idea in this book is to acknowledge that leadership in practice is often complex, filled with ambiguity, tensions and gaps between ideals and lived reality. Other modes of organizing – horizontal or vertical – might be more appropriate considering the task at hand and the qualities of the people involved. The appropriate mode of organizing may however be debated and contested depending on people's experiences, ambitions, identity, culture, and so forth. Following the last chapter on alignment and misfits we noticed how radically deviating views between individuals could cause confusion, dissatisfaction and conflicts and make organizations less functional as a result. This calls for reflection, collective sense-making and communication. In this chapter we focus on how misalignments can be identified, clarified and to some extent improved on at a group level, that is, how the organization can collectively engage with these issues. In the next two chapters we deal with this on an individual level, first addressing leaders and then, in Chapter 13, reflexive followers. But in this chapter we call for shared discussions on how to organize leadership and consider alternatives for *reflexive group work*. We discuss how reflexive group work can focus on different but important organizational issues, for example what degree of hierarchy does the organization in question need in order to work well – is there a need for a clear division of HIPs and LIPs at all (apart perhaps from a HIP filling a moderate management/administration function)? If so, what type of hierarchy – and LIPs - does the organization need? Or what type of position is it reasonable for subordinate employees to take? We present a few useful examples that might help managers and others to develop a more reflexive view on the various modes of organizing and how to approach leadership-followership.

We start by introducing a framework for understanding the unity or fragmentation of views of (non-)leadership as well as the emotional strength attached to these views. Following this, we introduce a dialogic view on how to encourage an open and reflexive dialogue on leadership and other modes of organizing, including some practical examples of how these principles are to a certain degree practised in contemporary organizations. The chapter ends with a short summary of our key points.

UNDERSTANDING HIPS' AND LIPS' DISCRETION REGARDING MODES OF ORGANIZING

How should one as a (potential) HIP understand and relate to people's (perceived) need for leadership? Historically, managerial perspectives on the issue have dominated in the leadership literature, giving the manager/HIP strong authority and discretion to interpret and define the situation mainly according to his/her preferences – a perspective well captured in Goffee and Jones' (2000) concept 'tough empathy': 'Tough empathy means giving people what they need, not what they want' (p. 68). In others words, do not give in to what the LIPs want if it is not in line with what you as a manager/leader think is right for them and in harmony with your true self, especially if they wish for a 'softer' leader: '… we do not believe that empathy of inspirational leaders is the soft kind described in so much of the management literature' (Goffee & Jones, 2000, p. 68). Here the HIP is supposed to know best.

However, as said many times before, followers and followership are central to leadership, where followers' attributions, acts and identity positions are key to understanding how to establish productive leader-follower relationships. The perceived need for leadership – if/what/how/when – is a social construction, based on, for example, the current and historical interplay between the manager and his/her current and former colleagues, superiors and subordinates. Leadership is not an objective fact but a matter of how a society in general and more specifically people interacting with one another create beliefs, ideas and meanings around leadership, that is through defining and evaluating certain practices in a specific way and then defining actors in relation to leadership ideas and values.

At a local organizational level this interplay is sometimes smooth and harmonious, but sometimes there are conflicts and tensions between how managers and their subordinates view the need for managerial interventions that result in misalignments and clashes. In the previous chapter we saw, for example, how various forms of misfit between HIPs and LIPs caused friction and problems in three of the four cases. George Green represented a case of value misfit, Benjamin Book a case of misalignment of constructions while in the case of Milt Masterson we saw significant meaning breakdowns. More generally, there are strong indications that various forms of misfit are very common – there is, for example, a rather low correlation between how HIPs and LIPs see their relationship (Cogliser et al., 2009). This raises questions such as whether one should depart from the manager's or the subordinates' view as a starting point to decide what – if any – leadership acts are appropriate. Of course a dialogue is important here, either to find a compromise between interests or explore who is right, that is, who has the most thoughtful view.

Social constructions are sometimes rather preliminary, and thus not so stable. But others are more robust – being shared and reproduced by many. Logically, ideas that are shared by many are more likely to be reproduced than those shared by a few and varying between individuals. Furthermore, ideas that people are emotionally committed to are typically harder to challenge, replace or modify than ideas with weaker feelings attached to them. This is clearly evident from various more or less revered convictions in religion, politics, ideologies or other -isms. This is relevant for leadership; the success of acts depends upon their emotional appeal. Leadership thus involves some emotional labour and leaders are sometimes even conceptualized as 'mood managers' (Ashkanasy & Humphrey, 2011). If a leadership attempt is targeted at people who share a strong and emotionally loaded counter-picture of what leadership is needed, there is probably a lower likelihood that they will voluntarily take on a follower identity (DeRue & Ashford, 2010), compared to a situation where they share the manager's/leader's view.

To sum up this section, and some ideas also addressed in previous chapters, so far:

- Leadership – as the perceived need for it – is socially constructed.
- From a HIP perspective, one needs to take the LIPs' ideas/perceptions of the need for leadership seriously, given the partly voluntary nature of a leader-follower relationship.
- An idea/perception that is shared by many and people feel strongly about is harder to challenge, replace or modify compared to those shared by fewer and/or with less emotions attached to it.

Strategies for balancing HIPs' and LIPs' perceptions

From a managerial perspective, it might be tempting to just follow one's own convictions and preferences in terms of leadership style and interventions. After all, managers are hired and paid to take responsibility for the results and performance of their units, and might feel expected to know what to do in terms of 'leading' their subordinates – 'It's my way or the highway!' This idea is typically represented in the majority of managerial leadership literature where it is more or less expected that the manager or leader takes charge and is in control. It is also fuelled by popular contemporary discourse such as 'authentic' leadership (see Chapter 3) or 'tough empathy' (above), both departing from the manager's/leader's 'true' self and understanding of the situation. Here a problematic assumption is that the HIP has a superior understanding of the situation and what leadership is needed and practised. As we saw in the previous chapter this can often be disputed – the HIP may be ignorant or have poor judgement. What is 'right' or 'effective' leadership in many workplaces is actually a matter of quite different opinions, sometimes openly disputed, although understandings in a workplace are often implicit and not always espoused. Strong or confused views are problematic, and we hope to encourage new practices where ideas and assessments of leadership and its alternatives are brought forward and discussed.

Recognizing the significance of social and cultural contexts however, the view of the manager or leader as the natural hub around which everything else revolves may be quite problematic, not least when the subordinates express a contrasting view on what leadership acts are needed. As emphasized frequently in this book, leadership implies a certain amount of willingness and voluntarism on behalf of the follower. If the LIPs' leadership expectations diverge too much from the leadership offered by the HIP, this identity position is less likely to be taken. It follows that it is highly significant for a potential leader to develop a good understanding of how the potential followers see the need for leadership. But does understanding the LIPs' need – or lack of need – for leadership also automatically mean adapting to it?

Authors like Goffee and Jones (2000) would likely answer 'no' to that question. The answer can be more nuanced. If the LIPs' perceived need for leadership stands in sharp contrast to the view of the HIP, the LIPs feel strongly about the matter and the feeling is widely shared within the group (strong consensus among the potential followers), it *might* – also from a managerial/HIP perspective – be more viable to adapt to it, than persisting with the HIP's view and trying to force the LIPs into a follower position they will likely be averse to, resist or just ignore. The HIP may be wrong, but even if s/he is right then it does not help if LIPs do not accept this, at least not if they are in agreement and take a firm stance, like George's subordinates back in Chapter 10.

On the other hand, uncertainty, dissonance and disagreement among potential followers about what, if any, leadership is needed will potentially make a one-sided adaption to the LIPs less obvious as an effective way to handle the situation. This might also be the case when the LIPs are in agreement, but have a lukewarm interest in leadership. If they do not seem to care that much, and there are tensions and disagreement within the group, then there is even more discretion for the manager/HIP to choose leadership interventions as s/he see fit without risking too much opposition, conflict and resistance. It is of course still uncertain whether the LIPs will actually buy into the leadership efforts and their responses may vary.

The discussion above can be conceptualized in a heuristic model by intersecting two dimensions that influence the positioning of HIPs in relation to subordinates/followers. We see this as an influence that affects the possibility for HIPs to ignore the view of subordinates/followers without risking resistance and failed leadership efforts.

The first of these two dimensions refers to followers' cognitive and/or emotional attachment to their views – ideas and interpretations – of leadership. According to our model, the attachment can be either strong or weak. When LIPs have a strong attachment to their view – regardless of whether they favour (a specific version of) leadership or something else – it might be a good idea for HIPs to recognize that their discretion is limited. If LIPs strongly prefer autonomy or group work, then a HIP insisting on prophesying, working with LIPs' feelings, preaching values and morals, etc., will appear odd. In some organizations, such as the police and the armed forces, there may be strong views about the significance of visible leadership (or other HIP forms, centralized decision-making, kicking ass, etc.), while other groups, such as professionals (e.g. doctors, lawyers, scientists), may feel strongly about the significance of avoiding or downplaying leadership and relying more on alternative modes of coordination.

The other dimension highlights the extent to which there is consensus among followers or views of leadership are more fragmented and contested. A shared view may result from strong traditions, common organizational history, lower employee turnover, organizational culture and professional norms, for example. When there is a broadly shared view among LIPs – regardless of whether they feel strongly about leadership or not – it is probably difficult to simply disregard that view if the HIP wants to avoid conflict, refusal or resistance. A broadly shared view normally narrows down the level of discretion and range of options about how to exercise leadership.

Combining these dimensions produces four different positions in terms of HIP discretion, as shown in Figure 11.1.

1. *Moderate HIP discretion.* A strong attachment coupled with a low degree of consensus among subordinates. In this position LIPs have strong feelings about leadership although there is disagreement about its relevance and variety. The strong attachment among LIPs suggests that HIPs have to adapt to a particular view, but since LIPs disagree on this view – in terms of the relevance and variety of leadership/non-leadership – the room for manoeuvre opens up somewhat and we label this position as 'moderate HIP discretion'. HIPs may feel moderately free in terms of how to do/not do leadership since the disagreement and contested view among LIPs reduce the risk of strongly unified resistance. At least it seems unlikely that a particular kind of leadership or non-leadership would be met with heavy resistance. This is not unusual in mergers and acquisitions, for example where people come together from different organizations and have different experiences of leadership. This normally provides some leeway for HIPs in terms of leadership positions. This can perhaps also be seen in work groups consisting of a heterogeneous workforce in terms of education, profession, identity, background, gender, age, etc.

2. *Limited HIP discretion.* A strong attachment combined with a shared view among subordinates produce limited HIP discretion. A shared view among LIPs about leadership/no leadership makes it difficult for HIPs to push for a contrasting view, at least without the risk of clashes and conflicts. A high degree of consensus among

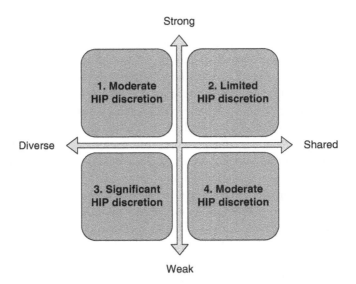

Figure 11.1   LIPs' views on leadership and its effects on HIP discretion

followers on an issue they also feel strongly about normally provides them with strong leverage in terms of influence in relation to HIPs. This illustrates a situation where HIPs normally have to adapt to and accommodate the interests and wishes of LIPs rather than proceeding solely on the basis of the HIP's own convictions and ideas about leadership. Embarking on leadership or non-leadership (other modes), based on personal convictions and leadership ideals without recognizing LIPs' views may produce frustration and conflict. We can think of professional organizations such as those in higher education where the professionals prefer to work based on horizontal modes of coordination – with the emphasis on autonomy and peer relations and networking – rather than leadership (or other vertical modes of organizing). Doing leadership in this context may clash with subordinates' professional interests. But again there are organizations, for example the police and the military, where people may feel strongly about the need for decisive leadership (possibly better described as management or exercise of power) in difficult situations. Avoiding leadership or relying on horizontal modes of coordination would likely produce much frustration, conflict and bad results in these organizations.

3. *Significant HIP discretion.* This position combines weak attachment from LIPs with disagreement about the significance of leadership/non-leadership. Disagreement among LIPs about varieties of leadership or non-leadership and a weak interest might provide HIPs with the broadest range of options in terms of leadership, what we call significant discretion. This normally presents a situation that entails less risk of resistance among LIPs as they place less emotional attachment in this as well as disagreeing about its relevance and proper form. This can be illustrated with boards, expert committees and temporary organizations that gather specialists from different areas, functions or organizations. People who are given temporary assignments or assigned to temporal organizations may not express strong demands on leadership/non-leadership and may accommodate a more open view. Overall, this means that there is greater discretion on behalf of HIPs to decide on whether some varieties of leadership makes sense or not and accordingly how to proceed.

4. *Moderate HIP discretion.* In the situation where there is a shared view among LIPs with a weak attachment to leadership, the range of options for HIPs is limited compared to position 3 above. On one hand HIPs have significant discretion since LIPs have a weak attachment and are thus possibly receptive, but this is moderated by the other dimension; HIPs need to adapt to what is shared among LIPs. The space for influence is moderate. This may be the case with some professional service organizations where work typically relies strongly on more horizontal modes of coordination and there are low expectations – people not thinking much about it because of the nature of their work – of leadership. Managers are self-evidently supposed to do management in terms of planning, administration, resource allocation and the like rather than leading, for example, complex engineering work.

From this reasoning we think that, given that the need for leadership is contested and negotiated over time, it seems reasonable to depart from the LIPs' understanding of what leadership they think they need. It may be quite productive to recognize and acknowledge the views of LIPs, especially if they feel strongly about what leadership they are in need of (if any) and if that view is widely shared within the group. Of course there is a possibility that the LIPs have got it all wrong and their view may be clouded by self-interest and a wish for more leeway and less direction and control, for example a quest for individual autonomy that might make the organization more dysfunctional. In addition, their overview of their work situations might be limited and suffering from information asymmetry in comparison to HIPs. Goffee and Jones (2000, p. 68) clearly separates subordinates' 'wants' from 'needs', but the 'wants' of the subordinates can actually also be their sincere 'need' for leadership, and the 'need' according to their manager/HIP can be nothing more than his or her 'wants'.

In the long run, a perceived mismatch between the 'supply' and 'demand' of leadership will most likely impede or even disable a working HIP-LIP relationship. The model in Figure 11.1 might serve as a useful tool for a HIP trying to understand his/her degrees of freedom when it comes to choosing between different modes of organizing and/or variants of leadership. It can therefore be seen as a means for facilitating engagement in reflexive group exercises aimed at identifying forms of interactions and group relational dynamics.

HOW TO ENCOURAGE COLLECTIVE REFLEXIVITY AND A GENUINE DIALOGUE ON MODES OF ORGANIZING?

We have hopefully now gained some understanding of the relational dynamics between HIPs and LIPs when it comes to the degree of commitment and diversity regarding ideas on modes of organizing. In some cases LIPs have a firm understanding and this is difficult to change. In most cases, however, there are opportunities for HIPs and LIPs to engage in reflection and dialogue and produce a shared understanding. An important question is how can a constructive dialogue be encouraged around these issues?

One way to approach a constructive dialogue is to draw upon Habermas' (1984; 1987) concepts of communicative action, communicative rationality and in particular the notion of ideal speech, concepts that form the basis for what Fryer (2011) calls facilitative leadership. Ideal speech occurs when (Habermas, 1990):

- Every subject with the competence to speak and act is allowed to take part in the discourse.
- Everyone is allowed to question any assertion whatever.
- Everyone is allowed to introduce any assertion whatever into the discourse.
- Everyone is allowed to express his (or her) attitudes, desires and needs.
- No speaker may be prevented, by internal or external coercion, from exercising his (or her) rights (the four points above).

The facilitative leader should therefore ensure that these conditions are met when interacting with his/her organizational members. But others need to be on board and actively contribute, not only to the ideal, but also to the conditions being fulfilled. The HIP may be central, but this is not a one-woman show.

We recognize of course that for a seasoned practitioner used to organizational politics, dysfunctional meeting traditions and/or limited resources in terms of time and money, these conditions might be viewed with scepticism and regarded as a naive academic utopia. Also, critical scholars such as, for example, Knights and Willmott (1992) highlight that even if a shared understanding can be reached between leaders and followers through such a 'negotiation', it tends to be achieved from different and unbalanced bargaining positions, where the HIP typically has better access to symbolic and/or material resources compared to the LIPs. In addition, Woods (2004) points out that even if there is a seemingly open and genuine dialogue, some boundaries and rationalities are nevertheless often still regarded as non-negotiable.

We recognize all these imperfections, but still claim the value and virtue of striving towards 'ideal speech'; an improved, but imperfect dialogue in a Habermasian sense is after all better than no dialogue at all. Departing from a democratic ideal and a less imposing way of leading may also be pragmatic:

> It is one thing for misty-eyed critical management theorists to speak of the virtues of workplace democracy, but if hard-bitten pragmatists like Peter Drucker (1993) are also preaching the need for participative organizational forms, there may be something for facilitative leadership to hook on to. (Fryer, 2011, p. 39)

This is especially the case if the situation is understood as 'limited or moderate HIP discretion' in line with Figure 11.1. It may be wise to pay attention to the LIPs' views because even if a HIP thinks they are wrong and sticks to his/her way of doing things without the support or at least consent of the LIPs, it will often come at a cost in terms of discontent, obstruction or resistance, as we could see in some of the cases in Chapter 10, especially in the cases of George and Benjamin.

As pointed out before, alignment of meaning in organizing is often productive for organizations. But as suggested, alignment of meaning is rarely something that occurs automatically or without some effort. It often calls for 'meta-leadership' in terms of influencing processes aimed at achieving alignment. These can take the shape of explicit and implicit ongoing negotiations among involved parties (HIPs, LIPs, MIPs and NIPs). Fryer's (2011) notion of facilitative leadership can serve as an inspiration. Facilitative leadership should be regarded as a progressive way of exercising leadership. In our view and terminology, this way of organizing comes closer to group work than leadership. However, it can be of high value for an organization's collective reflexivity to engage in this type of dialogue now and then (as opposed to Fryer's ideal of a continuous way of 'leading') – as an act of meta-leadership – in order to reflect upon how things work and could work better in terms of leadership/followership or other modes of organizing.

Simple questions can be put on the agenda:

- How do we work here in terms of leadership, management, exercise of power, group work, autonomy, use of networks?
- Is there too much or too little and is the quality good, acceptable or bad in relation to each of these?

- What are the needs and wants of leadership? In terms of visions, values/morals, emotional problems, workplace spirit and pedagogical support?
- Is there too much or too little and is the quality good, acceptable or bad in relation to each of these?
- How are things functioning in terms of HIPs, MIPs and LIPs? Do we need to work on asymmetries and symmetries? Upgrading or downgrading the significance of the HIP?

Even if there inevitably are people who hold back their views or do impression management and there is no agreement, it is likely that some clarification and food for thought can emerge. Ongoing leader-/followership or other work with modes of organizing may be facilitated. Outcomes such as the one realized by Justin in Chapter 10, where he learns that his co-workers neither expect nor want much leadership, may be accomplished.

FORMS OF REFLEXIVE GROUP WORK

There are a lot of different techniques used in leadership training. These include exercises, cases, games, role-playing, simulations, and group exercises. Here we focus on what enables group-oriented reflections and learning that acknowledge different stakeholders such as subordinates and thus exhibits certain dialogic and participatory elements reflecting Fryer's (2011) facilitative leadership. A number of group activities and methods can be drawn upon to facilitate learning and shared views on potential modes of organizing. For example, multisource feedback from the workplace is occasionally provided in order to improve leadership interactions. However, feedback about people's behaviour is seldom provided within the regular work context and even if it is it may not always result in learning. This is often explained by the difficulty of finding time and room for reflection and self-analysis and because people may be defensive and unwilling to take negative or questioning feedback in a constructive way. People who are defensive and insecure often avoid or ignore feedback about their weaknesses, even if this is framed as 'room for improvement' or 'potential for development', as the consultancy language often terms it. Also, people who think that events are predetermined by external forces may be less likely to view feedback as a way to improve their skills. Perhaps senior executives – successful in achieving a higher position – develop a sense of confidence that causes them to ignore or discount criticism?

Even so, providing feedback from multiple sources has become popular and is often used in a variety of organizations, especially large ones. It is sometimes called '360-degree' or 'multi-rater' feedback. Such multisource feedback can be drawn upon for different purposes, although the primary aim is to assess the strength and developmental needs of managers. The idea is to provide feedback from a person's (e.g. a HIP's) closest work environment, usually including superiors, subordinates and colleagues. Sometimes extra-organizational actors such as customers, partners and suppliers are also involved. It can be part of a formal review process, with effects on salary and promotion, but usually the less formal side, leading to insights, development and changed behaviour, is in focus. The actual effects on employee/organizational performance are debated (e.g. Hazucha et al., 1993; Pfau & Kay, 2002), but if taken seriously it can provide a basis for reflexivity and alignment of meaning.

Often these types of feedback sessions are organized internally, but there are also examples where HIPs let external actors conduct the evaluation. One such example is when the CEO of the Swedish national broadcasting company, Swedish Radio, Cilla Benkö, let the nation's leading magazine for managers – *Chef* ('Manager') – perform their 'manager test' on her and publish the result, including her interpretations of it.[1] The test is a limited 360, with more 'upward feedback' since it focuses on current and former subordinates' views and does not include superiors or peers.

After rather positive feedback highlighting her straightforwardness, effectiveness and vision and some less positive feedback concerning lack of humility, top-down approach and micro-management, she commented on the result:

> Interesting reading where I recognize some parts … Sure, I understand that people that are unhappy with me rarely give me direct feedback, so now when *Chef* presents a different view I have to go back and think about why our views deviate. (Cilla Benkö, CEO Swedish Radio)

If an exercise like this can facilitate individual and collective reflexivity – as indicated by the quote 'I have to go back and think about why our views deviate' – around how an organization is run and managed, led or not led, it can serve its purpose in line with the ideal of a more reflexive take on leadership. It is important to note, however, that the effectiveness of multisource feedback depends not only on the type of feedback provided but also on how it is presented to managers. For example, commonly managers receive feedback but have to interpret it without support, such as a group that facilitates dialogue about its meaning. Studies suggest that feedback workshops with facilitators are more effective in terms of influencing and developing behaviour (Seifert et al., 2003). This is good news for the leadership development industry.

We see feedback to individual managers about their leadership (and other aspects of their work) as important, but even more relevant for well-functioning organizations is to address the wider spectrum of modes of organizing: the 6M framework. One can imagine everyone in a unit going through how work is organized in terms of the uses of leadership, management, power, groups, networks and autonomy. What functions well and less well? What are the strong and weak spots? What is too much or too little or what are the different types of problems with quality in, for example, leadership, use of networks and space for autonomy? Perhaps there is a perceived need for more management (planning, order, structure, output control) and less leadership? Or, should we be relying more on leadership and minimizing bureaucracy? Or, can we have people working less in isolation and more in collaborative groups? Or, is group work sometimes perceived as being part of a chain-gang, were people feel that the group is an obstacle rather than a source of synergy effects? How come? Can we improve? Or should we reduce group work and ask for, for example, powerful managerial interventions rather than lengthy group discussions?

Reflexivity thus not only focuses on leadership, but leadership in relationship to the various modes of organizing characterizing the organization, or potentially characterizing it in the future. The interface between leadership and other modes is important to consider. A well-functioning workplace is not, as we have emphasized, only about a great HIP leading LIPs. This needs to be supplemented and balanced with initiatives, influencing processes and coordination from other sources.

Similarly with versions and aspects of leadership and followership as suggested by, for example, the 5P framework (or another list pointing at important domains and styles of leadership). How are HIPs and LIPs relating to any possible need for visions, morals, emotional support, workplace climate and learning? How are these functions or domains being taken care of? By whom? How can leadership be developed and/or supplemented with horizontal modes of organizing?

SPECIFIC AND INSTITUTIONALIZED GROUP ACTIVITIES FOR REFLEXIVITY

What we have addressed above is partly to be carried out on an ongoing, non-formal basis. People in a variety of interactions talk about these issues, perhaps also through actions influencing workplace norms and awareness. Employees can emphasize their followership or autonomy and that of their HIPs and colleagues through behaviour in meetings and by whom they approach (or do not approach) on specific issues. Is the manager (HIP) a centre of attention and very much present in decision-making and feedback giving, or do people often go to others or make decisions themselves and only occasionally involve the manager? There are various constructions of organizational cultures in terms of leadership-significance versus leadership-minimalism. This can be dealt with with on an ongoing, emergent, informal and implicit basis and done through small means (causal remarks, framing of issues in a particular way, use of irony). Reflexivity may also be expressed in these subtle ways.

But reflexivity may also be planned and explicit. It may be put on the agenda and people encouraged to consciously discuss leadership and other modes of organizing. Explicit reflection exercises, where the group meet now and then and discuss how the organization in question is led, managed, coordinated and supported, as well as the balance between people feeling autonomous versus managed, can infuse new perspectives and ideas and facilitate reflexivity. It can help with an understanding of different alternatives and positions and help to avoid dysfunctional misalignment of meanings.

But as said before, facilitating reflexivity is not a one-time exercise. Nor is it a matter of single episodes or of just becoming conscious about how to act. Ongoing everyday organizational conduct is even more important; structures, organizational culture, and organizational identity all play utterly important parts in facilitating reflexivity around leadership and alternative modes of organizing. Some basic examples include:

- Selective recruiting, such as actively looking for people with a capacity for reflexivity and encouraging them to communicate their observations and ideas.
- Group design and staffing, for instance designing teams in such a way that people with reflexive capabilities and different perspectives are included.

- Socialization, such as encouraging new hires to question processes, routines, organizations, as well as their own and others' assumptions and perspectives.
- Reward systems that symbolically and materially support reflexive behaviour.
- Conduct meetings and workshops with Habermas' conditions for ideal speech as an inspirational guide.

These practices are partially implemented in one of the world's most prestigious organizations: McKinsey & Company. The firm has an important principle or corporate value that they refer to as 'obligation to dissent'. According to their website it means:

> All McKinsey consultants are obligated to dissent if they believe something is incorrect or not in the client's best interests. Everyone's opinion counts. While you might be hesitant to disagree with the team's most senior member or the client, you're expected to share your point of view.

In theory, regardless of hierarchy, loyalties or dependencies, you are expected to speak up if you think a colleague, superior or client is wrong or about to make a mistake. It can be something as 'simple' as a minor error in an Excel-sheet or something as profound as the key recommendation or main message in the final PowerPoint deck.

McKinsey's selective recruitment, sophisticated staffing processes, and strong element of socialization (e.g. encouraging and teaching new recruits regarding the obligation to dissent) could constitute a good basis for a reflexive organization. The people they hire tend to have the necessary cognitive abilities. On the other hand, they may also be eager to fit in and realize that critical reflection will probably be fairly narrowly targeted. 'The client's best interests' sounds good, but the meaning of this is probably a matter of uncertainty and dispute, or may be simplified to just being about 'the bottom line'. The client's best interests may also be ethically problematic and sometimes there is a conflict between the consultancy organization – and their employees' well-being – and the client's wishes. 'The client' also tends to mask the variety of interests and interpretations within a client firm.

Encouraging efforts at dissent is not necessarily the same as getting people to question their own assumptions and the firm's institutionalized 'truths'. And if we compare the 'obligation to dissent' with Habermas' (1990) conditions for ideal speech, we can firstly note the sublime difference between 'allowed' and 'obliged' to dissent. In the firm it is required as part of being a consultant. In a Habermasian sense it is a right. Furthermore, the obligation to dissent is usually expected to be 'fact based', as are most forms of communication in management consultancies at this level. You need to prove that you are right and that someone else is wrong by looking at the 'facts'. Going back to Habermas, not only 'facts' but values and the sincerity of statements and positions are to be targeted for communicative action, where anything that appears questionable is a legitimate target of disputing validity claims. The fact-driven culture – often based on rigorous quantitative analysis – of many of the large consulting firms is seldom a fertile ground for arguments such as 'this may be morally problematic' (if not quantified in a solid business case). And again, as in all organizations, there are some 'holy cows' that you had better not start to question if you would like your career to prosper. There are, after all, limitations to how much radical, out-of-the-box thinking your colleagues and superiors can take.

One such area could be how the client's projects and the firm are run in terms of the 6Ms or the 5Ps (problem-solving in the service of clients is usually regarded as less sensitive to being questioned or being opinionated about). But still, the basic idea behind the 'obligation to dissent' is worth bearing in mind when thinking about how one can foster a more inclusive and reflexive view on leadership and other modes of organizing, and in so doing minimizing the risk of dysfunctional misfit between and among HIPs, LIPs and MIPs, as discussed in the previous chapter. As we have seen above such misfits are not uncommon. Many people do perceive leadership as ineffective (Bryman & Lilley, 2009; Cunha et al., 2009). Engaging in broader reflecting and communication among the involved actors is probably more often fruitful than simply trying to make leadership more effective through a narrow focus on the HIP who is supposed to do leadership.

SUMMARY

In this chapter we have discussed and provided various 'tools' and examples that might serve as inspiration for practitioners who wish to extend and promote their organizations' capability to collectively reflect on different modes of organizing, including leadership. An important issue to consider is the balance between explicit group work and more implicit, ongoing 'negotiations' regarding modes of organizing. Both might serve the purpose of increasing the understanding of various positions/meanings and provide means for increased alignment between diverging views. In the next chapter we will continue by discussing how reflexivity on an *individual* level can be encouraged and facilitated.

Again, it is important to note that reflexive group work is not a 'once and for all' type of exercise. It is something that needs to be done continuously. It can be done proactively or reactively (e.g. when some form of problem has been identified). It can also take the shape of explicit 'negotiations' or more implicit mutual acknowledgement. The organizational needs for coordination, support and control will of course also change over time so it is futile to think that they can be identified, agreed upon and fixed once and for all, even if such solutions have been preceded by careful analysis and a constructive and reflexive dialogue between all involved. But we still think that it is important to at least have some mutual understanding – and in the best case agreement – on the main features (e.g. in terms of 6M and/or 5P) when it comes to how a given organization should be led, managed or not.

NOTE

1. http://chef.se/chef-testar-sveriges-radios-vd-cilla-benko/

12
Reflexive and Unreflexive Leadership

In this chapter we look at the theme of reflexivity or lack thereof among people holding a senior position, primarily as managers but most of our views are also relevant for informal authorities (e.g. leading professionals, experienced and resourceful non-promoted people acting as informal leaders).

As said in Chapter 2 we see reflexivity as a broader orientation where people not only reflect on a limited topic, deal with a tricky situation or think about feedback they have received, but think more deeply about issues, including their own framework, assumptions, expectations, and favoured vocabulary. Reflexivity means being able to examine and, if motivated, transcend established templates for how to think and act. Although all people reflect to some degree and have at least a rudiment of capacity and interest in reflexivity, there are enormous variations. This is partly a personal matter, but situation also matters. With hard work pressure, stress and anxieties over failures and conflicts, even many with significant reflexive capacities may become unreflexive and limit their thinking to instrumental concerns. How can I reach my objectives? This question takes centre stage while deeper thinking about *how* one is thinking and considerations of problematic or questionable objectives or requirements escape attention. Unfortunately, much managerial and organizational work often pushes people to develop a limited capacity for and interest in reflexivity.

In this chapter we develop the topic of reflexivity based on some cases[1] that are discussed in depth. We start with illustrations of the unreflexive leader (or in some cases unreflexive HIP) and then move on to some more impressive and hopefully inspirational examples.

UNREFLEXIVE LEADERSHIP

Interestingly enough, our almost twenty years of in-depth studies of managerial life and work indicate that managers are often limitedly thoughtful about what they do, the way they are and what relations they are involved in. Some of our cases also indicate limited reflexivity – managers often have rather basic and contradictory views of themselves and their leadership (Sveningsson & Alvesson, 2016). In addition, managers often have high regard for their own ability, motives, ambitions, and practices, while subordinates tend to be less impressed. Of course, most people are reflexive to a degree – and so are our two case examples below – but there are often significant elements or aspects of most HIPs' work, including leadership, that score low on reflexivity, and it is to these we now turn.

A middle manager preaching coaching while practising directive interventions

Kim is a middle-aged manager with over ten years' experience in a senior role in a global manufacturing company (Alvesson & Jonsson, 2016). She combines a traditional line manager role with an overall integrating role in which she also coordinates other line mangers. Kim likes to be a coaching leader but also recognizes that some situations demand other styles: 'sometimes you have to be a manager'. She enjoys reading about leadership and coaching. Over the years Kim has also participated in several leadership and mentoring programmes, both initiated by the company and of her own accord. In the following extract from a conversation with Kim, we hear reflections about leadership and whether coaching is different from being a leader:

> I think leadership questions are interesting so I try to read as much as possible. Something that particularly interests me is this coaching element of leadership. In the role I have towards one of my co-workers, I want him to use me as a sounding board, but he shouldn't get the answers from me. I want to ask questions to make him think.

> When you read books about coaching … they can be extreme, in my opinion. Because they say that everything you do should be based on that and I'm not there yet. Maybe I'll get there some time. But I think a mix is preferable.

Kim strongly inclines towards the ideal of coaching, finding that this 'particularly interests me'. She indicates that this should be central although not 'extreme' in terms of leadership. She also emphasizes the importance of participation and responds to a question about what she thinks distinguishes good leadership from bad by stating that:

> A leadership style where you don't listen to the organization, or to your people, when you think you know best because you're the manager. I don't like that at all …
> I think leadership needs to be different in different situations. There are situations when the manager has to go in and say: No, we're doing it this way. But for the most part, when you've got a little time, then it's better that the group or the organization comes up with the answer, because then they'll commit.

Here, we can spot a clear and coherent view of 'leadership'. Occasionally, there are reasons for exceptions and it needs to be a mix, but Kim's view appears to be strongly in favour of coaching and participation. Mostly it should be the group or the organization – not the manager – that comes up with the answer. Kim expresses some awareness of variation, talking about the importance of adapting leadership and the impossibility of having *one* leadership style. This is to an extent in contrast with the company's efforts to achieve a uniform style of leadership:

> Different situations require different kinds of leadership ... I want to coach but this is not the same kind of situation as when I work with the people in my organization. Here I'm the person responsible for our organization and I'm talking to another person and making demands on them. And that means I'm not in a position to develop them, so it's not my style of leadership. That's what I mean when I say you can't just have one style of leadership. I don't believe you can.

Put another way: developing the employees and leading/managing the work are two quite separate things. At the same time, in our many interviews with Kim this view of the necessity of having a mix is sparsely expressed compared to the principles of good leadership, particularly coaching and participation, for example, when she claims that it is important to take on different roles as a leader and not least to: 'make the managers let go of things in the organization and not do all the work themselves. They should let people in the organization help them to do things and to grow and increase the level of motivation further down'.

Here we get an impression of a certain level of reflexivity. Kim reads a lot, but is not uncritical about certain ideals; she believes there are limits to the use of a coaching leadership style. Some mix is inevitable and you have to look at the situation.

But if we carefully observe Kim's actions in various situations we get a quite different picture. Kim's leadership *practices* are generally loosely coupled or even inconsistent with the (diverse) ideas and meanings expressed. Kim's self-image as a coaching leader is also difficult to discern in practice. Despite Kim's avowed love of coaching, this seems to be at odds with an otherwise natural tendency to speak up and take over. Kim seems to respond to situations by exercising 'stimuli-response leadership' where issues are dealt with based on a spontaneous reading of the situation, without much sign of careful reflection or an integrated, coherent idea or framework guiding an overall leadership ambition.

We will look at two interactions where leadership is – or could be – displayed.

The first is a meeting between Kim, in her role as line manager, and people from another part of the organization, who are responsible for spare parts. The purpose of the meeting is to agree on a price for an upgrade package. Kim confronts her co-workers with the fact that they do not have a full command of the central question and that they are unable to supply an answer within a reasonable time:

> This is absolutely crucial. It's unbelievable. I mean, you must know which level you're going to place yourselves on? What are you talking about? We need to have an idea of what this is going to cost. Surely you're well enough prepared to know what price you charge today?

This intervention may be read as reprimanding but, as is often the case when it comes to 'leadership', it can also be seen in other terms, as educational for instance, if slightly harshly expressed. Kim is pointing out the importance of the price and having a clear idea of this fundamental issue. But even if leadership as the management of meaning does not necessarily call for softness, perhaps this is more a case of Kim favouring exercising power: co-workers probably feel that Kim is inclined towards KITA (kick in the ass). There was no evidence of Kim's espoused trademark – coaching – or claimed tendency to give co-workers 'a very free hand'. She could, in principle, have been more interested in their thinking, experience of problems, and reasons for prioritizing issues other than the price. At least we could image something less than an opposite move from the espoused coaching-participation. If Kim then still saw the price question as vital she could try 'leadership manipulation' to coach them into zooming in on the price question. Instead of pursuing that line of action a more direct, power-oriented approach was taken, despite Kim's claim to dislike this approach and her emphasis on the need to listen to people.

Another case gives a similar impression of practice as disconnected from the espoused ideal. In a discussion with a project leader, Robyn, who was responsible for ending the product that Kim as a line manager is responsible for, Kim starts by stressing that the project leader has done a good job, thus supporting the project leader in the work.

> I must say, Robyn, I feel very comfortable having you in charge here. I think that you are lifting every … and see what's underneath, you are involving everybody, I really appreciate that.

But signs that Kim believes that Robyn is doing far too much without realizing it soon contradicts the satisfaction she expressed. Kim also gives Robyn some advice about how to make sure the project avoids criticism or failure – perhaps with the intention of trying to steer the project:

Kim: One risk when you do something this big, and as cost-functional as this, is that you will probably be criticized from time to time.

Robyn: I accept that.

Kim: You have my full support, but I think that you are taking a very broad teacher role here; we can never be 100 per cent. We need to clarify to the organization that this is much, much, much more than we ever did before. Let's try to capture as much as possible, but there will be things that are not handled correctly, and then we will have to do some of the work again.

Robyn: I see it pretty much like any other project. There are failures in the testing or in the parts, and then you have to reschedule or plan to do something more special. And recover.

Kim: But this is worse, because you are the first. This is not like any ordinary development of a product, because we have a lot of experience in this area. This is something totally new, and I think you are fully aware of this. I think that we need to push that in the organization. Some will be captured under the communication; the expectation level should be set right. I will definitely make sure that the engineering department here in the city fully understands that this is a huge task. But the expectations ...

While on the one hand Kim expresses full confidence in Robyn, on the other she appears to think Robyn is unaware of fundamental difficulties. Kim believes it is important to explain the situation and how Robyn should act, and does not really accept Robyn's relaxed and confident attitude. Robyn appears to be calm and sees the project as being like any other, while Kim is concerned about Robyn's broad teaching role and that the whole thing is 'much, much, much more than we ever did before' and 'something totally new'. Even after Robyn has responded that this is like any other project, Kim claims that 'This is something totally new, and I think you are fully aware of this', directly contradicting Robyn's statement. The assertion about how things are, the helpful tips and raising the awareness of problems are central. There is also a fairly strong effort to direct Robyn. Kim says 'we need to ... clarify... push that' but this seems to signal what *Robyn* should do. There is no coaching, only efforts to do directive leadership (or perhaps rather management). Whether Kim's directed style is motivated or not, is hard to tell. It may be a motivated deviation from Kim's espoused ideal, and it is not a clear contradiction of the participation ideal either – as Kim's tries to influence meaning and make Robyn see issues in a particular light, rather than directly instructing her to do something specific.

But it is interesting that during the eight meetings and interactions we observed we did not notice much, if any, of the coaching style or the participation ideal that Kim often preaches, or at least sees as the guiding star for being a good leader. Kim dislikes a leadership style based on strong leader-driven work, where 'you think you know best because you're the manager', as she puts it. But Kim actually appeared to have little doubt that she knew best and insisted on expressing that view in her acts as a leader (or HIP) in the two episodes above. Nor was the ideal of giving people very free hands obviously expressed in practice.

We can see that while Kim saw coaching-participation leadership as the core approach and the occasional – sporadically motivated – departures from that as a good mix, the actual mix involved peripheral coaching-participation, and 'the manager knows best' approach at the core. In Kim's case there are signs of reflexivity when thinking about leadership and its complexities, including the limits to coaching, but the practice often contradicted this and indicated that non-reflexivity was guiding a great deal of the practice.

A principal implementing standards and shaping things up in a school

A US state dealing with school problems decided to implement increased standardization of the curriculum and instructions. It also established rigid benchmarks for student promotion and threatened to close low-scoring schools (Hallett, 2007, 2010). In this context, Mrs Kox was seen as a rising star. As an assistant principal at an improving school, she learned the business ideal of accountability. She loved this education because 'business people have a different orientation to improvement. They have a better sense of urgency' (Interview).[2]

The school board believed Kox was a good match for accountability mandates because 'she's very opinionated and has very high standards'. She was seen as 'very tough' and as having a 'no nonsense' approach (Interview). Test scores played a role in the decision to hire Kox. The school performed better than the city average but fell short compared to its sister school Baxter Elementary. Importantly, the board also viewed Kox as a strong leader because she guided the school into the new era of accountability, had exhaustive knowledge of education policy, was tireless, and held firm to her convictions. She emphasized that she thought results, rather than being liked by everybody, to be central for her work. Senior management gave her outstanding reviews and enthusiastically renewed her contract. Excellent leadership, one may think. But going beneath the surface reveals a more complicated story.

Costen was a large school, with 90 teachers and 1,600 students from diverse backgrounds. For years, the school responded to heterogeneous student needs by creating a system of high autonomy and low surveillance. Teachers created their own work routines. Some teachers were rigid authoritarians; others used reward systems to promote good behaviour. Many relied on a teacher-driven, skills-centred style; others used an inquiry-based method. The teachers at the school described the previous principals in very positive terms: 'they hired good people who they let do their jobs …' (Interview). And despite an increased emphasis on accountability, teachers could 'do their jobs' without intervention.

For Kox accountability provided a 'rational theory of how' schools should operate. She told the researcher:

> They'd [the teachers] been running the school without a principal for six months. Everyone took full advantage of running in every direction that they chose to. Well, that's not going to happen with this administration. [Referring to teachers flooding her with reimbursement requests]. If you want to make any purchases with a reason, you submit a roster of what you need to purchase and you get approved and then you get reimbursed. I mean, if you allow no system in place, 100 people out there doing shopping on their own … can't function that way. (Interview, in Hallett, 2010, p. 60)

Kox liked to get involved in the work and say, 'What's going on here? This is what we're going to have to do', rather than just allowing the teacher to do it. She gave flesh to accountability through her surveillance of classroom and student management, grading, and curriculum and instruction. While previous administrations rubber-stamped grades, Kox scrutinized them. Recalling a meeting, Kox said teachers were 'panicking' and that one was 'very worried because she had never seen anyone review her grade book for the last 26 years' (Interview).

Teachers felt frustrated, many resigned, and over time, as they created meanings around the changes to draw upon as a means for political action, they tried to protect the prior order by mobilizing against Kox. They gathered a large number of complaints into a 119-page volume titled Turmoil at 'KOX'sten School.

> I plastered her [Kox's] name all over this city. Everybody I could think of I sent that book to. And the book was just magnificent ... It had, oh God, maybe a good 40 odd letters from various teachers... And through the whole process, all I kept hearing was 'You can't make principals change ... Let's just ride her out and eventually she'll be gone.' I was just like 'No, no.' The reason it's so difficult to combat leadership is that everybody runs scared. (Interview) (Hallett, 2010, p. 65)

One may view Kox as a slave to accountability, as an empowered entrepreneur who brought accountability to Costen, fighting conservative and sloppy teachers spoiled by lack of accountability, as a task-oriented despot (the teachers' view), or as an intrepid leader (the board's view) (Hallett, 2010, p. 67).[3]

It is thus not easy to find the optimal, 'correct' view of Kox's leadership – if indeed that is the best term for capturing her work. The resistance from the teachers' side can be viewed as an outcome of being spoiled and too autonomous, partly an outcome of previous management at the school, which could be described as laissez-faire, delegatory, trust-based or supportive of autonomy. Opposition does not necessarily mean that a manager is wrong or practising ineffective or unmotivated leadership. For example, acting as a psychotherapist or a party-host may not be the most appropriate leadership ideals if the task is to rapidly improve performance. However, if opposition is maintained or strengthened, then it is or becomes 'wrong' in the sense that it creates too much discontent and disturbance and most likely leads to less than optimal results.

The case suggests that there was little leadership in the sense that most teachers did not accept the idea of the management regime that the principal tried to implement. The teachers saw themselves as autonomous, working based on judgement, preferences and their own individual style. They were typical non-followers. They complied with requirements to some extent, but compliance was based more on what they saw as the exercise of power than rational management. One response was the use of counter-power. Willing followership and the acceptance of subordination gradually gave away to resistance and fighting. The idea was to get rid of the principal or at least to force her and senior levels to make significant compromises. Kox on her side had great faith in management and vigorously tried to get the teachers to work to the standards and tests as designed. There were some leadership efforts – trying to get teachers to accept the ideas and logic of moving from a laissez-faire, relaxed system to a culture of accountability and high standards. But this did not work and the management and power modes became dominant. Interestingly enough, the senior level, the school board, who were less familiar with the reception of Kox's style, very much saw Kox in leader terms: engaged, convincing, persistent with an ability to get people to follow.[4]

The case illustrates some un-reflective leadership effort. A particular management system was enthusiastically adopted with limited concern for organizational history and cultural context. Meanings clashed: the principal and school board viewed specific procedures, standards and measurements as carriers of accountability and the means to better results, while teachers saw them as rigid and serious restraints on professional judgement and viewed autonomy as they key to good results. Reflexivity would mean careful consideration of the meanings of those to be influenced, efforts to find a common ground of understanding based on negotiations of meanings as well as a willingness to evaluate and re-consider one's framework and ideals. Not much of this was apparent for the school principal in this case.

REFLEXIVE LEADERSHIP

A middle manager taking action

The case here is a middle level manager in a French bank who took action against what were seen as unfair and unproductive new assessment rules (Courpasson et al., 2012).[5] This was triggered by a board decision to punish two branch managers of small branches located in poor rural areas. A note had been sent to all 24 branch managers ranking them from best to worst. The note stressed shortcomings and asked for explanations.

Max, a young, well-educated, promising manager of a large branch, was shocked and saw this note as neglecting and violating the bank's – Bank – traditions: 'They spent time in meetings talking about trust and commitment and cooperation and friendship, the power of the "Household" (the company) and all of a sudden, wham, a cold note identifying two branches'. Max was convinced that an outsider, more precisely from the marketing department, had written the note.

In Bank's organizational culture, branches accounted for their results collectively rather than as individual entities. People talked about a culture of sharing things, 'we do not really compete with each other; we strive to find germane places for everybody', one manager said. In that 'communitarian' context, the note broke these tacit agreements.

Max very quickly understood that the note revealed emerging tensions between two commercial cultures within Bank: those of the 'street savvy banker' and the 'skilled head of market segment'. He decided to act because he thought that it was 'ethically unfair and overly political' to identify two specific underperforming branches. He contacted six close colleagues to obtain their opinions. Max carefully chose these colleagues on the basis of personal affinities, but also, as he said, as representing 'some of the best performing branches. I did not want to give the impression that weak fellows were protecting themselves from the necessities of doing a job. On the contrary, the best among the best were saying "no" to what we considered a personal attack'. Max's colleagues quickly agreed to join him. They formed what Courpasson et al. (2012) call an 'enclave', more precisely an enclave of resistance that opposes decisions arising from prevalent power systems and processes but still acts according to the systems' rules.

Frank, an enclave member, explained that Max's authority and charisma were important, together with the emerging sense of solidarity and collective action that was triggered by the note. Enclave mobilization also resulted from a refusal to let the new 'marketing people' impose their views on the CEO. Max took notes of enclave members' discussions and suggested that he write a synthesis that would be sent to the others for approval before it was sent to the CEO. He took the leadership because he was particularly aware of the cultural conflict, as he was at the centre of the branches' network. The group sent a 15-page response signed by the seven enclave members to top management, bypassing conventional hierarchical channels. In their report, they mainly elaborated on the fact that Marketing's note did not offer collaborative opportunities. In the introduction, they wrote, 'The initial note sounds authoritarian and strives to impose new criteria without having even discussed the issue with us. This is not acceptable'. Furthermore, the report mentions, 'We suggest that we discuss with the board the very important topic of branches' performance criteria'. They wanted to collaborate with the initiators of the system they opposed. However, they did not call for a truce; the report also reads, 'If no discussion is possible, we have decided that we would not proceed with annual evaluations of our local collaborators'. This is, in most corporate contexts, a strong message – a clear signal of willingness to use power.

The CEO initially responded angrily, finding this 'outrageous', but could not ignore the fact that something important was happening. He also realized that the resistance was not capricious: 'I knew they were regularly discussing, meeting together, and that they mobilized around their buddies. I also knew they made it a fundamental issue between them and the marketing director and staff. I did not want to encourage that but I understood that it was serious. We couldn't carry on as if nothing had happened'. (Courpasson et al., 2012, p. 808).

After some meetings, including with Max and the marketing director, the CEO decided to create a task force made up in an effort to establish a dialogue between two opposing groups of actors. Max was appointed leader of the task force. Part of the background to this was that the CEO interpreted Max's leadership and the formation of a resistance group as a result of the bank's specific culture – having people take initiatives, make autonomous decisions, and above all, take care of the company. All in all, the CEO began to see the resistance as credible and to accommodate it; from this perspective, he could easily read Max's leadership as proof of his involvement in the bank's community: 'Well, I wasn't surprised. I know him so well. He is simply the best'.

Eight months after the first meeting, Dan, the marketing manager, resigned and became regional head at another bank. He explains it as follows:

> That's not a thing we are used to, people contesting something not contestable. The fact was that a couple of branches were strikingly underperforming, and we wanted explanations from the managers. And they said no, and the boss was afraid of, I don't know, a strike or something. Moreover, the contest was led by a pretty influential guy, and the boss was not ready to have a fight with him. (Courpasson et al., 2012, p. 809)

Courpasson et al. highlight some elements of this successful intervention by subordinate managers. Enclave insurgency dramatized the situation; the enclave leader offered credible interpretations of events, prompting individuals to mobilize and helping the enclaves to form a strong group. This move led to a temporary re-alignment of the power relations at Bank. Sending a well-argued report not only allowed resisters to publicize their concerns, it also showed their willingness to take over the agenda. Although resisters acted with political subtlety and were able to justify their claims and offer concrete solutions, they nevertheless addressed topics that were normally encoded as being in the top managers' power domain. Here the members of the enclave took on new roles.

After initial surprise and irritation, top managers responded to these actions by retaking the lead and organizing further work. The CEO eventually decided to coproduce new policies in line with the new configuration of roles resulting from the productive resistance processes. Thus, at Bank, Max played a more influential role in the production of new assessment criteria than the marketing experts did. He had to defend the enclave members' view and demonstrate that he was acting for the collective good. The task force helped the CEO to restore his position as 'the boss'. It also smoothed some tensions that arose from growing opposition between the branches and central marketing, although the marketing director resigned (Courpasson et al., 2012).

In this case Max worked highly reflexively. He carefully assessed the initial note and its significance in light of organizational culture. He also considered his own role and decided to transcend his formal mandate. He contacted people in his network, and discussed and evaluated his view on the subject matter. On finding that his colleagues shared the view he decided to act further. He invited people to join a group and was a primus motor and spokesperson for the group. This initiative together with Max as a peer with a leader role made him a central actor. Collective action based on aligned understanding and aligned objectives was key to the process. The people involved realized their formal subordinate position but this did not significantly affect their action, which was a strong effort to make an impact on the organization. Some use of power was mobilized to show top management that if they rejected the idea of seriously discussing issues there would be consequences – the refusal to carry out certain work. The group recognized the authority of the CEO and senior management, but were not overly compliant, aiming to form a temporary relationship that was more MIP- than LIP-like. Also the CEO was forced/agreed to take a MIP (medium influencing position) in relationship to Max and his group. The establishment of a group responsible for new policies meant that the group mode of organizing also characterized corporate management issues beyond the resistance enclave work. In this case Max acted carefully in a reflexive way: transcending his role, working horizontally as well as vertically, exercising authority, but also showing respect for hierarchy (the manager-subordinate relationship) and balancing group- and individual-based modes of organizing. Networks and selective use of power were also part of his set of considerations and doings, moving outside of a follower position in order to have an impact upwards on the entire company. One may say that Max 'MIPified' hierarchical relations in this project.

A head of a hospital clinic dealing with suicide and economic issues

Another example of reflexive leadership is Stella, a physician and head of a hospital clinic with 130 employees. Her everyday behaviour and decisions are informed by careful ethical and cultural reflection and she tries to have a consistent impact on her staff in terms of meanings, values and thinking. She sometimes works very long hours, and is engaged both in management and also in everyday patient care, partly to have close contact with and first-hand knowledge of the quality of the care provided. She is convinced that this will allow her to influence the staff in a better and more credible way than managers who concentrate solely on management/leadership and stay out of medical work. Despite a heavy workload, Stella takes time with terminal patients when the staff are – or pretend to be – busy or emotionally stressed by the anxieties of a lonely death. Of course, Stella is not unaffected by this either and has less time than anyone else, but she thinks this is important in order to set a good example, taking her leadership role seriously. She tries to take time to answer any questions from nurses, even if they do not concern the patients she is in charge of. She is aware that employees pay attention to what she does, at least if it goes beyond the conventional behaviour of people in her position.

Stella communicates consistently that the clinic needs to operate in a cost-efficient way and requires people to think through and justify expensive and not obviously necessary purchases and use of materials – explaining that if the clinic does not use the entire budget it will most likely lead to another part of the hospital functioning better because the resources will be reallocated to them. As Christmas gifts for the staff she bought products from charity organizations supporting developing countries. For catering for the clinic's educational meetings including all staff, she asked for an ecological buffet and brown bags to save the food that was not consumed. All this signals an ethical awareness and in particular a strong and systematic influence going beyond conventional efforts to do leadership. There are strong signals to encourage people to think beyond a narrow horizon. Of course, much of this is not uncontroversial. Hospital management often asks heads of clinics to concentrate on management. Many believe budgets should be spent. The responses nevertheless indicate that most of the staff have very high opinions of Stella and celebrate her and her work. Members of her staff proposed Stella as the female leader of the year in Swedish healthcare and she received an honorary recognition. Employees often respond to her with praise and appreciation (e.g. with emails saying 'you are the best' and even 'we love you').

It is worth noting the stamina, consistency, reflection, originality, sacrifice, integrity, willingness to deviate from expectations and conventions, the taking of some risks (of subordinates' collective or hospital management's disapproval), and the use of symbolically effective means, that is, acts and talk that are congruent and make a difference. The influence is almost exclusively about everyday reframing and not about programmes and campaigns or the allocation of specific resources for organizational development work. Change is done as an integrated part of managerial and medical work. Stella clearly deviates from many of the managers we have studied, many of whom are confused about their leadership, seem to have moderate impact and often cause some irritation among subordinates.

Next we find two examples of Stella's specific leadership interventions, both in the form of email correspondence to all employees in the unit:

Illustration 1. Dealing with a sad event

Hello everyone,

During the last month we have had a patient with severe heart failure. He has been cared for on several occasions and has also – against our advice – discharged himself from the hospital. Last night he chose to go home against the advice of the night nurse and this morning he was found in his home, he had chosen to take his own life.

I have spoken with many of you today. But rather than having a general meeting with the whole clinic you can come to me to talk if you want. Of course, we shall talk with each other, support each other and discuss the patient and the care he received on the one hand, but also how fragile life can be and how difficult it is to choose life everyday, with all that comes with that in terms of joy and pain, on the other.

Every year around 1,500 [Swedish] people choose to take their life – there's probably an unreported number of suicides that is hidden behind here as well, car accidents, drowning, etc. Of these, only a minor part, 20%, have had any contact with health care, mostly psychiatry or primary care. This means that most people that take their lives have not talked to anyone about their intentions before committing the act. One often talks about the calm – even joy – that some people with depressions and years of anxiety can experience when the decision to commit suicide is taken.

Physically severely ill patients have a statutory right to refrain from life-supporting treatment. Patients that are in the end stages of a neurologic disease, for example, can receive help with closing a necessary respiratory care. This is not seen as 'active euthanasia' but part of the relief that the palliative care offers.

The patient in our case had several very difficult somatic disorders and a bad prognosis for survival with active treatment and had previously chosen not to participate in hospital care. Subsequently he had a clear mind about what he wanted to do with his life. Suicides can be explained by looking at patients' previous life choices.

Even so this comes with sorrow and anxiety for all of us, especially those that have had contacts with the patient during the time of care. Many thoughts come to us – about the meaning of life, about death and about our own professional role. We will certainly need to talk a lot about these things with each other.

In this situation it is important that you remember your confidentiality. Of course you should talk about this with your dear and near. They need to know the cause of your ruminations and downheartedness. However, talk about it without revealing details of age, gender, disease, ways of committing suicide or other things that are protected by confidentiality. Under no circumstances should this be spread in social media. And you should refrain from talking to people outside your family or health professionals – because then we surpass ethical limits as well as what is lawful.

I will report this to the head physician who decides about what should be done and the clinic will perform an incident report. I will also follow this up with the patients' relatives. You are welcome to talk to me about this at any time.

Take care of yourself! And continue to do a good job as you always do!

Illustration 2. Underscoring the productive use of resources

Dear all,

I'm sorry that you receive this several weeks after its completion. It needed checking and analysis. The conclusion is that we improved the result with more than 12 million SEK (about 1.3 million euro) in relation to budget! The numbers are unbelievable ... The difference between the budgeted and factual cost is almost 10% less, or more than 13 million.

What lies behind this?

This has primarily to do with that we implemented the obliged cuts in staff very fast and that had an impact over the whole year. This involved close colleagues that had to leave their positions with us – and that is always sad! – but for them personally it meant a possibility of speeding up the process of getting a new job. If we had waited it might have been more difficult for them to get jobs they wished for, and that would have increased worries and perhaps also been a significantly higher adjustment for those that are not with us anymore.

We also implemented consumption changes related to our environmental objectives. We had less waste of food and more control over the laundry and storage in general. We also significantly reduced the cost for staff due to vacancies. It has been difficult to find temporary nurseries during the whole year. We also had less administrative staff.

Expenses for drugs decreased significantly as we have been good at changing routines in how we manage drugs. This is also due to the physicians increasingly writing prescriptions for generic drugs ...

Besides this we also do a lot of voluntary work during our leisure time. The clinic management doesn't demand this but the commitment that you all show that makes this clinic so incredibly fantastic contributes to our growing as persons and as a clinic.

Why is finance important?

You have all heard the expression "monopoly money", "it disappears in a black hole" and all kinds of foul expressions in relation to finance in the public sector. It seems that it is bad to talk about being financially effective but I say once more: All the money that can be saved through more effective ways of working will contribute to more healthcare where it is needed. To spend money without any gains for the patients means to withdraw care and treatment for someone else. We have shown that it is possible to make sustainable savings that doesn't mean that we are all "just running faster". Our organization contributes to less stress and to increased control over our own work situation. It is also nice to avoid saving on things that are beneficial for the patients. We don't have to suspend activities that we think are necessary and meaningful. We are not subjected to "moral stress" that may occur when you are forced to make savings that affect patients.

You are all part of the reason that this has been successful and that we continue to develop as a clinic – while also having so much fun.

Thanks – once more – for the past year and for being so tremendously fantastic!

Often managers communicate good messages in orchestrated settings – CEOs may for example be excellent at giving a PowerPoint presentation in front of a large audience. Carefully crafted messages may be much better than communication in everyday or non-planned situations, where counterarguments are raised or unexpected issues turn up. Emails may be more impressive than the average interactions. But in Stella's case the emails are in line with other impressions of her practices.

Comments

These examples of leadership interventions show a high degree of reflexivity. Stella carefully thinks about the wider picture and at the same time focuses on the core issues. The frame is broad and considerate in both cases.

In the first illustration she puts the issue – the suicide – into a perspective which is both societal and existential. She confirms the anxieties, sorrow and possible feelings of guilt or inadequacy of those involved, but also tries to reduce them by putting things in a wider context. She points out that the patient probably knew what he was doing and, if so, the sad outcome was probably inevitable. She establishes credibility and trust by mentioning that she also had met the patient, but can move between empathy with him and the people that nurtured him, putting the case in a broader and more distancing context. Stella reduces the drama and emotional charge of the suicide by using knowledge and experience of people who have committed suicide.

The intervention thus demonstrates empathy and support and offers a framework for a more intellectual handling of the situation. Stella also expresses openness and willingness to talk with those struggling with the events and the general need for care and support. The email also highlights the legal issues and how internal procedures are used to make sure mistakes are avoided.

The second illustration focuses on something that can be viewed as the opposite of the suicide example, at least topic-wise. Positive news about budget outcomes is almost as far as you can get from dealing with the death of a patient. Still, there are dimensions that are similar in how Stella is addressing the issues.

Stella emphasizes that this is a shared concern. Everyone is contributing, everyone should think carefully about these issues and everyone plays a part in the outcome. The systematic thoughtfulness about how to use resources is underscored. Difficult decisions have to be made, but making them early is better than waiting. Stella makes people aware of revenues and costs, and highlights uncertainties, contradictions and fluctuations, but underscores that the clinic is not a victim to external forces such as allocated resources; they can do quite a lot to control the situation. She also underscores that many people do a lot of voluntary work, which is not required, but doing so contributes to making the clinic so extraordinarily fantastic. The norm of doing something extra is thus promoted and linked to the excellent performance and reputation of the clinic. This and its employees stand out and should be seen as a strong source of pride for all involved.

Stella also emphasizes the significance of a sound economy. Saving money for the benefit of other aspects of healthcare in the county and not using the budget for herself is sometimes viewed as stupid. In the email the opposite view is powerfully expressed. It is irresponsible and unethical to spend all the money allocated if it is not necessary, as this means fewer resources are available for healthcare somewhere else. Stella tries to expand the meaning horizon and highlight a fundamental ethical principle of taking broad responsibility and considering the ethical aspects if one thinks about the unapparent consequences of actions.

Stella also expresses warm and positive feelings towards others for contributing to excellent results, mainly in terms of the financials, to very positive developments in the organization, to a positive and joyful work climate, and for being fantastic people. The latter may seem ingratiating and an exaggeration but given the credible overview of the accomplishment it comes out as a reasonable assessment – and probably one that triggers a wealth of positive emotions and identity-responses among recipients of the mail.

As we read the two examples above, they are exemplary in terms of leadership as management of meaning. There are elements such as clarifying meanings and understandings, underscoring important values and priorities, emphasizing community and 'we' feeling, taking broad responsibility, combining emotional support with knowledge and intellectual clarity and sharpness. The leadership is anchored in accomplishments and practices and avoids the usual clichés and standardized jargon often used in leadership contexts. Reflexivity is also shown in the handling of quite difficult topics in broadly similar ways. There is situation-specificity – dealing with an emotionally difficult problem and respectively a positive budget outcome – but also a framework and a style that are supportive of an organization scoring highly in terms of both care and emotional support on the one hand, and financial effectiveness on the other. Stella shows examples of all the 5Ps: there is a sense of a low-profile vision in terms of having an excellent, cost-efficient clinic, an underscoring of important values like care and economy (broader responsibility), emphasis on positive spirit and reasons for it, acknowledgement of the emotional strains of the difficult work and time for people in need of her. She is very pedagogical in explaining how things hang together and clarifying meanings around patients' suffering and choices as well as the significance of always being cautious and thoughtful about costs. Her communication stimulates the broadening of mindsets and consideration of meanings and values outside conventional concerns.

SUMMARY

In this case we have addressed two examples of non-reflexive leadership and two of reflexive leadership. There are no formulae for the former or the latter. It is also important to consider that reflexive is not always viewed as much better than non-reflexive, at least not by everyone. The superiors of Max and Stella experience frustrations that they are sometimes difficult because they are not just loyal followers, they take initiative and are inclined to disobey if they consider superiors' ideas and decisions wrong while Kim is viewed as a reasonable and good manager by her superiors and Kox received rewards and praise for being an excellent leader from her superiors.

Our point is not to evaluate the entire spectrum of leadership qualities, which is a complicated issue as there are so many criteria and ideals and a wealth of various viewpoints from different actors. We can note that Kox was very committed, consistent and followed a strong line of action to work against the laissez-faire ideas that had characterized the school. But given the strong resistance of the teachers her attitude appears rigid and tunnel-visioned. There is a one-sided belief in the right approach combined with a limited ability to critically assess this and consider alternatives to the strict implementation of the preferred management model and close scrutiny of people sticking to it. The strong reliance on management means that alternatives such as a high degree of autonomy and/or perhaps group work do not really enter the picture for Kox. There are also shortcomings in terms of leadership. Leadership – as compared to management, power and horizontal modes of organizing – is not necessarily to be preferred as the only or main mode of organizing. Strong efforts to influence the ideas, values and understandings of the subordinates would had been one option. Here, space for mutual influencing of ideas and adjustments could have led to a shared set of understandings.

The case of Kim partly illustrates an opposite problem. Non-reflexivity is mainly a matter of contradiction between espoused ideals (coaching/participation) and practice (directing/manager domination). Little serious thought is given to leadership guiding work. Leadership – to the extent Kim is doing this rather than using management and power – appear to be more situation-driven and erratic than integrated and systematic.

There are many sources and modes of non-reflexivity but, as illustrated by these two cases, two common ones are being caught in a specific model for HIPs, respectively being disconnected and fragmented in the relationship between leadership ideals and practice. According to our extensive experience these two modes are common among managers (Sveningsson & Alvesson, 2016).

On the more positive side, the two cases of reflexive leadership both illustrate the virtue of broadly and carefully thinking through one's position and line of influencing and thus acting in a fairly systematic and focused way, being aware of problems. Reflexivity means the consideration of a set of ideals and logics. In Max's case it is a matter of doing leadership, being an active follower/subordinate, remaining relatively flexible about the followership (downplaying but acknowledging subordination) and being prepared to be autonomous in the way he thinks and acts. The mobilization of network resources and group work both contributed to the effectiveness of the initiative. In one sense Max used a wide set of the 6Ms, including power and group work, in a clever way and thus demonstrated the type of high-level reflexivity argued for in this book. One could even say that Max demonstrated and confirmed the value of our framework.

The other reflexive case, Stella, illustrates superior leadership in a more confined way – partly because the material we focus on concerns specific interventions. These demonstrate the consideration of a wide set of key elements (emotions, knowledge and cognitions, showing care, ethics and effectiveness, focusing on the performance of the units) but also the broader picture. Stella's communications influence an organizational culture where thoughtfulness, the need to consider meanings and values, and to form community and identification are key. These values are focused on but also enacted in the communication. Leadership drawing upon and combining the 5Ps is clearly demonstrated in a way that is integrated, coherent and provides direction. There are strong ingredients of the pedagogue, the pastor, the psychotherapist and the prophet. There is less of the party-host – the topics do not entirely invite this P to be so visible – but the positive and joyful spirit associated with being part of such a fantastic clinic also exhibits some party-hosting impact.

NOTES

1. Three of these cases have been published elsewhere and are also the result of other scholars' empirical research. The first case 'Kim' has previously been described in Alvesson and Jonsson (2016). Regarding the second case 'Kox' and the third case 'Max', credits should go to Hallett (2010) and Courpasson et al. (2012) respectively.
2. All empirical material is from Hallett (2010).
3. The remaining text in this section represent the authors' interpretations and comments, going beyond Hallett's text.
4. It is possible that the resistance to Kox's style was reinforced by her being a female. As mentioned in Chapter 3, there are some indicators that females have more problems when appearing authoritarian. However, as most of the teachers, including the most negative ones, were females, there is no easy or straightforward gender explanation for the resistance to Kox (Hallett, 2007).
5. This section is based on Courpasson et al. (2012). The final paragraph presents the comments of the authors of this book.

13

The Reflexive Follower (LIP)

Leadership is relational and acceptance of a follower-position is a necessary element of leadership. We briefly addressed this in Chapter 7 and continue in this chapter with an additional focus on reflexive followership. Whenever we address leadership the followership dimension is more or less included, but leadership talk often implicitly encourages people to take the leader view. Leadership is viewed as a matter for the leader. There are therefore good reasons to highlight followership, regardless of whether one views leadership as predominantly leader-driven, a co-construction involving both HIPs and LIPs or mainly follower-driven. The role of followership is more significant according to the last two views. But even passive followers are still crucial as their degree of responsiveness or non-responsiveness decides the fate of leadership efforts. LIPs need to notice and be impressed by the authenticity of or let themselves be transformed by the HIP trying to do authentic or transformational leadership.

In this chapter we initially mobilize our overall model as an antidote to what still dominates leadership studies and, in particular, the leadership industry: the view of followers as sheep. Following that we discuss how people supposed to be compliant with followership can make informed choices about this, both within and outside a followership position. Such informed choices are key in reflexivity. Central here is often how followers manage their relations – vertically and horizontally.

COUNTERACTING THE SHEEP VIEW

Often leadership theories and even more so the leadership industry embrace what could be referred to as the 'sheep view' on followership. The leader leads, the others follow almost mindlessly and without much will or ability. The idea is that the leader is the centre of the organizational universe and has far-reaching impact. Of course everybody realizes that leadership is about interaction and relations, but the initiative and force is typically seen as strongly with the leader. In most leadership and management education or development, individual managers are taken out of their normal work context and placed in an educational setting where they are supposed to be equipped with knowledge, tools, feedback, group discussions and generally improved abilities. They are then sent back to their workplaces and supposed to act in new or improved ways, thereby creating positive and significant effects. The subordinates are expected to be led in a new way, and to respond and improve accordingly – becoming more energetic, confident, happy and collaborate better. Their improvements are viewed as an outcome of the improved leadership accomplished through the education and development of the manager's leadership skills.

Sometimes people who advocate this view allow for variation in terms of leadership and followership. Roles may not be consistent or rigid. According to a popular slogan, everybody is a leader; sometimes you lead, sometimes you follow. How true – but quite a lot of the time you do neither; you interact horizontally. In the leadership industry, including some 'progressive' leadership versions, there is a one-dimensionality in terms of leading/following, where always everything 'good' is viewed as 'leadership'. But we do most organizational activities without being directly engaged in leadership or followership. We adapt to organizational bureaucracy, think and act in line with organizational culture, occupational and technical knowledge, professional ideals and requirements from people around us. Many of these people are not necessarily leaders or followers and are more likely colleagues, customers, suppliers, clients, pupils, patients, etc. Leadership may play a role in all this – a HIP arguing for worker integrity rather than treating the customer as a king may affect the degree of customer orientation and associated service level when interacting with a grumpy customer – but it is not necessarily highly significant.

As leadership is about influencing people, how those who are supposedly influenced understand and respond to the intentions and behaviour of the HIP aiming to exercise leadership is central. All this means that we need to be cautious about the sheep view. Most people easily express agreement with this standpoint: of course people at work are not sheep, subordinates are active and competent. The literature talks about more or less mature, active followers. But the fundamental assumptions and framing within leadership literature tell another story. Most leadership thinking still departs from at least a soft version of the followers-as-sheep view, illustrated by the emphasis of the great majority of the leadership industry on single managers being targeted for development/improvement. Implicit and dominant assumptions are based on the peculiar idea that the leader leads; others are followers that follow. The entire vocabulary reflects and invites an assumption of sheep-like non-leaders. So in practice most enthusiasts for leadership share some version of the sheep view.

And it would be naive to reject this altogether. As with most metaphors, followers as sheep may sometimes offer insights. Sometimes people do take strongly asymmetrical and relatively passive follower positions. Some people have fantasies about and strong expectations of senior people, in particular in top positions (Gabriel, 1997). Crowds cheering for political leaders are common. In companies junior managers look up to charismatic and powerful CEOs and are strongly responsive. As a manager in a US firm somewhat brutally expressed sensitivity to the senior person's will and messages, 'When the boss goes to the toilet we all get the shits' (Jackall, 1988, p. 23). So the sheep metaphor is not necessarily wrong or misleading but the general idea of the leader as the shepherd and the others as the sheep is not always the most informative.

And when subordinates seem to act like sheep, one may ask, why is this and, more productively, what can be done about it? As we have tried to clarify, there are often other potential positions than that of the follower. Effective organizing often calls for people to think carefully about alternative modes of organizing, and from the LIP point of view to consider both alternatives to leadership (ELR) and alternatives within leadership relationships (ILR). An ideal to be considered and promoted is reflexivity *within* and *beyond* a follower positioning.

As an aside, the sheep metaphor may also be used to illuminate much executive and manager behaviour. Jan Wallander (2002), presented at the very beginning of the book, remarked that most CEOs he knows are very fashion-oriented ('like teenage girls when it comes to new jeans') and inclined to follow the example of others. Wallander compares executives to a group of sheep chewing grass in a field. Then one sheep learns that it's grassier on the other side of the hill, so he goes over. After 15 minutes the other sheep are also there, all chewing grass in the new spot. And there is a strong tendency that managers, consultants, and HR workers jump on the newest leadership fashion and imitate one another.

It may sound harsh, but perhaps the leader-sheep 'leading' follower-sheep is not an entirely unfair picture of parts of contemporary organizational life. The idea could be used as input for reflection in many organizations. Are we sometimes more sheep-like than we would like to think? Thoughtlessness is a strong element in organizational life (Alvesson & Spicer, 2016).

But, and this is the main point of this section, followers are not necessarily best viewed as sheep compared to a leader-shepherd, who is assumed to be superior in terms of abilities and drive.

FOLLOWERSHIP AND CHOICE

In this book we have emphasized that leadership/followership is partly about voluntary compliance when it comes to those doing the following, that is, LIPs seeing themselves as followers rather than 'just' subordinates, colleagues, peers. Followership is not necessarily enthusiastic and committed, but there is still acceptance of the relationship and a degree of positive reception. As argued throughout the book, the LIP as a follower is prepared to accept ideas, values, meanings communicated by the HIP, i.e. the leader. Willingly or reluctantly you may realize that you are not as smart, experienced, creative, well educated, rhetorically skilled or have as good an overview as your manager or an informal authority with much to say. As a follower you tend to be convinced and/or recognize the significance of shared meanings and understandings and the role of a HIP, that is a leader, in having a strong say about these. One may 'define the leader/follower dyad as only one in which each accepts his or her role with apparent willingness …' (Seers & Chopin, 2012, p. 61). The more willingness the more followership.

It is reasonable to consider the response not only within the relationship as a whole – with more or less fixed positions – but also in specific interactions (leadership acts), where every interaction in principle provides followers with the opportunity to be a follower – or respond in another way.

As much of this is not conscious it cannot fully be a theme for consideration – many interactions have to be run quickly and smoothly and people at work do not have the time or cognitive resources to think carefully about all of them. Most things we do are habitual or routine. But the nature of the overall relationship as well as more significant interactions and episodes could – and we think *should* – be targeted for more conscious reflection and thus choices. The definition of leadership (a leadership relationship) could then include the idea that there is an acceptance of the leadership effort by a follower in many, perhaps even most, interactions. The follower is then defined as someone who regularly or at least frequently takes a followership position when exposed to leadership acts or practices. Of course, sometimes this position is not taken – the follower rejects some leadership interventions, as s/he may not follow all the time. This can be a matter of resistance, neglect or simply other concerns taking over. Often there is also a degree of interaction and mutual influence. Still, a leadership process means those in a followership position responding positively to the influencing efforts of the leader.

Key in order to make the leadership relationship productive is the reflexive orientation of not only the HIP but also the LIP. As emphasized, leadership is always about a leader/follower relationship; without a high degree of alignment in the relationship there is not so much functioning leadership, only aspirations and efforts. Followership is more or less reflexive. Our book aims to support 'more' and counteract 'less' reflexivity. Therefore, we like to promote the reflexive follower as an ideal. This means selective and careful choice in terms of both the degree of the influencing position taken and its nature. Questions to be carefully considered by the LIP may then include: Are you mainly influenced or do you (also) do a high degree of influencing? What type of LIP position appears to be appropriate – and/or avoided? What type of responsibility is reasonable?

There is less free choice when it comes to the alternative LIP positions, that is, subordination or target of power compared to followership. The HIP can insist on subordination or to some extent drive his or her will through, using formal and informal methods, in order to ensure obedience. This does not rule out some disobedience and the subordinate may be more or less subordinate, that is, being minimalistic or committed to subordination or putting up some or even considerable resistance (Collinson, 2005). But followership is something that includes a strong element of choice and thus calls for some reflection before taking this largely voluntary position in any given situation. The LIP may think that he/she does the job as required, but without accepting the manager's efforts to influence his/her thinking, values, mood or how s/he should see her/himself. Arguably, many accept and are subordinate in line with contracts and instructions, but without obviously being followers. The HIP can tell a LIP what to do, but never instruct him or her what to think or feel.

Of course often the choice of followership is not carefully reflected upon, but if there is a serious issue or something feels wrong then more conscious work is normally going on and sometimes there are departures from followership. A central element is thus the choice of the LIP *not* to do followership and to take another position instead: as a subordinate or as a target of power or in any of the horizontal organizing modes. The LIP may ask for instructions or specific targets, rather than meanings, values and coaching. LIPs may also want tough or resourceful people who take command, that is, power (as defined in this book) more than management or leadership. We will provide an example later in this chapter. The LIP may thus choose, at least to a certain degree, between the three LIP positions.

In very practical terms, imagine that the HIP suggests an idea or argues for a value, for example 'the customer is always right' and a supplementary construction of reality, such as creating meaning by saying that 'the competition in this business is extreme, like meeting a guy with a knife in an alley', to back up a claim about the importance of doing absolutely everything possible to keep the customers happy with the firm. There is no obviously specific instruction or use of power but rather an effort to get the LIP to buy into a particular meaning. But there is also an expectation that the LIP should act in line with this understanding and guideline. The LIP-responses may range from the reflexive follower to the compliant target of power and reason along the lines set out below.

The reflexive follower

The reflexive follower may think: Does this make sense? Should I take this on board? Even if these questions do not lead to sleepless nights they typically trigger a quick interpretation and possible reflection. Any leadership act is cognitively processed and is based on meaning.

Sometimes there is an immediate acceptance and followership positioning. The leadership act appears convincing, either because of the HIP's charisma, excellent idea or persuasive set up and tactics. There is a genuine follower response. Sometimes there is a more hesitant or thoughtful response. The LIP may not be spontaneously convinced. S/he may think: 'Perhaps not; this does not sound particularly convincing or helpful. But it may make sense if it is revised or if I get this explained further.' What are the options? One possibility is to raise doubts and ask for justification or to debate the issue and see what comes out of it? 'Perhaps the HIP can then convince me? Perhaps we need to have a dialogue around this?' Sometimes the HIP may offer strong arguments or there may be a revision of the leadership effort based on the co-construction of the issue at hand that the LIP (and HIP) then accepts and follows. If the formal subordinate has a strong say, s/he may actually do the leadership – becoming a HIP over even a formal superior or the influencing work might even be evenly distributed within a group of MIPs (bank manager Max in the previous chapter exemplifies this.) But we assume that the initiative and major influence comes from the superior or other HIP and that the LIP has a minor say, asking for justification or modification of the major message. So it leads to or reproduces followership.

If this is not the case the if LIP remains unconvinced and does not – after some serious reflection – take a follower position in a potential leadership relationship, that is, s/he is influenced in a voluntary way and may address the issue in one or several of the following ways.

The unreflexive follower

'Yes, of course my leader is right, as more or less always. I should not doubt the customer's wisdom or feel confused about what to do. If we lose customers we will soon be out of business. I will follow the idea of customer-orientation and everything will be simpler and more straightforward.'

The subordinate

'I do as the HIP suggests. She is the manager and has overall responsibility for this; she may have the full picture and it is easiest to do as suggested', thus interpreting the statement more as an instruction to be complied with by a subordinate. Whether the LIP fully believes or accepts it is not the issue. This is a *subordinate* positioning.

The target of power

'I reluctantly do as the HIP says. Even though it is proposed as a suggestion, the HIP is in a strong power position and I am eager not to be in an unfavourable position because the boss finds me difficult or something unwanted happens. She may lose her temper. My temporary contract may not be prolonged or I may be allocated some unattractive tasks if she does not see me as a good and loyal employee doing things in the "right" way. I have little choice but to comply, although I would prefer not to as I don't really believe in or care that much about following the stupid idea of customers as kings and do find the "guy with a knife in the alley" metaphor over the top.' This is a *target of power* position, quite different from the follower role (as we define it).

Moving outside a HIP-LIP relationship

Alternatively, a person may avoid the LIP position, divert attention away from the HIP and consider other sources of support instead: the group, another person in the network or thinking through issues with the help of her own judgement, reading a book or thinking through experiences and lessons from a similar situation. Here MIP or NIP replaces LIP, as in the case of Justin's and George's subordinates who were unwilling to be exposed to leadership in Chapter 10 and bank manager Max in Chapter 12. The person seeks more horizontal sources of guidance: values and ideas from the group or from an external person in the network; or decides to take the issue into his or her own hands. 'How much and what type of customer orientation is reasonable?' 'How harsh is competition really?' 'Should I be extremely customer focused (in one way or another) or do I work in line with my professional judgement of quality instead?' 'Can we afford to frustrate one or two customers?' Of course, such more horizontal work and guidance is not possible in all situations. But even if a HIP asks for something and backs this up with leadership, management and power (or a mix of them), often the LIP can use some other mode to deal with the situation.

Most managers would probably accept the performance of a disobedient subordinate if the person was somehow able to solve a problem with good results through other routes than doing precisely as the HIP suggested or directed.

LIPS GOVERNING HIPS?

Conventional thinking assumes that the HIP exercising power, doing management and leadership, influences LIPs in a fairly straightforward way. There is of course the co-construction literature, often blending various actors in a joint process of alignment, direction and other positive things, sometimes emphasizing leadership practice, for example relational leadership or shared leadership. But as pointed out before, in every case where there is no or limited asymmetry, we find the leadership vocabulary mis-leading and confusing. We prefer to talk about group processes instead, that is, a mode of organizing based mainly on horizontal influencing. Here (formal) managers and (formal) subordinates may be involved, but not in the capacity of HIP/LIP. Formal roles like manager and subordinate are ignored or downplayed. This tends to happen frequently – partly because (formal) subordinates are better informed about issues and argue their cases convincingly, making the interaction more or less symmetrical. This is a regular finding in careful observations of people at work, at least in certain Western contexts (e.g. Lundholm, 2011; Rennstam, 2007; Schaefer, 2014).

This is often missed in dominant texts, partly because the language used orders people into clear categories of leaders and followers and then this crude categorization is taken for granted in thinking. But also the superficiality and ideological bias of large parts of the academic literature mean that key aspects are missed. Questionnaires and interviews with only one party dominate and this leads to limited empirical material compared to more ambitious studies based on a combination of interviews with the various people involved and/or observations of leadership efforts in practice.

Still there is often also influencing across positions that are, on the whole, asym-metrical. An interesting idea is who is actually influencing whom, and who is doing so the most. A Swedish study asked managers 'who is your most significant source of feedback?' The answer was the subordinates (co-workers) (Kairos Futures/*Chef*, 2006). The managers in the study did not say their own superior managers, as the leadership literature would predict. As we are guided by feedback this is key to understanding leadership.

As feedback is a significant influencing mechanism, in particular in a leadership context, the finding indicates that leadership may not function as typically assumed, at least in some countries. Managers' sensitivity to subordinates' views reduces the scope for leaders to lead followers. One could actually argue for the opposite of leaders being on top of things and followers only responding. What is typically – at least within the leadership industry – viewed as leaders leading followers could be reversed: 'followers' (formal subordinates) 'lead' 'leaders' (formal managers). For example, 'followers' may more or less subtly direct HIPs into emotional support by approaching the HIP about problems or conflicts and asking for advice. Or they may agree upon and push for suggested lines of actions. Also a passive response – like falling asleep or looking bored or sceptical when targeted by a presumed transformational leader trying to sell the corporate vision – can be quite an influential activity. In the cases of George and Justin in Chapter 10, subordinate feedback made them take a rather passive and cautious position in terms of leadership and other HIP interventions.

At the same time, the significance of follower-feedback should not be overemphasized. As the reader realizes, there is enormous variation, and we need to consider the complexity and considerable differences when it comes to leadership and other modes of organizing. There are other elements in addition to feedback. Individual subordinates may be followers more than sources of feedback – or both at the same time. Feedback may only moderately change the recipient of the feedback – people are not always so sensitive or cannot change that much. The subordinates being the most important source of feedback may be an outcome of there being so many more of them than the manager's own outnumbered superior(s). Ten subordinates may offer much more and much better feedback than a single superior manager. Often subordinates have rather different interests and views, so they do not necessarily form a coherent whole; instead their feedback may be varied, inconsistent and vague. This limits how much the LIP can steer the HIP.

Nevertheless, it is important to note that managers typically – once again in some cultures or industrial or professional contexts – are sensitive to the views of their subordinates. In particular, followership is important and constitutes a great deal of the leadership.

The reflexive follower is not only careful about specific interactions and contributes in a thoughtful way, but also does quite a lot in terms of the formation of leadership relationships and/or the HIP-engagement in other modes of organizing. The six modes of organizing are part of the repertoire of the subordinate employee's *influencing positionings*. The LIP (or MIP) then provides feedback or influences in other ways so that the wanted form or combination of forms of modes of organizing is realized or at least encouraged. S/he seldom has full discretion, but through his/her own acts the LIP can try to move in the preferred direction. Some steering from below is typical and can to greater or lesser degrees be thoughtful, systematic, persuasive and influential.

This can be done both vertically and horizontally, in line with the 6Ms. *Vertically* the HIP is approached by the LIP who is trying to create or facilitate the right mode of organizing. The subordinate employee may take a rather clear but not passive LIP position, and indicate to the HIP the value and relevance of a specific relationship. This can follow the HIP/LIP pattern, but can also involve group work, autonomy and networks. One asks for leadership/management/power that supports the mode one finds relevant and superior. This may involve autonomy – minimal oversight, delegating, mild result-checking management – or (temporary) leadership aiming to support self-sufficient individuals, or group work or the use of networks. One may for example ask for delegation or permission or resources to use network resources (e.g. contacting people outside the chain of hierarchy or requesting money to go to professional conferences). Alternatively, one may ask for more leadership, better management or the exercise of power. The latter is often perhaps addressed in other terms or directed more to others. People being lazy, bullying or engaging in subtle forms of sexual abuse, are perhaps not best handled through leadership or management, but there are also – as we will see in the next section – examples where subordinates want strong 'leaders' – in our terms power-holders – acting more forcefully than influencing through meanings or doing rational management.

Also, the nature of leadership can be influenced by LIPs inviting or steering leaders into the wanted form or practice of leadership. LIPs may indicate their demand – explicitly or implicitly – for vision, values, emotional support, a pleasant workplace climate and/or pedagogical support (i.e. the 5Ps). Not everything can be delivered – as most HIPs have their shortcomings, strengths, preferences and own ideas about what is important – but few HIPs are blind and deaf to what is communicated by their LIPs.

This can be done in many ways. *Horizontally*, subordinates do not address a HIP formally but act directly outside a LIP/HIP position and take direct responsibility. You do not ask for permission and bypass a salient LIP position, but act directly in order to shape the workplace. One may work with others in a group, agree how things should work and bypass or minimize the impact of a HIP. One may decide to be autonomous, in no need of 'hand-holding' and mainly work outside the reach of the HIP, engaging in LIP/HIP interactions only marginally or symbolically (Lundholm, 2011). Or one may systematically cultivate network relationships and optimize supportive resources outside the people in one's own unit (manager and closest colleagues). This will indirectly form leadership, management and power targeting, making these modes less significant. Of course, there will always be a combination of approaches, and the success of people in subordinate positions who try to influence work will vary. Resourceful professionals and tight worker collectives may be key agents, often being more likely to influence a person than his/her senior people (manager or informal local authority). However, it is important to realize at the same time that many employees are still less significant when it comes to shaping the modes of organizing in operation, reacting rather than being proactive in relation to HIPs.

LIPs, MIPs and NIPs who significantly affect modes of organizing may do so for better or worse. Efforts to engage in other modes of organizing than the conventional ones are not necessarily anchored in careful thinking or 'good' values or lead to good results. Sometimes subordinates are driven by narrow self-interests, for example by considerations of comfort and easy work, and with a limited sense of responsibility for the organizational whole. Many do limit their efforts at work (Paulsen, 2014), sometimes for good reasons (much work is meaningless), sometimes without good motives or considerations (limited work morale or lack of understanding about the underlying value of the work). Often LIPs may have fantasies or anxieties that complicate their orientations and lead to immature rejections of authority (Sennett, 1980). Autonomous people or group work may lead to disasters. HIPs often have a broader overview and sense of responsibility in relation to legislation and various stakeholders. But the idea and ideal of reflexive followership may mean that the reflexivity of the employee whom the leadership industry (and most organizations and managers) expects to take a followership position is grounded in thoughtfulness. This can improve modes of organizing. In some cases then reflexive followership means that there is not much followership left.

The reflexive follower may get rid of herself as a follower, that is, by following less and working more autonomously or with the help of horizontal relations. Followership is only assumed in situations and relations where it is justified after careful thought. In this case one may talk of un-following.

But reflexivity may also lead to more or better forms of followership (or other LIP positions). Of course, sometimes followership may be seen as vital and something to be strengthened. Reflexive followership does not mean only being active and reducing vertical relationships. Sometimes one may think about situations and come to the conclusion that more leadership and followership is needed. This may include stronger vision, more leadership efforts to create a positive work climate or more consistency when it comes to shared values or understandings. Reflexive followership may mean that leadership is accepted, supported and reinforced, for example through combatting one's counter-dependencies to authorities, refraining from autonomy and resistance and becoming committed to the ideas, meanings and values proposed by the leader. Of course, the latter often comes automatically, but one can also work oneself into a follow-ership mode and encourage colleagues to do the same, that is by backing up the leader.

A CASE OF (UN?)REFLEXIVE FOLLOWERSHIP: ASKING FOR THE POWER MODE OF ORGANIZING[1]

The following case illustrates some interesting aspects of followership and perhaps LIP positioning more generally (Hentze, 1994). A relatively young manager from a German corporate group was appointed as the production director of a French subsidiary in the printing industry. One intention was to strengthen the bonds between different parts of the group. The new director was well educated and had modern ideas about participa-tive management. He replaced a very experienced French manager, M. Gaull, who had worked himself up from the bottom and had superior knowledge about many aspects of the production technology of the company. Gaull had a direct, paternalistic style, dealt with his subordinates on an individual basis, had clear ideas about what should be accomplished and was fairly outspoken both about what he perceived as positive and negative results. In our terms, one can say Gaull and his subordinates worked based on the exercise of power (with a dose of what is sometimes referred to as 'management by fear' in the pop-management literature), but also with strong respect. This can be seen as a mix of power and leadership. The new production director, Bernhard, was told several times about the personality and style of his predecessor and was well aware that he represented something very different. Bernhard believed in participative manage-ment and management by objectives; he explained the principles to his subordinates and started to implement this type of management. This was a typical case of manage-ment, not much leadership or power as we have defined the terms. After some time he was convinced that it had worked – production results did not indicate otherwise, a few managers left the company during his first months, but he carefully investigated their motives and concluded that they were not related to workplace issues. Bernhard thus gives the impression of being fairly high on reflexivity.

But then the CEO of the company, the production director's boss, received a letter from one of the production director's immediate subordinates, an experienced manager that the production director had much respect for and with whom he thought he worked well. This subordinate manager, M. Dupont, having been in the company for a very long time, expressed great worry about the state of affairs as well as the future of the production department. He emphasized the good intentions and qualifications of the new production director, but compared him with the predecessor and this comparison was clearly in favour of the latter, whose direct, autocratic style and superior technical knowledge received great respect. People felt great uncertainty about the purpose of all the management meetings that the new director had initiated. This led to endless discussions without clear decisions: Dupont had observed that over the course of one month about a quarter of the managers' working time was spent in the management team meetings. People lacked directions and felt that they were asked to solve problems without much support or clarification about what exactly they were supposed to do. Uncertainty led to anxiety – under the previous director failure was expected to lead to direct consequences such as people being informed about their bad performance in very clear terms.

The failure of the new production director – at least in the eyes of Dupont – can to some degree be ascribed to a lack of congruence between his management style and the expectations and assumptions of the people around him. There was a cultural misfit. The LIPs expected decisiveness, technical expertise and a strong mastery of the situation from a senior manager. They were also used to responding to relatively detailed instructions from Gaull and to doing so on an individual basis. They were also prepared to accept being told about mistakes in blunt language. This can be viewed as a wish for a very different management style, perhaps best described as based more strongly on power and to some extent leadership.

Even though people broadly understood the principles of the new management style, they only did so on a superficial level and did not value it. Meetings and discussions were seen as endless talk that seldom led anywhere, took time and energy away from 'real work' and were a bad 'surrogate' for the director informing people what to do. Group discussions also worked against a deeply engrained understanding of responsibility as an individual matter. As expressed in the letter to the CEO by the frustrated manager: 'at the end of the day we are only responsible for our own area of work'. This indicates a strong preference for autonomy, at least in relation to group work, within the overall frame of a desire for the exercise of HIP power and authority.

In this case the frustrated subordinate manager – and presumably most others in the unit – wanted power to be the major mode of organizing. Although the powerful and autocratic former manager Gaull caused some anxiety, he mainly gained respect. Subordinates appreciated his style and thought the exercise of power to be superior and to facilitate good work and results. His technical knowledge was excellent and created an important basis for respect. He probably scored highly on authenticity – people felt they knew him, he was perceived as direct and honest and very inclined to express his opinion. The emphasis of the new manager Bernhard on management and group work did not go down well – subordinates thought it time-consuming, insufficient and often a waste of time compared to the previous style. Subordinates also felt that he was imper-sonal, without humour or emotions, Dupont said. This made people uncertain and nervous. In authenticity terms, Bernhard scored low in the eyes of the LIPs. Leadership in our (and most leadership scholars') sense of the term did not really surface in Bernhard's managerial work apart from efforts to be pedagogical and teach people about participative management, which did not seem to get through. The preaching of values and vision, small talk, coaching, psychotherapy and other meaning-focused acts would probably not fare too well in this case. Respect for former manager Gaull also meant to some extent that leadership was most likely exercised and backed up by subordinates' followership (and they probably felt it was natural to follow his authority).

The case deviates from what one would expect the large majority of the leadership literature to predict, apart from authenticity theory in a limited way. It can also be viewed as rather old-fashioned and out of tune with the times and the desires of people in many contemporary Western organizations (except perhaps traditionally hierarchical organizations such as the military and the police). But we believe it is not that uncom-mon for people in organizations actually to want a degree of hierarchy and to obey people clearly in power. Very competent people with authority and a strong power base often create a mix of fear and respect that is very powerful in the exercise of influence. It may, of course, be counterproductive. In the case discussed, people seemed to be rather stuck in a specific mode of organizing (power) and bad at working with or considering alternatives. The dependence on the former manager Gaull was strong, and when he left people became bewildered. Authority-dependence is a serious weakness in the long run, as people become followers to an excessive degree and cannot cope well when the central character is not there. His replacement could not fill the void.

On the other hand, the subordinate manager Dupont cannot necessarily be viewed as an unreflexive follower. He seems to have thought carefully about the situation and made some astute interpretations of the problem. That he also acted upwards and took the initiative to discuss the problem indicates some degree of autonomy. One does wonder, however, why he did not approach Bernhard in the first instance. The issue of whether Dupont was trying to place himself in the position of taking over the job could be considered: his communication to the CEO indicates that a more Gaull-like person may be needed for the role. Perhaps Dupont himself? Reflexivity is not necessarily about the general good of the organization, but may be a quality promoting a person's own self-interest and organizational politics. Reflexive 'Machiavellians' can be found in LIP as well as HIP positions.

The case is thus not clear-cut in terms of follower (un)reflexivity. Perhaps the ingrained stasis of orientations to the unit's modes of organizing had fostered a partial lack of ability that co-exists with some clear sighting of the corporate situation and a good sense of the kinds of organizing principles that do not work in the organization, at least not in the short run? As is often the case, reflexivity is not an easy phenomenon – neither as a practice nor as something can we easily evaluate. In the case of Dupont, reflexive eagerness to diagnose and raise problems and consider a wide set of aspects is clearly there. On the other hand there is an inability to act in a reflexive way in specific situa-tions. If there are long and unproductive meetings, this is partly also a consequence of the inability of low-level participants to contribute to the organizing of the situation. It is not necessarily the case that meetings are, more or less by their very nature, a waste of time. The problem is often that those participating do not work actively enough to make them productive.

The case illustrates how ideas, preferences and competencies in various modes of organizing may clash. It is interesting to note that for the production director the clear articulation of the subordinates' frustration came as a shock, despite his efforts to be pedagogical and carefully consider and assess the situation. Simply trying to be reflective may not be enough.

SUMMARY

In this chapter we have followed up our overview of followership in Chapter 7 and addressed the problems and possibilities of reflexive followership. We believe that introducing, encouraging and circulating this notion could be a good thing in many organizations. While it is not a panacea, reflexive followership could be a useful value or slogan. There is often a tendency to believe that leadership is so important, that leaders lead followers and that followers do not do much independent thinking outside their ascribed and adapted roles. But the sheep metaphor for followers is not always relevant or valuable. It may actually be more relevant to many managers, in particular when trying to do leadership according to the latest fashion.

Organizations call for well-functioning organizing processes where everyone is more or less involved in productive interplay. As addressed in Chapters 10 and 11, aligned meanings around leadership and the other 6Ms are crucial. The case above clearly illustrates this. Reflexivity means thinking outside the box, including the followership box. Different perspectives and critical thinking are important, not only for how to be a 'good' follower, as large parts of the followership literature preach, but also in terms of if, when, and how much one should be a follower. Sometimes followership is called for and a productive HIP/LIP relationship is established. But sometimes it may be better *not* to turn to the HIP's vision and values, or their transformative, charismatic or authentic personality or appearance for guidance and meaning.

Extra-leadership relationships may occasionally be more productive: the 'follower' then aims for subordination to management (transactional relations), accepts and supports the exercise of power (engages in and encourages obedience) or emphasizes horizontal forms of organizing – relying on group work, autonomy or utilizing external networks for support and guidance. In other cases leadership may be viewed as important and productive. This can be supported by the reflexive follower who tries to take what is assessed as an optimal active-passive position, providing feedback to the HIP about the forms and expressions of leadership that are needed, and subtly or more explicitly indicating the needs for prophesying, psychotherapy, party-hosting, pedagogical interventions or preaching. A mature, thoughtful relationship with authority is important. Both immature dependence and counter-dependence need to be considered and minimized.

In other, and more general, words, the reflexive follower should take a broader and more ambitious perspective on the workplace and contribute actively to the formation of good modes of organizing at work. This can be done by influencing oneself, one's HIP and also other LIPs. The reflexive follower should therefore not be regarded as an opponent, but as a useful *ally* to the reflexive leader.

NOTE

1. The entire descriptive part of this section is based on Hentze (1994). We have added the interpretations at the end of the section.

14
Conclusions: Reflexivity, Trap-awareness and a Suggested Way Forward

This chapter illuminates some common obstacles to reflexivity in leadership. Many people probably emphasize a lack of time as crucial, but we take a different stance. We see ability, interest and priorities as more significant. The significance of social support and the degree to which organizational cultures are stimulating reflexivity also needs to be mentioned. The explanations for un- or low-reflexive leadership seem endless and we have covered many in the previous chapters. We zoom in on four obstacles that we refer to as 'traps' – partly following up on and deepening, partly extending themes from earlier chapters. These traps are often framed as ideals that appear to support leadership at its best, but as is the case with many nice-sounding ideals they often have the opposite effect. In this chapter, we also summarize our key points and draw our conclusions. We start the chapter with a brief overview and summary of our key points and subsequently highlight the traps and some productive principles for reflexive leadership.

KEY POINTS: 6M, 5P, ELR AND ILR, HIPS AND LIPS AND OTHER POSITIONINGS

As we have consistently argued in this book, leadership is important in many organizations but the concept needs to be cut down in size so that it does not cover everything or encourage fluffy attitudes. Good concepts aid thinking and clarification and avoid the pitfalls of covering everything and nothing. Distinctions are important here. In the field of leadership it is vital to consider alternatives and combinations. We think that the 6M and 5P models we proposed give a broad overview, are comparatively clear and helpful and can also aid managers and others thinking about leadership in fragmented and practical situations where one might have a hard time remembering abstract and complicated terms.

Together with the 6Ms, the 5P types of leadership can offer a map for considering alternative routes. A good map is not exact or complete but it should be fit for purpose and helpful for the user. This model offers a combination of acknowledging and indicating complexity and highlighting key issues in a pragmatic and simplifying way.

Considering alternatives to and within leadership arguably means that both extra-leadership and intra-leadership alternatives are on the agenda. In particular, the HIP, but also the LIP, needs to ask: is this a situation/relation motivating leadership or an alternative M(ode) of organizing?

Vertical and horizontal relations and interactions must both be considered. In many settings, the 'leader leading follower, top down' view and the 'everybody is engaged in leadership' are both too simplistic. Most workplaces in the West are positioned somewhere between the two extremes and both need to be considered. The potential relevance and value of strong asymmetry as well as an emphasis on horizontal, equal relations should be borne in mind, not as abstract principles but as alternatives to choose from depending on the specific workplace situation. Even if managers and other senior people (full professors at university departments, leading professionals in law firms) are HIPs (in the sense that they regularly exercise high influence) there are occasionally departures. A temporary knowledge hierarchy based on the specific work issue at hand may take over from the regular hierarchy based on formal position or general status. As we have emphasized, HIPs and LIPs are categories within relations and they are also situationally sensitive.

Well-functioning organizations call for effective vertical and horizontal relations and processes, where the people involved are sometimes more into HIP/LIP verticality and sometimes move outside this and try to work on more horizontal bases, that is, MIPifying (mid-level position), as in the case of bank manager Max in Chapter 12. Sensitivity for how people in organizations work best and attention to the specific work problems are vital. A too strict focus on leadership tends to exaggerate the vertical dimension: the idea that asymmetrical relations are always superior may be one-sided. The leadership industry is generally insensitive to what cannot be plugged into a leader-follower scheme. But the world is not made up of only two kinds of people, leaders and followers. Sometimes this categorization makes sense and is productive but sometimes it is not.

The question of how central leadership (and other HIP positions) is and what mode for organizing to aim for is very much a matter of who, when, how, and of locating one's work situation wisely within the 6M and 5P frameworks. Most HIPs and LIPs have a major or favourite position in a specific setting or relational context, but most also vary their orientation depending on situation-specifics.

If leadership is aimed for, that is, is viewed as more important and effective than power, network, autonomy, etc. then there is still a wealth of choices. Our key point is that it can be wise to consider vision, moral values, education/learning, emotional support and workplace climate as major aspects and focuses of attention. We have popularized these into five types of leadership work: prophesying, preaching values, psychotherapeutic intervention, party-hosting and pedagogical work. These leadership activities are not necessarily the task of a HIP in the sense of their being a formally senior person. The latter – the manager or some other in a high position (chairperson, recognized senior professional) – tends to carry some extra weight and have a stronger impact, but, e.g. pedagogical support, therapeutic interventions and party-hosting can equally well be offered by people in horizontal group settings.

A CASE FOR MORE REFLEXIVITY AND FEWER CHECKLISTS

The reader may want more specific guidelines than those we suggest in this book. Transformational, authentic, Level 5, etc. all offer a formula for superior leadership. More practitioner-oriented literature usually offers lists of 5–10 bullet points for how to do effective leadership. These are seductive; they oversimplify, deny complexity and may mislead rather than productively guide the recipe-hungry uncertain manager or other leader-wannabe eager to make it. It is probably no coincidence that a number of leadership researchers interviewed said that they find the theories in circulation of limited relevance and usefulness, at least in their own organizations (Bryman & Lilley, 2009).

We are only pointing out that relying on simple recipes, concepts that capture essentials in a simple way or natural laws about good leadership are futile. They are more likely to create problems for the narrow-minded HIP (or LIP) than to be helpful. What is needed is people who like and are capable of thinking, using their own judgement, being sensitive to and open-minded about local processes, and act accordingly. This is not a specific recipe, it's an overall ideal of reflexivity.

This is, as we have said, very much a collective process. A HIP – often a person with more resources, normally with a managerial/senior position, and usually a better overview – has a primary responsibility and is often crucial. But for good leadership to function, everyone involved needs to think carefully about and communicate this. The ERL as well as the IRL alternatives need to be understood and clarified, partly in dialogue between the parties. This can be accomplished explicitly: through formal meetings, consultancy interventions, education, and quantitative and qualitative feedback in various directions. But often it is more implicit and ongoing, through informal, subtle feedback and signalling. This is how modes of organizing are often negotiated.

SOME COMMON TRAPS: POSITIVITY, PSYCHOPOLITICS, AUTHENTICITY AND HUBRIS

Being aware and actively working – individually and in groups – with options of organizing is a good general principle, but it is of course often easier said than done. It is important to craft and develop a more reflective attitude in order to steer away from traps. There are, as we have indicated, many of these; here we highlight four common but difficult ones.

The positivity trap

In the leadership industry, as well as in many organizations, an ideology of being positive prevails. Most popular leadership concepts radiate the uplifting: transformational, authentic, support, emotional intelligence, etc. A common norm in workplaces is that we should be positive, optimistic and refrain from moaning and groaning and pointing out problems. Being positive has many advantages and people appreciate HIPs who are able to create a positive workplace climate and act in emotionally positive ways. An emphasis on an appealing vision, nice-sounding values, and on possibilities rather than obstacles is often advocated. Many celebrate positive leadership which aims to make people happy at work. Collinson (2012) refers to this as 'Prozac leadership'. There is of course a downside to this. It often reinforces leaders' – and others' – reluctance to address difficult problems, and a tendency to dismiss disturbing news and future diffi-cult possibilities, leaving little or no space for more questioning perspectives (p. 100). This may easily create problems. President George W. Bush (the younger) liked positive news. His staff, including senior people, was discouraged from communicating negative messages. So information about problematic conditions was softened and problems sometimes downplayed. This seemed to contribute to insufficient preparations for hur-ricane Katrina within the Bush administration (Collinson, 2012).

Also, in the IT consultancy firm CCC, the norm of being positive dominated. HIPs emphasized the need to think positively and see opportunities rather than problems. One common statement was: only raise a critique if you have a solution! This may minimize the moaning and groaning that plagues many workplaces and also encourage creative thinking. Critique plus proposal for improvement is good, critique plus con-tinued complaining is not. This norm of being positive seemed to contribute to a strong sense of community and a positive workplace climate that benefited people internally but also relationships with customers and collaborations in consultancy projects. But when a recession came, HIPs and others at CCC ran into severe problems. Positive thinking made them slow to realize the seriousness of the situation. This is just tempo-rary, no reason to panic, was one response. So the firm was very slow in responding and adapting to the shrinking assignments available, that is, by firing people. An emphasis on positive relations and skills in communicating uplifting news reduced the ability to be instrumental and to create crisis consciousness (Alvesson, 2000).

These examples of course highlight a basic dilemma. It is very easy to buy into a specific leadership ideology and see its value. In retrospect – after Katrina and the deep year-long recession that followed for CCC – it is also easy to see that the players here were too optimistic and that positivity can marginalize critical assessment and realism (Alvesson & Spicer, 2016).

The solution may seem to be very situational; be positive when it is required and switch over to criticality and realism when conditions call for this. But being so flexible and adaptable is seldom possible. If one is very much into creating positive outlooks and emotions, one needs skills, mind-sets, vocabulary and cultural expectations and values that ground this. It is like a core competence, a worldview, part of your identity – both as a HIP and as a LIP – and a part of organizational culture. Smiles and outbursts like 'we are all great, aren't we' or 'see this as an opportunity' may sound shallow and false if they are not grounded in a richer set of behaviour.

There are no easy solutions. One way to remain thoughtful about this is to be aware of the disadvantages of any ideology being dominant. Being positive sounds – positive. It is, in the same way as many popular leadership ideas, appealing and seductive. But being aware of the downside is fundamental. The 'true' interests, capacities and identities of the people involved – HIPs and others – may not be in line with the ideal. Some organizations and professions also have limited opportunities to solely focus on positivity. For example, selective critical thinking is important for universities, tax authorities, law firms and others where analytical scrutiny is part of the core competence.

In most cases, however, positivity may be an option. And the communication of positive aspects is important in influencing people; so, a certain amount is often fine. Many might get better results if they increased the dose somewhat.

At the same time, it is important to have access to a counter-position – positivity may be a source of problems. These may range broadly. At one extreme, there is the risk of increasing the narcissism of all involved – too much gratification and positive feedback in a 'loving' or mutually affirming relationship may lead to a boosted but weak sense of self. At the other, you have a sense of fake positivity – with the habitual spreading of good messages that sound shallow and dishonest. Finally, there is the lowered ability to see and deal with problems.

Access to counter-positions is key in reflexivity. As preached in this book, it is vital to master various perspectives, at a minimum more than one. It is important to avoid getting stuck in one ideal and one superior vocabulary. Concepts such as Prozac leadership are valuable as a warning signal. It is easy to remember and, at least occasionally, the very positive HIP (or LIP) may remind him- or herself that this is not only a blessing but may also be a trap.

The psychopolitics trap

Much leadership is linked to psychology. Apart from the ideal of positivity and happiness, there are broader issues associated with human relations at work. Relating to people in the right way is viewed as key for good leadership. This strong contemporary emphasis on people, their needs, feelings and relations is not unproblematic. It is related to a narcissistic culture where people's sense of self is strongly in focus and in constant need of attention and confirmation (Lasch, 1978). But confirmation may only reinforce the appetite for and dependence on ego-massage. Followers and leaders could easily become caught in a joint dependency on mutual confirmation, where positive feedback in both directions becomes a key priority. Leaders are in need of followers to confirm them and followers want leaders to give them attention, praise and support. Zaleznik (1997) argues that what he calls 'real work' – focusing on products, markets and customers – may be marginalized by managers spending too much time 'smoothing over conflict, greasing the wheels of human interaction ...' (p. 56).

Time is limited and not everything can receive attention. The substance of organizational work may suffer if there is a strong focus on how people feel and relate to each other rather than what they do or accomplish. Our impression is in line with Zaleznik's observation that many managers are strongly focused on having good relationships with their subordinates and become dependent on their explicit and implicit feedback signalling that they are good leaders. Managers often view this as a moral issue. Being a good person often means being good to and with subordinates. In many organizational contexts performance is hard to trace and measure, therefore output related feedback is limited, weak or uncertain – as a staff manager, specialist, development unit manager or university department head, there are seldom clear signs of your success – and substance or real work tends to become even more marginalized.

It is very tempting to attend carefully to people's needs and wants, and many managers are disinclined to break with this norm in relation to their immediate subordinates unless they are disliked or there are clear career benefits to doing so. Middle managers often go for scoring points in popularity contests in the form of employee satisfaction questionnaires. Senior management often has a slightly different attitude. Having a more distanced relationship with the majority of the workforce – mostly seen in terms of numbers and costs – they tend to focus more on bottom-line results in order to please shareholders, the board and analysts rather than their subordinates (e.g. business unit heads).

A way of trying to cope with the tricky issue of morality in the sense of being good to people versus maximizing profits is to twist morality so that it becomes adapted to the business logic. Jack Welch, in a communication to shareholders, insisted on the moral virtue of making some people redundant, arguing that it shows good management to routinely 'remove' the bottom performing 10 per cent of staff. Not doing so is likened to 'management failure', 'false kindness' and a form of 'cruelty' (Amernic et al., 2007, p. 1855). Collins (2001) also expresses the opinion that firing people who are not 'the best' is not a matter of ruthlessness but about the higher principle of creating excellent results. This is arguably better seen as an exercise of management or power, but there may be elements of leadership in explaining and justifying these practices to the survivors who are still suffering from the 'false kindness' and 'cruelty' of not having been fired, as yet.

The good workplace recognizes a mix of different legitimate interests that are often in conflict. It is of course not the case that single-minded profit-orientation is a blessing for people who are in badly performing units. They may do a good job, but are perhaps located in poorer regions or facing specific difficulties for which they are not responsible. And society must also allow for less resourceful groups and people to have jobs. There is often a conflict between concern for people and concern for performance and profits that needs to be considered and wrestled with. Both a strong inclination to emphasize party-hosting and psychotherapy at work together with an assumption that a strong performance measurement orientation will automatically lead to only good effects are over-simplistic and mean denying the contradictory nature of contemporary organizations and leadership. Problems associated with excessive profit and performance orientation are well recognized – issues around short-sightedness, exploitation, stress and pressure are easy to raise – but we also need to consider problems of psychopolitics, which are easily covered up by a leadership industry celebrating authentic, transformational leadership, emotional intelligence and other things well in line with a certain neglect of 'real work'.

The self-righteousness/authenticity trap

Another major pitfall in much leadership work is the inclination to engage in self-serving bias. It is good to feel good about oneself and one's intentions, values and accomplishments. Leadership ideologies that are seductive, easy to identify with and boost ego and self-esteem are popular. But they offer a mixed blessing in terms of being helpful at work. Often they reinforce a filter through which HIPs see their working world in highly selective ways, and in which positive clues are overemphasized and negative signs are repressed or marginalized.

We saw this in the case of Benjamin Book, discussed in Chapter 10. Book managed to establish a reputation for being an excellent leader and thus had devoted followers in his previous workplace – built on an authentic and caring style – but was unable to re-establish the same in his new organization. His new subordinates did not accept his claims to authenticity. This in spite of the fact that Book's new job as a CEO offered him scope to express himself and amplify the effects of his actions.

Generally, many managers like to pride themselves on having finely tuned values (Sveningsson & Alvesson, 2016). Sometimes this is an outcome of the flattering voice of the leadership industry, inclined to praise the manager who identifies him- or herself with the seemingly good values that permeate lectures and writings. Subordinates also tend to be careful about delivering honest, critical feedback, making it easy for managers to maintain a positive self-image.

Book was viewed by others as behaving superficially, showing few signs of integrity or honesty. This is bad in itself, but the problem was amplified by his own strong belief in and expression of his quality as an authentic leader.

As pointed out previously, there are several problematic assumptions and effects in relation to an exaggerated emphasis on authenticity when it comes to leadership. Ibarra (2015) points out three important issues. First, what self to be true to (we evolve as persons and different situations evoke different selves)? Second, too much transparency and disclosure tends to undermine the ('magic' and hence the) effectiveness of leadership acts. Third, a stubborn embracing of a favoured leadership style that might have worked before could be a disaster in the face of new challenges (as clearly illustrated by the case of Book above).

The hubris trap

A related problem is the one of hubris or excessive self-confidence. The leadership industry emphasizes the importance of leadership. As we have ironically pointed out, there is a great faith in leadership being the solution. Many think like this: What is the problem? Low innovation, ethical problems, low morale among employees, conflicts between ethnic groups or lack of integration of functions? Better/more/the right leadership is the solution.

There is a widespread hubris problem. Major problems in the private and public sectors are supposed to be solved through leadership. A prevalent hero-mythology and the celebration of a few cases, often presented in mass media in a glorified and simplistic way, where a single CEO accomplished miracles more or less on his (or occasionally her) own, easily lead naive and uncritical people to believe that leaders are highly significant and do or at least can accomplish a great deal.

But we can also observe hubris on a smaller scale. Many managers believe that they can have significant effects on LIPs through very small means. The open-door policy where LIPs can come and air their problems, the small talk with people, remembering their birthdays or giving them some praise, the occasional communication of some cherished value (working like a family, think of the customer as a king) are supposed to create a strong impact on others who are expected to benefit strongly from a few minutes of interaction with the HIP doing leadership (Alvesson & Sveningsson, 2003c). While this may happen, real influence is normally not that easy. It calls for care, consistency and ongoing thoughtful influencing work with uncertain and temporary effects. People often do appreciate some friendly words or a joke from a HIP, but that does not necessarily mean that the day has been saved or that they will walk that extra mile, work in more clever ways or something else remarkable.

For example, a form of hubris could be seen in a particular organizational change process where a middle manager was supposed to exercise leadership as part of a cultural change (Sveningsson & Larsson, 2006). The middle manager had taken part in a variety of leadership programmes and was well informed about leadership ideas, especially those related to broader strategic issues and of a more coaching and therapeutic variety. In expressing his view of leadership, the manager explained that: 'Good leadership involves explaining the objectives with the business in the horizon and then engage people to follow you'. The manager also explained that what mostly engages him is exercising leadership on projects related to customers and markets, also signalling an interest in strategic issues. He also believed that this was something that he was good at, something of a core competence: 'I make it work in groups. I get others to act. I'm not the one designing technical solution, others are better at that. I want a unified view of where we are going – that's my leader style'. This middle manager also looked upon himself as a reflexive leader: 'I reflect a lot upon what we need to achieve in the long term, with a five year period'. This is all fine, but careful observation of the manager in action would support a more modest self-view (Sveningsson & Larsson, 2006).

Such fantasies about greatness and actual or, given the right position, potential contribution are not uncommon in modern business life and pointedly it is often the case that fantasies of leadership – often framed in romanticized terms where the leader rules and governs – are formed by pompous and slightly narcissistic ideals of leadership. This is not to suggest that people have a narcissistic personality but rather that fantasies of leadership are encouraged and formed in specific organizational contexts in which such ideals are salient. The leadership industry regularly fuels such fantasies – it thereby makes its customers happy but it is often far from well-functioning. The latter calls for a more realistic view of oneself and one's accomplishments.

CONSIDERATIONS FOR THOUGHTFUL LEADERSHIP – SOME WAYS FORWARD

On being cautious about the leadership label: using differentiated vocabulary

Arguably, much of what is published under the label of leadership contributes to strengthening, rather than undermining, the ideology of leadership, thereby legitimizing and supporting a faith in leader-elites doing good things. Many researchers find a market for work using the popular signifier 'leadership' because it is fashionable. More broadly, leadership fits into a culture of grandiosity, where roles and activities are upgraded to sound impressive and boost status and self-esteem (Alvesson, 2013a).

Thus, many efforts to develop 'alternative' views partly break with and at the same time reinforce the domination of 'leadership' (Alvesson & Spicer, 2014). Nuances involved in the efforts to revise 'leadership' are easily lost as the major framing reinforces a hegemonic 'mega-discourse', weakening or crowding out others (Blom & Alvesson, 2015). This reinforces an understanding that the alternative to leadership is *leadership*, not peer relations, professionalism, autonomy, co-working, organizing processes, or mutual adjustment offering alternative framings and understanding than those the leadership vocabulary invites.

Crevani et al. (2010) argue that researchers should stick to and use the leadership word. The reason for this is its perceived relevance and strong appeal to practitioners.

> If we don't study this in terms of leadership our research will be void of all the aspects of power, domination ... normative assumptions, that comes with the word. Articulating and emphasizing such aspects in terms of leadership is to take our role as social scientists seriously. (p. 81)

We disagree; following Crevani et al. arguably means retreating from our responsibility as social scientists. The task is not to just adapt to what is fashionable and what the market seems to want and reward. Becoming relevant does not call for adapting, using or reinforcing a dominant mainstream vocabulary – that leads to confusion and wishful thinking. Leadership talk that is too wide and vague is fundamentally unintellectual – unfortunately such lack of intellectuality dominates large parts of the leadership industry. We cannot say that we have been entirely successful in avoiding all the problems either – it is not easy to avoid using ideas on leadership in loose and shifting ways. We have nevertheless tried to connect to the interest in leadership – and in doing so perhaps partly exploited the persuasive appeal of the term – but also striven to highlight alternative ways of thinking about leadership and other organizing modes, with some emphasis on the latter. Alternative viewpoints and concepts that better illuminate phenomena are less ideological, and facilitating more differentiated and nuanced ways of thinking and acting should in all respects – apart from opportunism – be preferred to overusing the leadership vocabulary.

Using the vocabulary introduced in this book may thus be useful both in making the reader more clearly aware of options for organizing and working more productively to grasp these, and creating some common understanding of leadership and alternative forms of organizing at a workplace level. Sharp concepts that are pragmatically helpful are important here. This is about counteracting the lazy use and reproduction of stand-ardized language that is taken for granted, and encouraging the active use of vocabu-lary that inspires thinking in novel ways. Such vocabulary aids communication and may facilitate more reflexive leadership and followership as well as helping HIPs and LIPs to find other, supplementary ways of working.

Counteracting the strong mainstreaming of leadership vocabulary for everything good and avoiding opportunistic (over-)exploitation of sexy, but confusing leadership talk are important. It is a part of the intellectual cleaning-up work that the fluffy lead-ership field is in such need of.[1] A degree of anti-opportunism and anti-stupidity man-agement is much needed (Alvesson & Spicer, 2016).

Working with meta-leadership

A second possible principle is to engage in meta-leadership. This means that one takes an overall view of organizational issues and acknowledges social relations and different lines of thinking and acting. Meta-leadership focuses on the context, and means scrutinizing the entire domain of modes of organizing and types of leadership. The idea then is to reach agreement about how to relate to different issues and try to clarify and influence overall understandings, values and priorities. Meta-leadership is *not* doing leadership focused on specific issues, that is, how people think, feel and relate to work tasks, customers, rules, personal development, but leadership focusing on *questions around* how are we doing things and how should we do them in terms of modes of organizing and (possibly) types of leadership. Meta-leadership may mean engaging in work towards a higher degree of alignment in meanings that we addressed in Chapter 10.

Meta-leadership may be structured around the 6M and/or 5P frameworks (but of course any other framework clarifying leadership alternatives – both ELR and ILR – can do). Meta-leadership aims to lead people into the right combination of the various Ms and/or Ps. Meta-leadership is about influencing people as to how to take and relate to a position in terms of leadership and the alternatives. It is not about accepting leadership interventions, but about the foundations for such acceptance. Meta-leadership may reinforce LIPs' subordinate, followership or target-of-power positions. Or meta-leadership may suggest a reduction in the expectations of leadership, instead encouraging autonomy, group work or reliance on networks rather than LIPs being followers.

Meta-leadership may thus increase LIPs' inclinations to followership or have the opposite effect. This may be accomplished by the HIP downplaying their own influ-ence and emphasizing the significance of autonomy and initiative. S/he may highlight a lack of technical and/or social expertise: 'Consider who really knows something about this and approach her' or 'If you have a personal problem go to your best friend or a shrink, I am not a good psychotherapist.' 'Here we encourage people that don't need hand-holding at work.' A true believer in leadership (as *the* all-embracing solution) may find such statements upsetting, but they could be part of a leadership strategy that encourages people to be less leader-dependent and more inclined to find other solutions than followership at work.

Balancing alignment with constructive dissensus

We have preached the significance of having an alignment of meanings of leadership, including followership and/or the alternative Ms (modes of organizing) as well as the types of leadership (5Ps). Without alignment it is difficult for a relationship to function well. It is like a marriage where people have different views of the arrangement: if one party is into romanticism and the other views this as an arrangement of economic convenience then there will be tensions. So clarification of understandings and working towards a common understanding are vital. If a subordinate believes that the leader is an expert in emotional intelligence and coaching (psychotherapist) and the leader feels like a visionary prophet, focused on the overall purpose and results, and dislikes being a shrink at work, things will not work. So, some efforts to find a common ground and to work on this on a more or less ongoing basis are necessary, as things change all the time.

But striving for shared meanings and consensus needs to be supplemented with at least occasional questioning of common understandings and practices. A consensus and harmony around optimal leadership and other modes may mean that criticality and reflexivity are reduced. Consensus reduces openness. People may prioritize 'psychopolitics', more eager to make relations work smoothly and adjust to each other's needs and wants for confirmation and cosiness over doing effective work and accomplishing good results. As mentioned above, 'real work' may suffer from too much psychology. The leadership industry often focuses on smooth human relations, frequently emphasizing emotional intelligence, service, authenticity, individual consideration, idealized influence. Leaders and followers being happy with and affirming one another may be at the expense of those supposed to benefit from their work, such as customers, shareholders, tax payers, patients, pupils and welfare clients.

Efforts to create alignment need to be supplemented with some space for and encouragement of critique and questioning. A concept here is productive or constructive dissensus. This means that one takes a critical view of what one is doing and encourages open, critical debates about what goes on and how one relates to leadership/followership and other modes of organizing. There are at least temporary efforts to break away from consensus and harmony and encourage more pluralistic thinking. This can be seen as a supplement to or a part of the meta-leadership – the latter is mainly oriented towards making everyone involved think about modes of organizing and forms of leadership ideals in similar ways. This is the main principle – shared understandings of organization and leadership are important. But occasionally, critical scrutiny and challenging of what is shared and perhaps taken for granted are vital – particularly as what was for a time reasonable and functional may be less so under changing conditions. Productive dissensus means that people are confronted with different views that stimulate dialogue and reflection in a way that consensus does not.

THE TIME ISSUE

'I don't have time to reflect' is a common statement. This often makes sense. Time and reflexivity hang together. But often in the opposite way from what is normally thought. One reason for a shortage of time is the absence of reflexivity: as people do not reflect much or well, they use their time badly and do not have time to reflect.

In everyday life, with its myriad of tasks and micro situations, most people cannot be particularly reflective most of the time. Routines and habits guide us. Sometimes we face difficult or unexpected problems that call for thought and thus reflection. But this is often narrow and instrumental: how to deal with this problem? As we have emphasized, reflexivity is broader and relates to how we develop good working principles for leadership and other modes of organizing, that is, what is our overall approach to problem-solving (pedagogical leadership, using networks)? Sometimes it is wise to realize that there are problems that cannot be solved – we have to live with some imperfections – or that are not worth putting in much effort to deal with.

Most of the time reflexivity is not on the agenda at work. And often it is not needed. Most work needs to be instrumental, focused, partly routinized and pragmatic. But it also needs to be balanced with reflexivity. Now and then HIPs and others need to think more deeply and broadly about how they tend to do things. This needs not only to involve fine-tuning a favoured style or way of solving specific problems, but also to include thinking about one's own thinking and that of one's co-workers. This can sometimes be done on an ongoing basis, sometimes in meetings or informal interactions with others at work, sometimes with colleagues outside work, for example at an after-work pub outing or sometimes alone during free time. As most people have plenty of time around working hours, for example travelling to and from work or relaxing during evenings or weekends, the statement that one lacks time for reflection is a hollow one. It is rather ability, interest or knowledge that is lacking. We hope that this book helps to strengthen the reader in all three respects.

Reflexivity can be accomplished in formal settings or informally. Management education, lectures, seminars, consultancy reports and systematic feedback can be helpful in putting reflexivity on the agenda. But a workplace culture where people encourage themselves and others to be thoughtful is more vital. This means that reflexivity can be promoted on an everyday basis and without much time being spent explicitly on it. A manager can ask people to think about using 'external leaders', chosen people in the network, besides him- or herself as sources of support, thereby encouraging LIPs to think through where best to turn. A HIP interested in psychological issues can talk about his own personal problems – health issues, depression, relatives who are sick or alcoholic, etc. – in order to facilitate a psychotherapy type of leadership. A manager can have a closed-door policy and encourage people to be autonomous or engage in-group work, signalling that not much leadership (typically calling for quite a lot of interaction) is needed.

Being reflexive takes time but may mean in the long-term that time is saved. Quality in reflexivity may, given circumstances such as HIPs' and LIPs' resources and interests or type of work situation, lead to productive modes of organizing and leadership being

achieved, saving time for busy people. In organizations time is often devoted to unproductive meetings and lengthy discussions. Managers may receive too much attention
and strong demands on their time, particularly if they and LIPs buy into the idea of the
centrality of leadership. Most popular leadership recipes call for very time-consuming
leadership. Also, followers expected to look to their leaders for vision, the right values,
inspiration, support, learning, conflict resolution, personal development, encouragement and moral guidance may find that the queue outside the boss's office is quite long
as there are a great many followers who think they need such leadership. This of course
leads to a shortage of time and limited reflection. There can easily be a spiral down-
wards. High demands for leadership (and other HIP actions) mean that the HIP
becomes busy, unreflective and over-occupied with meeting those expectations. Of
course, some managers may like and favour such demands from an identity point of
view in order to strengthen their feelings of importance and self-esteem. However,
rather than meeting these demands the reflexive leader is more inclined to steer LIPs
around this and create fewer leader-and-follower-intensive relationships. Spending
some time on reflexivity may be stressful, at least in the short run, but it is likely to
save so much time later on.

CONCLUSION: WORKING WITH THE RIGHT M

In this book we have suggested a framework and vocabulary for thinking about leadership
issues and highlighted that we need to consider and balance leadership with other modes
of organizing. You will not hear us repeat our key points here, with one exception – our
overall message about the need for people involved to consistently work on their reflexive
orientation to leadership and other Ms.

Good organizing, including acts of leadership, is very much a matter of finding the
version that works in a particular context, with a specific group of people (HIPs and
LIPs) and for a specific problem. Many treat matters as if there is an objective situation
calling for an objective response. An influential approach is situational leadership
theory, emphasizing the objective nature of the LIPs (subordinates, followers) determining the correct leadership style. Another idea is to emphasize the nature of the
problem calling for a specific response – command, management or leadership (Grint,
2005). But against this we can argue that many situations are highly complex and the
number of dimensions involved almost endless. For example, you may have mature and
autonomous LIPs – rather MIPs or NIPs if they really are competent and autonomous –
but there may still be variations in their functions. There may be variation within
the group but also on an individual basis, depending on the issue. A person may be
reliable and autonomous in most respects, but less mature when it comes to others, for
example administration or gender relations. For most people 'maturity' is not a trait; it
is issue-specific. Most of us are mature (self-confident, competent, interested) some of
the time and sometimes less so (uncertain, uncommitted, dealing with issues outside
one's expertise or comfort zone).

Another issue is the possibility of varied views on the subject matter. People in a work
relationship may define problems, context, themselves, others and the relationship in

quite different ways. A problem is not necessarily clearly tame or wicked for the people involved. People with different expertise and experience may see something as more or less complex or more or less relevant to be solved given their expertise and interest. They may also vary in how they see themselves in terms of HIPs, LIPs, MIPs or perhaps NIPs.

In addition, there may be great variation in how people see the availability of various Ms. Working on clarifying, developing and sometimes restricting alternative modes of organizing is vital. How do we make things work through a good combination of leadership, management, use of power, group work, network and autonomy? What pushes do we need to make: more or less leadership, perhaps supporting or limiting management, drawing upon or lessening the use of power, becoming better at effective group work or liberating people from the constraints of the team, developing and using networks or drawing more focus to the local setting and people in the workplace, encouraging autonomy or restricting options for people to do what they want?

Keeping questions like this on the agenda takes time, brainpower and energy but may save quite a lot in the long run. It 'only' calls for people to bear in mind and navigate a broad framework of considering a variety of modes of organizing and leadership.

NOTE

1. We can easily point to examples of how not only the leadership industry (commercial actors and groups promising leader improvement) but also more serious academics follow this line. One example is Western (2008) who makes a distinction between management and leadership (p. 39). Management is about efficiency and control, leadership is about moving forward, creating change through influencing. Then there is a chapter on the leader as a controller. Here 'the leader' does scientific management and subscribes to command and control. The chapter ends with reflections on how the leader as controller rationale was much admired by Hitler and Stalin and employed in their terror regimes (p. 89).

Appendix: Reflexive questions

In this appendix we provide a number of questions aiming for stimulating reflexivity. We primarily address people in working life with a managerial position or people with a strong informal standing in the workplace, exercising informal leadership, but also subordinates having experience of leadership and organizing issues may find the questions relevant. When the latter, 'I' may be exchanged with 'my manager'. Some are targeting followers and followership. In other cases, where we ask about leadership considerations, the reader or the teacher using the book in e.g. a MBA programme or a workplace development activity may choose to reformulate the questions so they focus on the subordinate's perspective instead. Most questions are broadly relevant across the book, but we have chosen to structure them in accordance with the chapter structure. Therefore, reflexive questions that can be addressed after reading chapters 2, 4, 5, 6, 9 and 10.

CHAPTER 2

- Am I truly reflexive concerning my work situation, views and beliefs or do I tend to be more narrowly reflective?
- What needs to be influenced in my work setting? Is it people's meanings, thinking or emotions, or perhaps behaviour? The former is the task for leadership. Are people into voluntary, engaged subordination acceptable or do LIPs feel they simply have to comply with requirements for behaviour?
- What do I mean when I refer to leadership? What do my potential followers refer to when they talk about leadership? Something specific or 'everything'?
- What is the necessary element(s) of my leadership interventions? Is it to provide direction, understanding of meaning or support? What should be emphasized and when? What is the 'demand' of leadership among the LIPs? Do they ask for/need leadership at all?
- What is the degree of pro- and re-activity in my leadership interventions? Am I taking the initiative or am I responding to a call from someone else? How can the influence processes be characterized and what directions seem to dominate in interaction?
- What is my specific focus of attention: people, task, activities, output, internal organizational issues, external factors (e.g. customers, competitors, suppliers, regulations), short- or long-term view? Why is this the case?
- What are the likely consequences – intended and unintended – of my leadership? Are there any unwanted side effects (increased dependence, resistance, waste of precious time) that might outweigh the intended productive effects?

CHAPTER 4

- How do my ideological orientations influence my understanding of leadership? For example, am I caught in certain ideals – visionary, strategic, coaching – that potentially seduce me? Are these ideals constraining my ability to understand alternatives to leadership?
- Which ideologies are reinforced or, alternatively, challenged by the way I understand and talk about leadership? Have I uncritically adapted management fashions (most people do) or do I take a more autonomous – reflexive – position in relation to many popular leadership ideals? Do I have ideas on leadership that are politically (in)correct?
- What alternative vocabulary – words, labels, and phrases – can be used instead of leader/leadership in order to describe the way I think about accomplishing influence.
- To what extent do I talk about and try to practise leadership for my own sake – such as self-promotion, ego boosting, seeking confirmation or social dominance – rather than for what may be most appropriate considering my organization's work tasks and situation? ('Never' may be the spontaneous answer but a more reflexive and honest answer may be different.)
- What results can I foresee of my leadership/followership? Is there some variation in terms of the short or long term and for various relevant stakeholders? For example, are there any indications – for instance commitment, morality, emotions, or understanding of a specific task – on how I influence people? Or am I perhaps less successful in influencing others? Or is it almost impossible to assess the results of my leadership/followership?
- On what – for example, formal position, knowledge, skills, high morals, natural authority, ambition, need to dominate – do I base my authority and right to lead others? Why should others follow me?

CHAPTER 5

- Does leadership create culture or does culture define and guide leadership? How can we understand the relation between leadership and organizational culture in our organization?
- In what way can we understand organizational culture as an alternative to leadership?
- Based on our organizational culture what is the room for and significance of leadership as a means for organizing work?
- If leadership still is deemed to have a purpose, how can this be exercised so that it works in concert with our culture? Perhaps there are areas or situations where it has an important role?
- To what extent are the use of management, power and leadership (or favoured horizontal modes of organizing) an uncritical and unreflexive outcome of taken-for-granted cultural beliefs and ideals?
- To what extent may there sometimes be a need for cultural non-adaptation and productive tension or the starting of work with re-definitions of what is natural, positive and reasonable to think and do? What are the risks and costs of upsetting people and creating conflicts?

CHAPTER 6

- Do followers co-construct or even construct leadership? Or do they tend to be passive recipients of leadership?
- What are the alternatives to followership? How is this related to reflexive followership and how can the latter be encouraged?
- Am I a follower in relation to a particular person (manager or informal leader)? If yes, is the followership based on being young and in need of guidance, dependencies, general faith in authorities, admiration, fear or something else?
- Or do I rather see myself as a (more or less equal) co-worker or more of a formal subordinate in relation to that person?
- If I am not seeing myself as a follower in relation to a certain person, why is this the case? For example, is this based on need for independence, general trouble with authorities, narcissism (I deserve to be followed rather than follow), power (I will not submit to anyone at the expense of my own influence), status (my ego and image will be damaged by taking a follower position) or something else?
- What are the specific characteristics of followership in my work unit in terms of the amount or degree of followership (and leadership)? For example, is followership more pronounced in particular jobs, areas and work tasks?
- What alternatives to followership – in terms of organizing work – may be considered in my work unit?

CHAPTER 9

- What is the profile in terms of knowledge, professionalism and commitment among my subordinates? When is leadership an appropriate means of influencing and when are other alternatives more appropriate? For example, how does the level of knowledge among employees affect the choice of mode of organizing?
- How do I allocate time for reflection/reflexivity in a typical workday? In what ways can I take charge of my time rather than being a victim of time constraints? For example, to what extent is my workday regulated by demands and expectations that are less important than leadership activities?
- In what ways do work-related demands and expectations change the relevance of leadership? For example, how does the increased digitalization of the workplace – e.g. communication and information – affect the possibility of accomplishing effective influencing processes?
- What characterize my relation – e.g. content, form, intensity, space for manoeuvring – to superiors? How does that affect the possibility – constraining, facilitating, or obstructing – of accomplishing leadership in relation to alternative modes of organizing?

CHAPTER 10

- In what ways – different dimensions – can we understand alignment and misfit in leadership processes? Can you think of any typical illustrations of either alignment or misfits?

- How can we practically work with clarifying and reducing misfits in leadership processes in order to improve leadership?
- What characterizes my relationship with superiors and subordinates in terms of influencing? What is the nature of the relationship in terms of interdependencies, interactions and questions discussed? Do I really know this or am I mainly guessing and potentially deceived by wishful thinking?
- To what extent and in what ways do I ambitiously and systematically reflect on the meaning and value of the relation to subordinates and superiors?
- To what extent do I consider diversity in terms of meaning and value of leadership among those somehow involved in leadership relations, i.e. both HIPs and LIPs?
- How may I improve the possibility of avoiding misalignments and misconstructions in terms of meaning and value? Do I need to?
- Am I prepared and able to adjust my leadership according to the preferences of the LIPs, even if it feels uncomfortable? Or do I stick to my preferred way of leading, even if it will cause some resistance? Am I persistent or adaptive?

References

Alvesson, M. (1995) *Management of Knowledge-Intensive Companies.* Berlin: de Gruyter.

Alvesson, M. (2000) *Ledning av Kunskapsföretag: En studie av ett datakonsultföretag.* Stockholm: Norstedts juridik.

Alvesson, M. (2004) *Knowledge Work and Knowledge Intensive Firms.* Oxford: Oxford University Press.

Alvesson, M. (2011a) Organizational culture: meaning, discourse and identity. In N. Ashkanasy, C. Wilderom & M. Peterson (eds) *Handbook of Organizational Culture and Climate* (2nd edn). Thousand Oaks: Sage.

Alvesson, M. (2011b) The leader as saint. In M Alvesson & A Spicer (eds), *Metaphors We Lead By. Understanding Leadership in the Real World.* London: Routledge.

Alvesson, M. (2013a) *Understanding Organizational Culture.* London: Sage.

Alvesson, M. (2013b) *The Triumph of Emptiness: Consumption, Higher Education and Work Organization.* Oxford: Oxford University Press.

Alvesson, M. & Billing, Y.D. (2009) *Understanding Gender in Organizations.* London: Sage.

Alvesson, M. & Björkman, I. (1992) *Organisationsidentitet och Organisationsbyggande: En studie av ett industriföretag.* Lund: Studentlitteratur.

Alvesson, M. & Empson, L. (2008) The construction of organizational identity: comparative case studies of consulting firms. *Scandinavian Journal of Management* 24, pp. 1–16.

Alvesson, M. & Jonsson, A. (2016) The bumpy road to exercising leadership: fragmentations in meaning and practice. *Leadership* (forthcoming).

Alvesson, M. & Kärreman, D. (2000) Varieties of discourse: on the study of organizations through discourse analysis. *Human Relations* 53(9), pp. 1125–1149.

Alvesson, M. & Kärreman, D. (2016) Intellectual failure and ideological success in organization studies: the case of transformational leadership, *Journal of Management Inquiry* 25(2), pp. 139–152.

Alvesson, M. & Lundholm, S. (2014) *Personalchefers Arbete och Identitet. Strategi och strul.* Lund: Studentlitteratur.

Alvesson, M. & Sköldberg, K. (2009) *Reflexive Methodology: New Vistas for Qualitative Research.* London: Sage.

Alvesson, M. & Spicer, A. (2011) *Metaphors We Lead By: Understanding Leadership in the Real World.* London: Routledge.

Alvesson, M. & Spicer, A. (2012) A stupidity-based theory of organizations. *Journal of Management Studies* 49(7), pp. 1194–1220.

Alvesson, M. & Spicer, A. (2014) Critical perspectives on leadership. In D. Day (ed.), *Oxford Handbook of Organization and Leadership.* Oxford: Oxford University Press.

Alvesson, M. & Spicer, A. (2016) *The Stupidity Paradox.* London: Profile.

Alvesson, M. & Sveningsson, S. (2003a) The good visions, the bad micro-management and the ugly ambiguity: contradictions of (non-)leadership in a knowledge-intensive company. *Organization Studies* 24(6), pp. 961–988.

Alvesson, M. & Sveningsson, S. (2003b) The great disappearance act: difficulties in doing 'leadership'. *Leadership Quarterly* 14(3), pp. 359–381.

Alvesson, M. & Sveningsson, S. (2003c) Managers doing leadership: the extra-ordinarization of the mundane. *Human Relations* 56(12), pp. 1435–1459.

Alvesson, M. & Sveningsson, S. (2015) *Changing Organizational Culture.* London: Routledge.

Alvesson, M. & Thompson, P. (2005) Post-bureaucracy? In S. Ackroyd et al. (eds), *Oxford Handbook of Work and Organization Studies.* Oxford: Oxford University Press.

Alvesson, M. & Wenglén, R. (2008) Master, mystery, mess or mediocre? Ambiguities in leadership constructions. *Working Paper*, Lund University School of Economics and Management.

Alvesson, M. & Willmott, H. (2012) Producing the appropriate individual: identity regulation as organizational control. *Journal of Management Studies* 39(5), pp. 619–644.

Amernic, J., Craig, R. & Tourish, D. (2007) The transformational leader as pedagogue, physician, architect, commander and saint: five root metaphors in Jack Welch's letters to stockholders in General Electric. *Human Relations* 60(2), pp. 1839–1872.

Anand, S., Hu, J., Liden, R. & Vidyarthi, P. (2011) Leader-member exchange: recent research findings and prospects for the future. In A. Bryman, D. Collinson, K. Grint, B. Jackson & M. Uhl-Bien (eds), *The Sage Handbook of Leadership* (pp. 311–325). London: Sage.

Antonakis, J. (2011) Predictors of leadership: the usual suspects and the suspect traits. In A. Bryman, D. Collinson, K. Grint, B. Jackson & M. Uhl-Bien (eds), *The Sage Handbook of Leadership* (pp. 269–287). London: Sage.

Antonakis, J., Ciancilo, A. & Stjenberg, R. (2004) Introduction. In J. Antonakis, A. Ciancilo & R. Stjernberg (eds) *The Nature of Leadership*. Thousand Oaks: Sage.

Ashforth, B. & Humphrey, R. (1995) Emotions in the workplace: a reappraisal. *Human Relations* 48(2), pp. 97–125.

Ashkanasy, N. & Humphrey, R. (2011) A multi-level view of leadership and emotion: leading with emotional labor. In A. Bryman, D. Collinson, B. Jackson & M. Uhl-Bien (eds), *The Sage Handbook of Leadership* (pp. 365–379). London: Sage.

Argyris, C. (1982) How learning and reasoning processes affect organizational change. In P. Goodman (ed.), *Change in Organizations*. San Francisco: Jossey-Bass.

Argyris, C. (1993) *Knowledge for Action: A guide to Overcoming Barriers to Organizational Change*. San Francisco: Jossey-Bass.

Argyris, C. (1994) Good communication that blocks learning. *Harvard Business Review* 72(4), p. 77.

Argyris, C. & Schön, D. (1974) *Theory in Practice: Increasing Professional Effectiveness*. San Francisco: Jossey-Bass.

Argyris, C. & Schön, D. (1978) *Organizational Learning: A Theory of Action Perspective*. Reading, MA: Addison Wesley.

Arvidsson, M., Johansson, C.R., Ek, Å. & Akselsson, R. (2007) Situational leadership in air traffic control. *Journal of Air Transportation* 12(1), pp. 67–86.

Avolio, B.J. & Gardner, W.L. (2005) Authentic leadership development: getting to the root of positive forms of leadership, *Leadership Quarterly* 16, pp. 315–338.

Barnard, C. (1938/1968) *The Functions of the Executive*. Cambridge, MA: Harvard University Press.

Barros, M. (2010) Emancipatory management. *Journal of Management Inquiry* 19, pp. 166–184.

Bass, B.M. (1985) *Leadership and Performance beyond Expectations*. New York: Free Press.

Bass, B. & Avolio, B.J. (1994) *Improving Organizational Effectiveness through Transformational Leadership*. Thousand Oaks: Sage.

Bass, B.M. & Avolio, B.J. (2000) *MLQ – Multifactor Leadership Questionnaire*. Redwood City, CA: Mindgarden.

Bass, B. & Steidlmeier, P. (1999) Ethics, character, and authentic transformational leadership behavior. *Leadership Quarterly* 10(2), pp. 181–217.

Batista, E. (2015) How great coaches ask, listen and empathize. *Harvard Business Review* 2, p. 22.

Beard, A. (2014) Leading with humor. *Harvard Business Review*, 92(5), p. 130–131.

Bendix, R. (1970) The impact of ideas on organizational structure. In O. Gursky & G.A. Miller (eds), *The Sociology of Organizations: Basic Studies*. New York: Free Press of Glencoe.

Bennis, W. & Thomas, R. (2002) Crucibles of leadership. *Harvard Business Review* Sept, pp. 39–45.

Biggart, N.W. & Hamilton, G.G. (1987) An institutional theory of leadership. *Journal of Applied Behavioural Science* 23, pp. 429–441.

Blake, R. & Mouton, J. (1964) *The Managerial Grid*. Houston: Gulf Publishing Company.

Blake, R. & Mouton, J. (1975) An overview of the grid. *Training and Development Journal* May, pp. 29–37.

Blom, M. (2012) Ledarskapsstilar i innovativa miljöer – en studie av hejarklacksledare, gurus, skyddsombud och helpdeskare [Leadership Behaviour in Innovative Environments]. In A. Richnér & J. Frishammar (eds), *Innovationsledning och kreativitet i svenska företag* [*Innovation Management and Creativity in Swedish Companies*] (pp. 98–109). Stockholm: IMIT.

Blom, M. & Alvesson, M. (2014) Leadership on demand: followers as initiators and inhibitors of managerial leadership. *Scandinavian Journal of Management* 30(3), pp. 344–357.

Blom, M. & Alvesson, M. (2015) All-inclusive and all good: the hegemonic ambiguity of leadership. *Scandinavian Journal of Management* 31(4), pp. 480–492.

Bolden, R. (2011) Distributed leadership in organizations: a review of theory and research. *International Journal of Management Reviews* 13(1).

Bolden, R., Gosling, J. & Hawkins, B. (2011) *Exploring Leadership*. Oxford: Oxford University Press.

Bond, C. & Seneque, M. (2013) Conceptualizing coaching as an approach to management and organizational development. *Journal of Management Development* 32(1), pp. 57–72.

Bouchard, T.J., Lykken, D.T., McGue, M., Segal, N.L. & Tellegen, A. (1990) Sources of human psychological differences: the Minnesota study of twins reared apart. *Science* pp. 2230–2250.

Boud, D., Keogh, R. & Walker, D. (eds) (1985) *Reflection: Turning Experience into Learning*. London: Kogan Page.

Bourdieu, P. (1992) *An Invitation to Reflexive Sociology*. Chicago: University of Chicago Press.

Branson, R. (2013) *Forbes*, 16 March, http://www.forbes.com/sites/erikaandersen/2013/03/16/11-quotes-from-sir-richard-branson-on-business-leadership-and-passion/#d668d447b272

Bryman, A. (1992), *Charisma and Leadership in Organizations*. London: Sage.

Bryman, A. & Lilley, S. (2009) Leadership researchers on leadership in higher education. *Leadership* 5(3), pp. 331–346.

Burns, J. (1978) *Leadership*. New York: Harper & Row.

Burns, J. (2003) *Transforming Leadership*. New York: Grove.

Calás, M. & Smircich, L. (1991) Voicing seduction to silence leadership. *Organization Studies* 12(4), pp. 567–601.

Calder, B. (1977) An attribution theory of leadership. In B. Staw & J. Salacik (eds), *New Directions in Organizational Behavior* (pp. 179–204). Chicago: St Clair Press.

Carli, L. & Eagly, A. (2011) Gender and leadership. In A. Bryman, D. Collinson, K. Grint, B. Jackson & M. Uhl-Bien (eds), *The Sage Handbook of Leadership* (pp. 181–194). London: Sage.

Carsten, M., Uhl-Bien, M., West, B., Patera, B. & McGregor, R. (2010) Exploring social constructions of followership – a qualitative study. *Leadership Quarterly* 21(3), pp. 543–562.

Chamorro-Premuzic, T. (2007) *Personality and Individual Differences*. Oxford: Blackwell.

Chamorro-Premuzic, T. & Furnham, A. (2010) *The Psychology of Personnel Selection*. Cambridge: Cambridge University Press.

Chapman, G. & White, P. (2012) *The 5 Languages of Appreciation in the Workplace: Empowering Organizations by Encouraging People*. Chicago: Northfield Publishing.

Chef (2015) Undersökning: Administration har tagit över ledarskapet [Chief executive: administration has taken over leadership] *Chef* 1 May.

Chemers, M. (2003) Leadership effectiveness: functional, constructivist and empirical perspectives. In D. van Knippenberg & M. Hogg (eds), *Leadership and Power*. London: Sage.

Clegg, S. (1989) *Frameworks of power*. London: Sage.

Cliff, J., Langton, N. & Aldrich, H. (2005) Walking the talk? Gendered rhetoric vs. Action in small firms. *Organization Studies* 26(1): 63–91.

Cogliser, C., Schriesheim, C., Scandura, T. & Gardner, W. (2009) Balance in leader and follower perceptions of leader-member exchange: relationships with performance and work attitudes. *Leadership Quarterly* 20, pp. 452–465.

Colbert, A., Judge, T., Daejeon, C. & Wang, G. (2012) Assessing the trait theory of leadership using self and observer ratings of personality: the mediating role of contributions to group success. *The Leadership Quarterly* 23(4), pp. 670–685.

Collins, B.J., Buurus, C.J. & Meyer, R.D. (2014) Gender differences in the impact of leadership styles on subordinate embeddedness and job satisfaction. *Leadership Quarterly* 25(4), pp. 660–671.

Collins, J. (2001) *Good to Great: Why Some Companies Make the Leap – and Others Don't*. New York: Harper Business.

Collins, J. (2005) Level 5 leadership: The triumph of humility and fierce resolve. *Harvard Business Review* July–August, pp. 136–146.

Collinson, D. (2005) Dialectics of leadership. *Human Relations* 58, pp. 1419–1442.

Collinson, D. (2011) Critical leadership studies. In A. Bryman, D. Collinson, K. Grint, B. Jackson & M. Uhl-Bien (eds), *The Sage Handbook of Leadership* (pp. 181–194). London: Sage.

Collinson, D. (2012) Prozac leadership and the limits of positive thinking. *Leadership* 8, pp. 87–107.

Cooper, R. & Burrell, G. (1988) Modernism, postmodernism and organizational analysis: an introduction, *Organization Studies* 9, pp. 91–112.

Conger, J.A. & Kanungo, R.N. (1987) Toward a behavioral theory of charismatic leadership in organizational settings. *Academy of Management Review* 12(4), pp. 637–647.

Conger, J.A. & Kanungo, R.N. (1998) *Charismatic Leadership in Organizations.* Thousand Oaks, CA: Sage.

Courpasson, D., Dany, F. & Clegg, S. (2012) Resisters at work: Generating productive resistance in the workplace. *Organization Science* 23(3), pp. 801–819.

Crevani, L., Lindgren, M. & Packendorff, J. (2010) Leadership, not leaders: On the study of leadership as practices and interactions. *Scandinavian Journal of Management* 26(1), pp. 77–86.

Cunha, M.P. & Cabral-Cardoso, C. (2006) Shades of gray: a liminal interpretation of organizational legality-illegality. *International Public Management Journal* 9(3), pp. 209–225.

Cunha, M., Cunha, R., & Rego, A. (2009) Exploring the Role of Leader—Subordinate Interactions in the Construction of Organizational Positivity. *Leadership* 5, pp. 81–101.

Cunha, M.P., Clegg, S. & Rego, A. (2013) Lessons for leaders: positive organization studies meets Niccolo Machiavelli. *Leadership* 9, pp. 450–465.

Cunliffe, A. & Eriksen, M. (2011) Relational leadership. *Human Relations* 64, pp. 1435–1449.

Czarniawska-Joerges, B. (1988) *Ideological Control in Non-ideological Organizations.* New York: Preager.

Dagens Industri (2009) Article in Weekend supplement 2009(2), 17 February.

Davis, A. & Kleiner, B. (1989) The value of humour in effective leadership. *Leadership & Organization Development Journal* 10(1), pp. i–iii.

DeCelles, K. & Pfarrer, M. (2004) Heroes or villains? Corruption and the charismatic leader. *Journal of Leadership and Organizational Studies* 11(1), pp. 67–77.

Deetz, S. (1992) *Democracy in an Age of Corporate Colonization.* Albany: Suny Press.

DeRue, S. & Ashford, S. (2010) Who will lead and who will follow? A social process of leadership identity constructions in organizations. *Academy of Management Review* 35(4), pp. 627–647.

De Cramer, D. (2003) A relational perspective on leadership and cooperation. In D. van Knippenberg & M. Hogg (eds), *Leadership and Power.* London: Sage.

De Hoogh, A., Greer, L. & Den Hartog, D. (2015) Diabolical dictators or capable commanders? An investigation of the differential effects of autocratic leadership on team performance. *Leadership Quarterly* 26(5), pp. 687–701.

Diaz-Saenz, H. (2011) Transformational leadership. In A. Bryman et al. (eds), *The SAGE Handbook of Leadership.* London: Sage.

Dobrow, J. (2014) *Natural Prophets: From Health Foods to Whole Foods – How the Pioneers of the Industry Changed the Way We Eat and Reshaped American Business.* New York: Rodale Books.

Drucker, P. (1983) *Concept of the Corporation.* New Brunswick, NJ: Transaction Publishers.

Drucker, P. (1993) *Post Capitalist Society.* New York: Harper and Row.

Dunér, A. & Wolmesjö, M. (2015) Interprofessional Collaboration in Swedish health and social care from a care manager's perspective: [Interprofessionell samverkan i svensk hälso-och sjukvård och social omsorg ur biståndshandläggares perspektiv]. *European Journal of Social Work* 18(3), pp. 354–369.

Eagly, A. & Johannesen-Schmidt, M.A. (2008) Leadership style matters: the small but important style differences between male and female leaders. In D. Bilimoria & S.K. Piderit (eds), *Handbook on Women in Business and Management* (pp. 279–303). Northampton, MA: Edward Elgar.

Eagly, A. & Johnson, B. (1990) Gender and leadership style: a meta-analysis. *Psychological Bulletin* 108(2): 233–256.

Eagly, A., Karau, S.J. & Makhijani, M.G. (1995) Gender and the effectiveness of leaders: a meta-analysis. *Psychological Bulletin* 117, pp. 125–145.

Eagly, A., Makhijani, M. & Klonsky, B. (1992) Gender and the evaluation of leaders: a meta-analysis. *Psychological Bulletin* 111(1), pp. 3–22.

Earley, P.C. & Mosakowski, E. (2004) Cultural intelligence. *Harvard Business Review* October.

Eden, D. (1984) Self-fulfilling prophecy as a management tool: harnessing Pygmalion. *Academy of Management Review* 1(9), pp. 64–73.

Engels, F. (1893/1968) *Letters to Franz Mehring*. London: International Publishers.

Erdogan, B. and Bauer, T. (2014) Leader-member exchange theory: the relational approach to leadership. In D. Day (ed.), *The Oxford Handbook of Leadership and Organizations*. Oxford: Oxford University Press.

Etzioni, A. (1961) *A Comparative Analysis of Complex Organizations*. New York: Free Press.

Fairhurst, G. (2007) *Discursive Leadership: In conversation with Leadership Psychology*. Thousand Oaks, CA: Sage.

Fairhurst, G. & Grant, D. (2010) The social construction of leadership: a sailing guide. *Management Communication Quarterly* 24(2), pp. 171–210.

Fairhurst, G. & Uhl-Bien, M. (2012) Organizational discourse analysis (ODA): examining leadership as relational process. *Leadership Quarterly* 23(6), pp. 1043–1062.

Festinger, L. (1957) *A Theory of Cognitive Dissonance*. Stanford: Stanford University Press.

Ferraro, F., Pfeffer, J. & Sutton, R. (2005) Economics language and assumptions: how theories can become self-fulfilling. *Academy of Management Review* 30(1), pp. 8–24.

Fiedler, F. (1967) *A Theory of Leadership Effectiveness*. New York: McGraw Hill.

Fleming, P. (2005) Workers' playtime? Boundaries and cynicism in a 'culture of fun' program. *Journal of Applied Behavioral Science* 41(3), pp. 285–303.

Fletcher, J. & Käufer, K. (2003) Shared leadership: paradoxes and possibility. In C. Pearce & J. Conger (eds), *Shared Leadership*. Thousand Oaks: Sage.

Foley, M. (2010) *The Age of Absurdity: Why Modern Life Makes it Hard to be Happy*. London: Simon & Shuster.

Forbes (2009) Four styles of leadership, 15 October, http://www.forbes.com/forbes/2009/1102/opinions-rich-karlgaard-digital-rules.html

Forbes (2012) Why most leaders need to shut up and listen, 9 February, http://www.forbes.com/sites/mikemyatt/2012/02/09/why-most-leaders-need-to-shut-up-listen/

Forbes (2013a) 6 ways effective listening can make you a better leader, 20 May, http://www.forbes.com/sites/glennllopis/2013/05/20/6-effective-ways-listening-can-make-you-a-better-leader/

Forbes (2013b) 10 reasons why humour is a key to success at work, 3 May, http://www.forbes.com/sites/jacquelynsmith/2013/05/03/10-reasons-why-humor-is-a-key-to-success-at-work/

Ford, J. (1981) Departmental context and formal structure as constraints on leader behavior. *Academy of Management Journal* 24(2), pp. 274–288.

Foucault, M. (1977) *Discipline and Punish*. New York: Vintage Books.

Foucault, M. (1980) *Power/Knowledge: Selected Interviews and Other Writings*. New York: Pantheon.

Fryer, M. (2011) Facilitative leadership: drawing on Jürgen Habermas' model of ideal speech to propose a less impositional way to lead. *Organization* 19(1), pp. 25–43.

Gabriel, Y. (1997) Meeting god: when organizational members come face to face with the supreme leader. *Human Relations* 50(4), pp. 315–342.

Gabriel, Y. (2005) Class cages and glass palaces: images of organizations in image-conscious times. *Organization* 12(1), pp. 9–27.

Garner, E. (2012) *The Art of Managing People*. Eric Garner & Ventus Publishing ApS. Bookboon.com

Geertz, C. (1973) *The Interpretation of Culture*. London: Fontana Press.

Gemmill, G. & Oakley, J. (1992) Leadership: an alienating social myth? *Human Relations* 45(2), pp. 113–129.

George, B. (2008) Failed leadership caused the financial crisis, *US News*, 19 November, http://www.usnews.com/opinion/articles/2008/11/19/failed-leadership-caused-the-financial-crisis

George, J. (2000) Emotions and leadership: the role of emotional intelligence. *Human Relations* 53(8), pp. 1027–1055.

Giddens, A. (1991) *Modernity and Self-identity: Self and Society in the Late Modern Age*. Cambridge: Polity.

Goffe, R. & Jones, G. (2000) Why should anyone be led by you? *Harvard Business Review* September, pp. 63–70.

Golden, D., Boyatzis, R. & McKee, A. (2001) Primal leadership: the hidden driver of great performance. *Harvard Business Review* December, pp. 42–51.

Goldsmith, M., Baldoni, J. & McArthur, S. (2010) *The AMA Handbook of Leadership*. New York: The American Management Association.

Goleman, D. (1998) *Working with Emotional Intelligence*. New York: Bantam Books.

Goleman, D. (2000) Leadership that gets results. *Harvard Business Review* March–April, pp. 78–90.

Gordon, R. (2011) Leadership and power. In A. Bryman, D. Collinson, K. Grint, B. Jackson & M. Uhl-Bien (eds), *The Sage Handbook of Leadership*. London: Sage.

Gouldner, A. (1960) The norm of reciprocity. *American Sociological Review.*

Graef, C. (1997) Evolution of situational leadership theory: a critical review. *Leadership Quarterly* 8(2), pp. 153–170.

Graen, G. & Uhl-Bien, M. (1995) Relationship-based approach to leadership: Development of leader-member exchange (LMX) theory of leadership over 25 years: applying a multi-level multi-domain perspective. *Leadership Quarterly* 6(2), pp. 219–247.

Greenwood, J. (1998) The role of reflection in single and double loop learning. *Journal of Advanced Nursing* 27, pp. 1048–1053.

Greenleaf, R. (1977) *Servant Leadership.* New York: Paulist Press.

Grey, C. (2005) *A Very Short, Fairly Interesting and Reasonably Cheap Book about Studying Organizations.* London: Sage.

Grint, K. (2005) Problems, problems, problems: the social construction of 'leadership'. *Human Relations* 58(11), pp. 1467–1494.

Grint, K. (2010a) *Leadership – A Very Short Introduction.* Oxford: Oxford University Press.

Grint, K. (2010b) The sacred in leadership: separation, sacrifice and silence. *Organization Studies* 31, pp. 89–107.

Grint, K. (2014) The hedgehog and the fox: leadership lessons from D-Day. *Leadership* 6, pp. 1–21.

Gronn, P. (2002) Distributed leadership as a unit of analysis. *Leadership Quarterly* 13(4), pp. 423–451.

Gronn, P. (2009) Leadership configurations. *Leadership* 5(3), pp. 381–393.

Gruenfeld, D. & Zander, L. (2011) Authentic leadership can be bad leadership. *Harvard Business Review* February.

Guillet de Monthoux, P. (1981) *Doktor Kant eller den Oekonomiska Rationaliseringen.* Göteborg: Korpen.

Habermas, J. (1984) *The Theory of Communicative Action, Volume One: Reason and the Rationalization of Society.* Boston: Beacon Press.

Habermas, J. (1987) *The Theory of Communicative Action, Volume Two: Lifeworld and system – A critique of Functionalist Reason.* Boston: Beacon Press.

Habermas, J. (1990) *Moral Consciousness and Communicative Action.* Boston: MIT Press.

Hallett, T. (2007) Between deference and distinction: interaction ritual through symbolic power in an educational institution. *Social Psychology Quarterly* 70, pp. 148–171.

Hallett, T. (2010) The myth incarnate: recoupling processes, turmoil, and inhabited institutions in an urban elementary school. *American Sociological Review* 75, pp. 52–74.

Hamlin, R.G., Ellinger, A.D. & Beattie, R.S. (2008) The emergent 'coaching industry': a wake-up call for HRD professionals. *Human Resource Development International* 11(3), pp. 287–305.

Hargreaves, A. & Fink, D. (2008) Distributed leadership: democracy or delivery? *Journal of Educational Administration* 46(2), pp. 229–240.

Harris, K., Wheeler, A. & Kacmar, M. (2009) Leader-member exchange and empowerment: direct and interactive effects on job satisfaction, turnover intentions, and performance. *Leadership Quarterly* 20(3), pp. 371–382.

Harrison, R. (1987) Harnessing personal energy: how companies can inspire employees. *Organizational Dynamics* Autumn, pp. 4–21.

Harter, N., Ziolkowski, F. & Wyatt, S. (2006) Leadership and inequality. *Leadership* 3(3), pp. 275–294.

Harvard Business Review (2012) The value of happiness: how employee well-being drives profits. January–February.

Hatch, M., Kostera, M. & Kozminski, A. (2006) The three faces of leadership: manager, artist, priest. *Organizational Dynamics* 35(1), pp. 49–68.

Hawkins, B. (2015) Ship-shape: materializing leadership in the British Royal Navy, *Human Relations* 68, pp. 951–972.

Hazucha, J.F., Hezlett, S.A. & Schneider, R.J. (1993) The impact of 360-degree feedback on management skills development. *Human Resource Management* 3(3), pp. 325–351.

Heifetz, R., Grashow, A. & Linsky, M. (2009) *The Practice of Adaptive Leadership: Tools and Tactics for Changing Your Organization and the World.* Boston: Harvard Business Press.

Heifetz, R. & Laurie, D. (1994) The work of leadership. *Harvard Business Review* Jan–Feb, pp. 124–134.

Heifetz, R. & Linsky, M. (2002) *Leadership on the Line: Staying Alive Through the Dangers of Leading.* Boston: Harvard University Press.

Helgesen, S. (1990) *The Female Advantage.* New York: Doubleday.

Hentze, H. (1994) My greatest failure. In D. Adam-Smith & A. Peacock (eds), *Cases in Organizational Behaviour*. London: Pitman.

Hersey, P. & Blanchard, K. (1982) *Management of Organizational Behavior: Leading Human Resources*. New Jersey: Prentice-Hall.

Hochschild, A. (1983) *The Managed Heart: The Commercialization of Human Feeling*. Berkeley, CA: University of California Press.

Hogan, R., Curphy, G.J. & Hogan, J. (1994) What we know about leadership: effectiveness and personality. *American Psychologist* 49(6), pp. 493–504.

Holmberg, I. & Tyrstrup, M. (2010) Well then – what now? An everyday approach to managerial leadership. *Leadership* 6, pp. 353–372.

Hosking, D. (2011) Moving relationality: mediations on a relational approach to leadership. In A. Bryman, D. Collinson, K. Grint, B. Jackson & M. Uhl-Bien (eds), *The Sage Handbook of Leadership*. London: Sage.

Houghton, J., Neck, C. & Manz, C. (2003) Selfleadership and superleadership. In C. Pearce & J. Conger (eds), *Shared Leadership*. Thousand Oaks: Sage.

House, R. (1977) A 1976 theory of charismatic leadership. In J.G. Hunt & L.L. Larson (eds), *Leadership: The Cutting Edge* (pp. 189–207). Carbondale, IL: Southern Illinois University Press.

House, R. (1996) Path-goal theory of leadership: lessons, legacy, and a reformulated theory. *Leadership Quarterly* 7(3), pp. 323–352.

Howell, J. & Shamir, B. (2005) The role of followers in the charismatic leadership process: relationships and their consequences. *Academy of Management Review* 30(1), pp. 96–112.

Hughes, L.W., Avey, J.B. & Nixon, D.R. (2010) Relationships between leadership and followers' quitting intentions and job search behaviors. *Journal of Leadership & Organization Studies* 17(4), pp. 351–362.

Hughes, R.L., Ginnett, R.C. & Curphy, G.J. (2006) *Leadership: Enhancing the Lessons of Experience* (5th edn). Boston, MA: McGraw-Hill.

Hunt, J. (1999) Transformational/charismatic leadership's transformation of the field: an historical essay. *Leadership Quarterly* 10(2), pp. 129–144.

Hunt, J.G., Boal, K.B. & Dodge, G.E. (1999) The effects of visionary and crisis-responsive charisma on followers: an experimental examination of two kinds of charismatic leadership. *Leadership Quarterly* 10(3), pp. 432–488.

Hunter, S., Bedell-Avers, K. & Mumford, M. (2007) The typical leadership study: assumptions, implications, and potential remedies. *Leadership Quarterly* 18(5), pp. 435–446.

Huzzard, T. & Spoelstra, S. (2011) Leaders as gardeners: leadership through facilitation growth. In M. Alvesson & A. Spicer (eds), *Metaphors We Lead By: Understanding Leadership in the Real World* (pp. 76–95). Abingdon: Routledge.

Iacocca, L. & Novak, W. (1984) *Iacocca: An Autobiography*. London: Bantam Books.

Ibarra, H. (2015) The authenticity paradox. *Harvard Business Review* Jan–Feb, pp. 4–9.

Isaacson, W. (2012) *Steve Jobs*. New York: Simon & Schuster.

Islam, G. (2014) Identities and ideals: psychoanalytic dialogues of self and leadership. *Leadership* 10(3), pp. 344–360.

Jackall, R. (1988) *Moral Mazes*. Oxford: Oxford University Press.

Jackson, B. & Parry, K. (2008) *A Very Short, Fairly Interesting and Reasonably Cheap Book about Studying Leadership*. London: Sage.

Jermier, J. & Kerr, S. (1997) Substitutes for leadership: their meaning and measurement – contextual recollections and current observations. *Leadership Quarterly* 8(2), pp. 95–100.

Kairos Futures/*Chef* (2006) Bäst på allt och aldrig nöjd [Best on everything and never pleased]. Stockholm.

Kjærgaard, A., Morsing, M. & Ravasi, D. (2011) Mediating identity: a study of media influence on organizational identity construction in a celebrity firm. *Journal of Management Studies* 48(3), pp. 514–543.

Kanter, R. (2008) Transforming giants. *Harvard Business Review* January, pp. 43–52.

Kärreman, D., Sveningsson, S. & Alvesson, M. (2002) The return of the machine bureaucracy. *International Studies of Management & Organization* 32(2), pp. 70–92.

Katz, D. & Kahn, R. (1952) Some recent findings in human-relations research in industry. In G.E. Swanson, T. Newcomb & E. Hartley (eds), *Readings in Social Psychology* (pp. 650–665). New York: Holt.

Katz, D. & Kahn, R. (1978) *The Social Psychology of Organizations* (2nd edn). New York: John Wiley.

Keller, R. (1992) Transformational leadership and the performance of research and development project groups. *Journal of Management* 18, pp. 489–501.

Keller, R. (2002) Transformational leadership, initiating structure, and substitutes for leadership: a longitudinal study of research and development project team performance. *Journal of Applied Psychology* 91(1), pp. 202–210.

Kelley, R. (1988) In praise of followers. *Harvard Business Review* 66(6), pp. 141–148.

Kelley, R. (1992) *The Power of Followership*. New York: Doubleday.

Kelly, S. (2008) Leadership: a categorical mistake? *Human Relations* 61(6), pp. 763–782.

Kelly, S. (2014) Towards a negative ontology of leadership. *Human Relations* 67, pp. 905–922.

Kerr, S. & Jermier, J. (1978) Substitutes for leadership: their meaning and measurement. *Organizational Behavior and Human Performance* 22, pp. 375–403.

Kets de Vries, M. (1994) The leadership mystique. *Academy of Management Executive* 8(3), pp. 73–92.

Kets de Vries, M. & Balasz, K. (2011) The shadow side of leadership. In A. Bryman, D. Collinson, K. Grint, B. Jackson & M. Uhl-Bien (eds), *The Sage Handbook of Leadership*. London: Sage, pp. 380–392.

Kets de Vries, M. & Miller, D. (1984) *The Neurotic Organization*. San Francisco: Jossey-Bass.

Khanna, T. (2014) Contextual intelligence. *Harvard Business Review* 92(9), pp. 58–68.

Khanna, T., Gulati, R. & Nohria, N. (1998) The dynamics of learning alliances: competition, cooperation, and relative scope. *Strategic Management Journal* 19(3), pp. 193–210.

Kirkpatrick, S.A. & Locke, E.A. (1991) Leadership: do traits matter? *Academy of Management Executive* 5(2), pp. 48–59.

Kirkpatrick, S.A. & Locke, E.A. (1996) Direct and indirect effect of three core charismatic leadership components on performances and attitudes. *Journal of Applied Psychology* 81(1), pp 36–51.

Kjærgaard, A., Morsing, M. & Ravasi, D. (2011) Mediating identity: A study of media influence on organizational identity construction in a celebrity firm. *Journal of Management Studies*, 48(3), pp. 514–543.

Knights, D. & Willmott, H. (1992) Conceptualizing leadership processes: a study of senior managers in a financial services company. *Journal of Management Studies* 29(6), pp. 761–782.

Korman, A.K. (1966) Consideration, initiating structure, and organizational criteria: a review. *Personnel Psychology* 1(9), pp. 349–361.

Kotter, J. (1982) *The General Managers*. New York: Free Press.

Kotter, J. (1990) *A Force for Change: How Leadership Differs from Management*. New York: Free Press.

Kouzes, J. & Posner, B. (1995) *The Leadership Challenge: How to Keep Getting Extraordinary Things Done in Organizations* (The Leadership Practices Inventory). San Francisco: Jossey-Bass.

Kovalainen, A. (1990) How do male and female managers in banking view their work roles and their subordinates. *Scandinavian Journal of Management*, 6, pp. 143–159.

Kunda, G. (1992) *Engineering Culture: Control and Commitment in a High-Tech Corporation*. Philadelphia: Temple University Press.

Ladegard, G. & Gjerde, S. (2014) Leadership coaching, leader role-efficacy, and trust in subordinates: a mixed methods study assessing leadership coaching as a leadership development tool. *Leadership Quarterly* 25(4), pp. 631–646.

Ladkin, D. (2010) *Rethinking Leadership: A New Look at Old Leadership Questions*. Cheltenham: Edward Elgar.

Larsson, J. & Vinberg, S. (2010) Leadership behaviour in successful organizations: universal or situation-dependent? *Total Quality Management & Business Excellence* 21(3), pp. 317–334.

Lasch, C. (1978) *The Culture of Narcissism*. New York: Norton.

Laurent, A. (1978) Managerial subordinancy: a neglected aspect of organizational hierarchy. *Academy of Management Review* 3(2), pp. 220–230.

Lewin, K. (1939) When facing danger. In G.W. Lewin (ed.) (1948), *Resolving Social Conflict* (pp. 116–121). London: Harper & Row.

Lewin, K. (1951) *Field Theory in Social Science*. New York: Harper & Row.

Lipman-Blumen, J. (2005) *The Allure of Toxic Leaders: Why We Follow Destructive Bosses and Corrupt Politicians – and How We Can Survive Them*. New York: Oxford University Press.

Llopis, G. (2014) Solving the leadership identity crisis to enable unseen opportunities. *Forbes* 1(13).

Lord, R., De Vader, C. & Alliger, G. (1986) A meta-analysis of the relation between personality traits and leadership perceptions: an application of validity generalization procedures. *Journal of Applied Psychology* 71(3), pp. 402–410.

Lovelace, K.J., Manz, C. & Alves, J.C. (2007) Work stress and leadership development: the role of self-leadership, shared leadership, physical fitness and flow in managing demands and increasing job control. *Human Resource Management Review* 17(4), pp. 374–387.

Lukes, S. (1978) Power and authority. In B. Bottomore & R.A. Nisbet (eds), *A History of Sociological Analysis*. T. London: Heinemann.

Lundholm, S. (2011) *An Act of Balance: Hierarchy in Contemporary Work*. Dissertation. Lund: Lund Business Press.

Luthans, F., Stajkovic, A.D. & Ibrayeva, E. (2000) Environmental and psychological challenges facing entrepreneurial development in transitional economics. *Journal of World Business* 35, pp. 95–110.

Lyons, J. & Schneider, T. (2009) The effects of leadership style on stress outcomes. *Leadership Quarterly* 20(5), pp. 737–748.

Machiavelli, N. (1993/1532) *The Prince*. Ware: Wordsworth Reference.

Magala, S. (2005) *Cross-Cultural Competence*. London: Routledge.

Manz, C. (1986) Self-leadership: toward an expanded theory of self-influence processes in organizations. *Academy of Management Review* 11(3), pp. 585–600.

Manz, C. & Sims, H. (1980) Self-management as a substitute for leadership: a social learning theory perspective. *Academy of Management Review* 5(3), pp. 361–367.

Manz, C. & Sims, H. (1987) Leading workers to lead themselves: The external leadership of self-managing work teams. *Administrative Science Quarterly* 32(1), pp. 106–128.

Maslow, A.H. (1943) A theory of human motivation. *Psychological Review* 50, pp. 370–396.

Maslow, A.H. (1954) *Motivation and Personality*. New York: Harper & Row.

Maxwell, J. (2001) *The 17th Irrefutable Laws of Teamwork*. New York: Thomas Nelson Publishing.

Mayer, J. & Salovey, P. (1997) What is emotional intelligence? In P. Salovey & D.J. Sluyter (eds), *Emotional Development and Emotional Intelligence: Educational Implications* (pp. 3–34). New York: Harper Collins.

Mayer, J., Salovey, P., Caruso, D. & Sitarenios, G. (2001) Emotional intelligence as standard intelligence. *Emotion* 1(3), pp. 232–242.

Mayo, E. (1949) *Hawthorne and the Western Electric Company: The Social Problems of an Industrial Civilization*. New York: Routledge.

McCarthy, G. & Milner, J. (2013) Managerial coaching: challenges, opportunities and training. *Journal of Management Development* 32(7), pp. 768–779.

McGraw, P. & Warner, J. (2014) *The Humor Code*. New York: Simon & Schuster.

McSweeney, B. (2006) Are we living in a post-bureaucratic epoch? *Journal of Organizational Change Management* 19(1), pp. 22–37.

Meindl, J. (1995) The romance of leadership as a follower-centric theory: a social constructionist approach. *Leadership Quarterly* 6, pp. 329–341.

Mintzberg, H. (1973) *The Nature of Managerial Work*. New York: Harper & Row.

Mintzberg, H. (1983) *Structures in Fives: Designing Effective Organizations*. Englewood Cliffs, NJ: Prentice-Hall.

Mintzberg, H. (2009) *Managing*. San Francisco, CA: Berrett-Koehler.

Mintzberg, H. (2012) That research on managing be developed. In S. Tengblad (ed.), *The Work of Managers* (pp. 327–328). Oxford: Oxford University Press.

Morgan, G. (1986) *Images of Organization*. Beverly Hills: Sage.

Mukunda, G. (2012) Leaders don't matter (most of the time). *Harvard Business Review* August, pp. 15–16.

Nadler, D. & Tushman, M. (1997) *Competing by Design. The Power of Organizational Architecture*. Oxford: Oxford University Press.

Naus, F., van Iterson, A. & Roe, R. (2007) Organizational cynicism: extending the exit, voice, loyalty, and neglect model. *Human Relations* 60, pp. 683–718.

Nelson, B. & Spitzer, D. (2003) *The 1001 Rewards and Recognition Fieldbook*. New York: Workman Publishing.

Northouse, P. (2007) *Leadership: Theory and Practice*. London: Sage.

Orfalea, P. (2005) *Copy This! How I Turned Dyslexia, ADHD, and 100 Square Feet into a Company Called Kinko's*. New York: Workman Publishing.

Ospina, S. & Sorenson, G. (2006) A constructionist lens on leadership: charting new territory. In G. Goethals & G. Sorenson (eds), *The Quest for a General Theory of Leadership*. Cheltenham: Edward Elgar.

Palmer, I. & Hardy, C. (2000) *Thinking About Management*. London: Sage.

Panepinto, J. (2015) Good leaders aren't afraid to be nice. *Harvard Business Review* April, http://www.afr.com/leadership/five-ways-leaders-can-stay-nice-20150409-1mh7h2

Paulsen, R. (2014) *Empty Labour*. Cambridge: Cambridge University Press.

Pearce, C. & Conger, J. (eds) (2003) *Shared Leadership*. Thousand Oaks: Sage.

Pelz, D. & Andrews, F. (1966) *Scientists in Organizations: Productive Climates for Research and Development.* New York: Wiley.

Peters, T.J. (1992) *Liberation Management.* New York: Alfred A. Knopf.

Peters, T. & Waterman, R. (1982) *In Search of Excellence.* New York: Harper Row.

Peterson, D. & Hicks, M.D. (1996) *Leader as Coach: Strategies for Coaching and Developing Others.* Minneapolis: Personnel Decisions.

Pfau, B. & Kay, I. (2002) Does 360-degree feedback negatively affect company performance? Studies show that 360-degree feedback may do more harm than good. What's the problem? *HR Magazine* 47(6), pp. 54–60.

Pfeffer, J. (1977) The ambiguity of leadership. *Academy of Management Review* 2(1), pp. 104–112.

Pfeffer, J. (1994) *Competitive Advantage through People: Unleashing the Power of the Work Force.* Boston: Harvard Business School Press.

Pfeffer, J. (2013) You're still the same: why theories of power hold over time and across contexts. *Academy of Management Perspectives* 27(4), pp. 269–280.

Pfeffer, J. & Salancik, G. (1978) *The External Control of Organizations: A Resource Dependence Perspective.* New York: Harper & Row.

Potter, J. & Wetherell, M. (1987) *Discourse and Social Psychology: Beyond Attitudes and Behaviour.* London: Sage.

Powell, G.N. (1988) *Women and Men in Management.* Beverly Hills: Sage.

Puffer, S. (1999) CompUSA's CEO James Halpin on technology, rewards, and commitment. *Academy of Management Executive* 13(2), pp. 29–36.

Raelin, J.A. (1989) An anatomy of autonomy: managing professionals. *Academy of Management Executive* 3, pp. 216–228.

Raelin, J. (2003) *Creating Leaderful Organizations: How to Bring Out Leadership in Everyone.* San Francisco, CA: Berrett-Koehler.

Raelin, J. (2011) From leadership-as-practice to leaderful practice. *Leadership* 7(2), pp. 195–211.

Raelin, J. (2014) Imagine there are no leaders: Reframing leadership as collaborative agency. *Leadership* 12(2), pp. 131–158.

Rennstam, J. (2007) *Engineering Work: On Peer Reviewing as a Method of Horizontal Control.* Lund: Lund University Business Press.

Riggio, R.E. (2014) You can lead, but are you a good follower? *Psychology Today* 16 March, https://www.psychologytoday.com/blog/cutting-edge-leadership/201403/you-can-lead-are-you-good-follower

Rijsenbilt, A. & Commandeur, H. (2013) Narcissus enters the courtroom: CEO narcissism and fraud. *Journal of Business Ethics* 11(2), pp. 413–429.

Robinson, V. (2001) *Student-centered leadership.* San Francisco: Jossey-Bass.

Rosensweig, P. (2007) *The Halo Effect … and the Eight Other Business Delusions that Deceive Managers.* New York: The Free Press.

Rost, J. (1991) *Leadership for the Twenty-first Century.* New York: Praeger.

Sandberg, J. & Targama, A. (2007) *Managing Understanding in Organizations.* London: Sage.

Sandjaya, S., Sarros, J. & Santora, J. (2008) Defining and measuring servant leadership behaviour in organizations. *Journal of Management Studies* 45(2), pp. 402–424.

Sandelands, L. & Drazin, R. (1989) On the language of organization theory. *Organization Studies* 10(4), pp. 457–478.

Sashkin, M. (2004) Transformational leadership approaches: a review and synthesis. In J. Antonakis et al. (eds), *The Nature of Leadership.* Thousand Oaks: Sage.

Schaefer, S. (2014) *Managerial Ignorance: A Study of How Managers Organise for Creativity.* (Dissertation). Lund: Lund University Press.

Schein, E. (1985) *Organizational Culture and Leadership.* San Francisco: Jossey-Bass.

Schön, D. (1983) *The Reflective Practitioner.* New York: Basic Books.

Schön, D. (1979) Generative metaphor: a perspective on problem setting in social policy. In A. Ortony (ed.), *Metaphor and Thought.* Cambridge: Cambridge University Press.

Schwartz, B. (1997) Psychology, idea technology, and ideology. *Psychological Science* 8(1), pp. 21–27.

Seers, A. & Chopin, S. (2012) The social production of leadership. In Uhl-Bien, M & Ospina, S (eds), *Advancing Relational Leadership.* Charlotte: Information Age Publishing.

Seifert, C.F., Yukl, G. & McDonald, R. (2003) Effects of multi-source feedback and a feedback facilitator on the influence behavior of managers towards subordinates. *Journal of Applied Psychology* 88, pp. 561–569.

Semmer, N.K. & Jacobshagen, N. (2010) Feedback im Arbeitsleben – eine Selbstwert-Perspektive. *Gruppendynamik und Organisationsberatung* 41(1), pp. 39–55.

Semmer, N.K., Jacobshagen, N., Meier, L.L. & Elfering, A. (2007) Occupational stress research: the 'stress-as-offense-to-self" perspective. In J. Houdmont & S. McIntyre (eds), *Occupational Health Psychology: European Perspectives On Research, Education and Practice*, Vol. 2 (pp. 43–60). Castelo da Maia: ISMAI.

Semmer, N.K., Tschan, F., Meier, L., Facchin, S. & Jacobshagen, N. (2010) Illegitimate tasks and counterproductive work behavior. *Applied Psychology: An International Review* 59, pp. 70–96.

Senge, P. (1990) *The Fifth Discipline: The Art and Practice of the Learning Organization*. New York: Doubleday.

Senge, P. (1996) The leader's new work: building learning organizations. In K. Starkey (ed.), *How Organizations Learn* (pp. 288–315). London: Thomson Business Press.

Sennett, R. (1980) *Authority*. New York: Vintage.

Shamir, B. (2007) From passive recipients to active co-producers: follower's roles in the leadership process. In B. Shamir, R. Pillai, M. Bligh & M. Uhl-Bien (eds), *Follower-Centred Perspectives on Leadership* (pp. ix–xxxix). Greenwich: Information Age Publishing.

Shamir, B. (2012) Leadership research on post-leadership research: Advancing leadership theory versus throwing out the baby with the bath water. In M. Uhl-Bien & S. Ospina (eds), *Advancing Relational Leadership Research: A Dialogue Among Perspectives* (pp. 477–500). Charlotte, NC: Information Age Publishers.

Shamir, B., Pillai, R., Bligh, M. & Uhl-Bien, M. (eds) (2007), *Follower-centered Perspectives on Leadership: A Tribute to the Memory of James R. Meindl*. Greenwich, CT: Information Age Publishing.

Shamir, R., House, R. & Arthur, M. (1993) The motivational effects of charismatic leadership: a self-concept based theory. *Organization Science* 4(4), pp. 577–594.

Sjöstrand, J-E, Sandberg, J. & Tyrstrup, M. (2001) *Invisible Management: The Social Construction of Leadership*. London: Thomson Learning.

Smircich, L. & Morgan, G. (1982) Leadership: the management of meaning. *The Journal of Applied Behavioural Science* 18(3), pp. 257–273.

Smith, B.N., Montagno, R.V. & Kuzmenko, T.N. (2004) Transformational and servant leadership: content and contextual comparisons. *Journal of Leadership and Organizational Studies* 10(4), pp. 80–91.

Smith, M.A. & Canger, J.M. (2004) Effects of superior 'big five' personality and subordinates attitudes. *Journal of Business and Psychology* 18(4), pp. 465–481.

Sosik, J. & Dinger, S. (2007) Relationships between leadership style and vision content: the moderating role of need for social approval, self-monitoring, and need for social power. *Leadership Quarterly* 18(2), pp. 134–153.

Spector, B. (2014) Flawed from the 'get-go': Lee Iacocca and the origins of transformational leadership. *Leadership* 10, pp. 361–378.

Spoelstra, S. & ten Bos, R. (2011) Leadership. In *Business Ethics and Contemporary Philosophy*. Cambridge: Cambridge University Press.

Stivers, C. (1993) *Gender Images in Public Administration*. Newbury Park: Sage.

Stocker, D., Jacobshagen, N., Semmer, N. & Annen, H. (2015) Appreciation at work in the Swiss armed forces. *Swiss Journal of Psychology* 69(2), pp. 117–124.

Stogdill, R. (1948) Personal factors associated with leadership: a survey of the literature. *Journal of Psychology* 25, pp. 35–71.

Stogdill, R. (1974) *Handbook of Leadership: A Survey of Theory and Research*. New York: Free Press.

Sturdy, A. & Fleming, P. (2003) Talk as technique – a critique of the words and deeds distinction in the diffusion of customer service cultures in call centres. *Journal of Management Studies* 40(4), pp. 753–773.

Sutherland, N., Land, C. & Böhm, S. (2014) Anti-leader(ship) in social movement organizations. *Organization* 21(6), pp. 759–781.

Sveningsson, S. & Alvesson, M. (2003) Managing managerial identities: organizational fragmentation, discourse and identity struggle. *Human Relations* 56(10), pp. 1163–1193.

Sveningsson, S. & Alvesson, M. (2016) *Managerial Lives: Leadership and Identity in an Imperfect World*. Cambridge: Cambridge University Press.

Sveningsson, S. & Blom, M. (2011) Leaders as buddies. In M. Alvesson & A. Spicer (eds), *Metaphors We Lead By: Understanding Leadership in the Real World* (pp. 96–117). London: Routledge.

Sveningsson, S. & Larsson, M. (2006) Fantasies of leadership: identity work. *Leadership* 2(2), pp. 203–224.

Sveningsson, S., Alvehus, J. & Alvesson, M. (2012) Managerial leadership: identities, processes, and interactions. In S. Tengblad (ed.), *The Work of Managers* (pp. 69–86). Oxford: Oxford University Press.

The Guardian (2014) Health sector crisis is a failure of leadership, 21 August.

The Telegraph (2011) Virgin's Richard Branson: Apple boss Steve Jobs was the entrepreneur I most admired, 6 October, http://www.telegraph.co.uk/technology/steve-jobs/8811232/Virgins-Richard-Branson-Apple-boss-Steve-Jobs-was-the-entrepreneur-I-most-admired.html

Thelin, A. & Wolmesjö, M. (2015) Tid att leva. En kunskapsöversikt om hur chefskap påverkar äldreomsorgens kvalité. [Time to live: a review of knowledge of how management impacts elderly care]. Rapport.

Thompson, G. & Vecchio, R. (2009) Situational leadership theory: a test of three versions. *Leadership Quarterly* 20(5), pp. 837–848.

Tichy, N.M. & Devanna, M.A. (1986) *The Transformational Leader*. New York: John Wiley & Sons.

Tourish, D. (2013) *The Dark Side of Transformational Leadership – A Critical Perspective*. New York: Routledge.

Tourish, D. (2014) Leadership, more or less? A processual, communication perspective on the role of agency in leadership theory. *Leadership* 10(1), pp. 79–98.

Tourish, D. & Pinnington, A. (2002) Transformational leadership, corporate cultism and the spirituality paradigm: An unholy trinity in the workplace? *Human Relations* 55(2), pp. 147–152.

Trice, H. & Beyer, J. (1993) *The Culture of Work Organizations*. Englewood Cliffs, NJ: Prentice-Hall.

Uhl-Bien, M., Marion, R. & McKelvey, B. (2007) Complexity leadership theory: shifting leadership from the industrial age to the knowledge era. *Leadership Quarterly* 18(4), pp. 298–318.

Uhl-Bien, M., Riggio, R., Lowe, K. & Carsten, M. (2014) Followership theory: a review and research agenda. *Leadership Quarterly* 25(1), pp. 83–104.

van Knippenberg, D. & Sitkin, S.B. (2013) A critical assessment of charismatic-transformational leadership research: back to the drawing board? *The Academy of Management Annals* 7, pp. 1–60.

Ventrice, C. (2009) *Make Their Day! Employee Recognition that Works: Proven Ways to Boost Morale, Productivity, and Profits*. San Francisco: Berrett-Koehler.

Wallander, J. (2002) *Med den mänskliga naturen – inte mot*. Stockholm: SNS Förlag.

Wallander, J. (2003) *Decentralisation: Why and How to Make It Work*. Stockholm: SNS Forlag.

Watson, T. (1994) *In Search of Management*. London: Routledge.

Wenzel, L. (2000) *Understanding Managerial Coaching: The role of Manager Attributes and Skills in Effective Coaching*. Unpublished doctoral dissertation, Colorado State University.

Western, S. (2008) *Leadership: A Critical Text*. Thousand Oaks, CA: Sage.

Woods, P. (2004) Democratic leadership: drawing distinctions with distributed leadership. *International Journal of Leadership in Education* 7(1), pp. 3–26.

Wright, P. (1996) *Managerial Leadership*. London: Routledge.

Wright, S. & McKinnon, C. (2003) *Leadership Alchemy: The Magic of the Leader Coach*. Toronto: The Coaching Project Publications.

Yukl, G. (1999) An evaluation of conceptual weaknesses in transformational and charismatic leadership theories. *Leadership Quarterly* 10, pp. 285–305.

Yukl, G. (2006) *Leadership in Organizations* (6th edn). Upper Saddle River, NJ: Prentice Hall.

Yukl, G. (2009) *Leadership in Organizations* (7th edn). Upper Saddle River, NJ: Prentice Hall.

Yukl, G. (2011) Contingency theories of effective leadership. In A. Bryman et al. (eds), *The SAGE Handbook of Leadership*. London: Sage.

Zaccaro, S.J. (2007) Trait-based perspectives of leadership. *American Psychologist*, 62(1), pp. 6–16.

Zaccaro, S.J., Kemp, C. & Bader, P. (2004) Leader traits and attributes. In J. Antonakis, A. Cianciolo & R. Sternberg (eds), *The Nature of Leadership*. London: Sage.

Zaccaro, S.J., Weis, E., Chen, T.R. & Matthews, M.D. (2014) Situational load and personal attributes: implications for adaptive readiness and training. In H.F. O'Neil, R.S. Perez & E.L. Baker (eds), *Teaching and Measuring Cognitive Readiness* (pp. 93–115). New York: Springer.

Zaleznik, A. (1977) Managers and leaders: are they different? *Harvard Business Review* May–June, pp. 67–68.

Zaleznik, A. (1997) Real work. *Harvard Business Review* 75(6), pp. 53–63.

Index